Southern Living

OUR BEST

CHRISTMAS RECIPES

Southern Living

OUR BEST

CHRISTMAS RECIPES

Compiled by
Jean Wickstrom Liles

Edited by Lisa A. Hooper

Oxmoor House®

Library of Congress Catalog Card Number: 94-066230
ISBN: 0-8487-1183-1
Manufactured in the United States of America
Tenth Printing 2001

Editor-in-Chief: Nancy J. Fitzpatrick
Senior Foods Editor: Susan Carlisle Payne
Senior Editor, Editorial Services: Olivia Kindig Wells
Art Director: James Boone

 Southern Living *Our Best Christmas Recipes*

Editor: Lisa A. Hooper
Foods Editor: Cathy A. Wesler
Copy Editors: Holly Ensor, Cecilia C. Robinson
Editorial Assistant: Rebecca Meng Sommers
Director, Test Kitchens: Vanessa Taylor Johnson
Assistant Director, Test Kitchens: Gayle Hays Sadler
Test Kitchen Home Economists: Beth Floyd, Michele B. Fuller, Elizabeth Luckett,
    Christina A. Pieroni, Kathleen Royal, Angie N. Sinclair, Jan A. Smith
Senior Photographer: Jim Bathie
Photographers: Ralph Anderson, J. Savage Gibson
Senior Photo Stylist: Kay E. Clarke
Photo Stylist: Virginia R. Cravens
Designer: Melissa Jones Clark
Production and Distribution Manager: Phillip Lee
Associate Production and Distribution Manager: John Charles Gardner
Associate Production Manager: Theresa L. Beste
Production Assistant: Marianne Jordan
Menu and Recipe Consultant: Jean Wickstrom Liles

Cover: *Lemon-Raspberry Cake (page 29)*
Back cover: *Smoked Hatcreek Quail (page 137)*
Frontispiece: *Beef Medaillons with Horseradish Cream (page 124)*

Table of Contents

Holiday Greetings

The magical season of Christmas holds different meanings for each of us. For some, it's a time of festive parties filled with food, carols, and laughter. For others, it's a quiet time for observing family customs. For most of us, though, Christmas is a combination of these pleasures—a season of special family times and goodwill.

As the holiday approaches, we pull out recipes that are craved as much for tradition as for flavor—Mother's stately coconut cake, Aunt Mary's moist cornbread dressing, or Grandmother's streusel-topped sweet potato casserole, to name a few. Think back to the familiar aromas and tastes of your childhood Christmases—fragrant fruitcake baking in the oven, buttery sugar cookies left for Santa, and creamy, pecan-laden fudge just waiting to be sampled. These wonderful sensations link each Christmas in a magic that remains the same year after year.

The treasured flavors represented in **Our Best Christmas Recipes** mean Christmas to the families who have shared their recipes with **Southern Living** since our first issue in 1966. Many of these recipes are requested for specific events such as holiday open houses, Christmas Eve dinners, or Christmas brunches. Others are handed-down favorites, connecting us to past generations and bringing fond memories of loved ones. And some have even been passed on to special friends as gifts from the kitchen. In fact, most of the recipes in this collection can be used year-round for any occasion.

We're proud that **Our Best Christmas Recipes** continues the tradition started by **Southern Living** nearly three decades ago—helping you celebrate the season with delicious recipes and gracious entertaining ideas. May our cherished recipes become part of your family's holiday traditions.

Jean Wickstrom Liles

Chocolate Decadence (page 226)

While compiling the contents for *Our Best Christmas Recipes*, Jean Wickstrom Liles spent countless hours poring through the recipe files at *Southern Living*, recalling the food staff's favorites from 1966 to the present. Each menu and recipe, carefully selected by Jean for its high rating, was retested and updated to reflect today's can and package sizes and cooking techniques. With this assurance, you can center all of your holiday celebrations around *Our Best Christmas Recipes*.

Jean, longtime foods editor at *Southern Living*, now consults with Oxmoor House, the book publishing division of Southern Progress Corporation.

Christmas Menus

Fit For the Silver Platter

Garland the table, decorate the chandelier, and light the candles—the holidays are here, and it's time to entertain! That means it's time to bring out the fine china and crystal for sharing Southern hospitality. And where there's a celebration in the South, there's plenty of good food and fond memories. No other time of the year brings such distinctive efforts from our kitchens. Celebrate the season with our spirited gatherings ranging from elegant feasts to lavish dessert parties.

"Elegance Comes Easy" menu. *Clockwise from top:* Vegetables Tossed in Olive Butter, Chicken Alouette, and, on plate, Cranberry Congealed Salad. (Recipes begin on page 20.)

Ring In the Holidays

Goat Cheese Rosemary
Artichoke Soup
Dijon-Crusted Rack of Lamb
Gourmet Wild Rice
Cardamom Carrots
Tossed Green Salad
Commercial French Bread
Red Wine   Water
Queen's Chocolate Cake
Coffee

Serves 6

The silver is polished, the linens are pressed, and the house is decorated for a small formal dinner party. For a nice change of pace, try serving a nontraditional holiday meal. You'll be relaxed and ready to enjoy the event if you take advantage of the handy make-ahead instructions we've included with most of these recipes.

Dijon-Crusted Rack of Lamb, Gourmet Wild Rice, Cardamom Carrots. (Recipes begin on page 15.)

GOAT CHEESE ROSEMARY

1 (3-ounce) package chèvre or other goat cheese
2 to 4 tablespoons chopped fresh rosemary, divided
⅓ cup olive oil

12 (½-inch-thick) slices French baguette, lightly toasted
Garnish: small fresh rosemary sprigs

Cut cheese into 12 (¼-inch-thick) slices. Sprinkle half of chopped rosemary in an 11- x 7- x 1½-inch baking dish; arrange cheese slices over chopped rosemary. Pour oil over cheese, and sprinkle with remaining half of chopped rosemary. Cover and refrigerate at least 8 hours.

Remove cheese slices from dish, reserving oil mixture. Place 1 cheese slice on each baguette slice; brush lightly with reserved oil mixture. Arrange baguette slices on an ungreased baking sheet. Broil 5½ inches from heat (with electric oven door partially opened) 1 minute or until cheese is warm. Garnish, if desired. Yield: 1 dozen.

ARTICHOKE SOUP

2 cups sliced green onions
½ cup chopped onion
¼ cup butter or margarine, melted
¼ cup plus 2 tablespoons all-purpose flour

2 (14½-ounce) cans ready-to-serve chicken broth
2 (14-ounce) cans artichoke hearts, undrained and chopped
¼ teaspoon ground white pepper
Garnish: minced fresh parsley

Cook onions in butter in a large skillet over medium-high heat, stirring constantly, until tender. Reduce heat to low; add flour. Cook, stirring constantly, 1 minute. Gradually add chicken broth; cook over medium heat, stirring constantly, until mixture is thickened and bubbly. Stir in artichoke hearts and pepper; cook until thoroughly heated, stirring occasionally. Ladle soup into individual bowls, and garnish, if desired. Yield: 7 cups.

Note: Artichoke Soup may be prepared ahead. Prepare as directed above, omitting garnish. Cover and refrigerate up to 24 hours. Reheat soup to serve. Garnish, if desired.

DIJON-CRUSTED RACK OF LAMB

¼ cup olive oil
3 tablespoons Dijon mustard
½ teaspoon salt
½ teaspoon dried thyme
1 clove garlic, crushed
1½ cups soft breadcrumbs

¼ cup butter or margarine,
　melted
2 (2-pound) racks of lamb
　(8 chops each)
Herb Sauce

Combine first 5 ingredients; stir well with a wire whisk. Combine bread-crumbs and butter; stir well. Trim exterior fat on lamb racks to ¼ inch; place lamb racks, fat side up, on a rack in a roasting pan. Brush mustard mixture over lamb racks. Pat breadcrumb mixture over tops and sides of lamb racks.

Insert meat thermometer into thickest portion of 1 rack, making sure it does not touch fat or bone. Bake at 375° for 1 hour or until thermometer registers desired degree of doneness (medium-rare 150° or medium 160°). Let stand 10 minutes before slicing. Serve with Herb Sauce. Yield: 6 to 8 servings.

Herb Sauce

1 (14½-ounce) can ready-to-serve
　beef broth
3 tablespoons minced onion
3 tablespoons minced carrot
1 tablespoon minced celery
½ teaspoon dried rosemary
½ teaspoon dried thyme

2 fresh parsley sprigs
1 large bay leaf
1 tablespoon cornstarch
1 tablespoon water
½ cup dry vermouth
1 tablespoon tomato paste

Combine first 8 ingredients in a small saucepan; bring to a boil over medium heat. Reduce heat, and simmer 20 minutes. Pour broth through a wire-mesh strainer into a bowl, discarding vegetables. Return broth to pan.

Combine cornstarch and water; stir until smooth. Add cornstarch mix-ture, vermouth, and tomato paste to broth. Bring to a boil; reduce heat, and cook, stirring constantly, 1 minute or until thickened. Yield: 1 cup.

Note: Lamb and sauce may be prepared ahead. Coat lamb racks with mustard and breadcrumb mixtures; cover and refrigerate up to 8 hours. Remove lamb racks from refrigerator; let stand at room temperature 30 min-utes. Uncover and bake as directed above. Prepare Herb Sauce as directed above; cover and refrigerate up to 2 days. Reheat to serve.

GOURMET WILD RICE

Wild rice isn't rice at all, but is a long-grain marsh grass native to the northern Great Lakes area.

⅔ cup currants
¼ cup brandy
1⅓ cups wild rice, uncooked

3 cups chicken broth
2 tablespoons olive oil
½ cup pine nuts, toasted

Combine currants and brandy; set aside. Combine wild rice and chicken broth in a medium saucepan; bring to a boil. Cover, reduce heat, and simmer 55 to 60 minutes or until rice is tender and liquid is absorbed. Stir in currant mixture, olive oil, and pine nuts. Yield: 6 to 8 servings.

CARDAMOM CARROTS

1½ pounds carrots, scraped and
  cut into very thin strips
1 tablespoon cornstarch
⅓ cup dry vermouth
½ cup butter
2 teaspoons grated lemon rind
¼ cup lemon juice

¼ cup orange juice
¼ cup honey
¾ teaspoon ground cardamom
½ teaspoon pepper
¼ teaspoon salt
2 tablespoons chopped fresh
  parsley

Cook carrot strips in a small amount of boiling water 4 to 5 minutes or until crisp-tender. Drain and plunge into cold water; drain well. Set aside.

Combine cornstarch and vermouth; stir well. Combine cornstarch mixture, butter, and next 4 ingredients in a large skillet; bring to a boil over medium heat, stirring constantly, until butter melts. Add carrot strips, cardamom, pepper, and salt; cook, tossing gently, until mixture is thoroughly heated. Stir in parsley. Yield: 6 servings.

Note: Cardamom Carrots may be prepared ahead. Cook carrot strips as directed above. Drain and plunge into cold water; drain well. Cover and chill. Prepare sauce mixture as directed above; cover and chill. To serve, combine carrot strips and sauce in a large skillet. Cook over medium heat until thoroughly heated. Stir in parsley.

QUEEN'S CHOCOLATE CAKE

⅔ cup semisweet chocolate morsels
2 tablespoons dark rum
½ cup butter, softened
⅔ cup sugar
3 large eggs, separated
⅓ cup ground almonds

¼ teaspoon almond extract
¼ teaspoon cream of tartar
Dash of salt
2 tablespoons sugar
¾ cup sifted cake flour
Chocolate Butter Frosting
⅓ cup sliced almonds, toasted

Don't be surprised by this cake's dense, creamy texture. It seems more like a cheesecake than a traditional cake.

Combine chocolate and rum in top of a double boiler; bring water to a boil. Reduce heat to low; cook until chocolate melts. Remove from heat; let cool.

Beat butter at medium speed of an electric mixer until creamy; gradually add ⅔ cup sugar, beating well. Add egg yolks, one at a time, beating until mixture is pale yellow (about 5 minutes). Reduce speed to low; add chocolate mixture, beating until smooth. Stir in ground almonds and almond extract.

Combine egg whites, cream of tartar, and salt in a small mixing bowl; beat at medium speed until foamy. Add 2 tablespoons sugar, beating at high speed until stiff peaks form. Fold egg white mixture into chocolate mixture alternately with flour, beginning and ending with egg white mixture.

Spoon batter into a greased and floured 9-inch round cakepan. Bake at 350° for 25 minutes or until a wooden pick inserted 1½ inches from edge of pan comes out clean. (Center may be soft and will be creamy when cool.) Cool in pan on a wire rack 10 minutes; remove from pan, and let cool completely on wire rack.

Spread Chocolate Butter Frosting on top and sides of cake; arrange almond slices on top of cake. Cover and chill thoroughly. Let stand at room temperature about 2 hours before serving. Yield: one 9-inch cake.

Chocolate Butter Frosting

½ cup semisweet chocolate morsels
2 tablespoons dark rum

¼ cup plus 2 tablespoons butter, softened

Combine chocolate and rum in top of a double boiler; bring water to a boil. Reduce heat to low; cook until chocolate melts. Remove from heat. Add butter, 1 tablespoon at a time, beating at high speed of an electric mixer until blended. Place mixture over cold water; beat until spreading consistency. (Frosting will lighten in color.) Yield: enough for one 9-inch cake layer.

Elegance Comes Easy

Acorn Squash Soup
Chicken Alouette
Vegetables Tossed in Olive Butter
Cranberry Congealed Salads
White Wine   Water
Chocolate Mousse au Grand Marnier
Coffee

Serves 6

Christmas is a season of sharing and celebrating. And there's no better way to do that than by hosting an elegant dinner party. This menu sparkles with holiday spirit, allowing you to entertain with ease and style by offering several dishes that can be prepared ahead. As guests finish the appetizer soup, set up the main course on the buffet. End the meal as distinctively as it began with Chocolate Mousse au Grand Marnier.

Acorn Squash Soup (page 20)

ACORN SQUASH SOUP

3 acorn squash
3 carrots, scraped and sliced
1 medium onion, sliced
3½ cups canned ready-to-serve
  chicken broth, divided
⅓ cup water, divided
2 tablespoons butter or margarine
1 tablespoon all-purpose flour
½ cup sherry

1 teaspoon salt
½ to 1 teaspoon black pepper
½ teaspoon ground nutmeg
⅛ teaspoon paprika
Dash of ground allspice
Dash of ground red pepper
1 cup half-and-half
Garnish: fresh thyme sprigs

Cut each squash in half lengthwise; remove seeds. Place halves, cut side down, in a shallow pan; add hot water to pan to a depth of 1 inch. Bake, uncovered, at 350° for 55 minutes or until tender. Drain squash halves on paper towels, cut side down. Scoop out and reserve pulp; discard shells.

Cook carrot and onion in boiling water to cover 12 to 15 minutes or until very tender; drain. Combine half of carrot mixture, half of reserved squash pulp, ½ cup chicken broth, and half of water in container of an electric blender; process until smooth. Repeat procedure with remaining carrot mixture, pulp, ½ cup chicken broth, and water; set aside.

Melt butter in a Dutch oven over low heat; add flour, stirring until smooth. Cook, stirring constantly, 1 minute. Gradually add pureed mixture, remaining 2½ cups chicken broth, sherry, and next 6 ingredients; bring to a boil over medium heat. Cover, reduce heat, and simmer 1 hour, stirring occasionally. Stir in half-and-half; cook just until thoroughly heated. (Do not boil.) Ladle soup into individual bowls; garnish, if desired. Yield: 11½ cups.

CHICKEN ALOUETTE

Puff pastry comprises many layers of dough and butter. During baking, the moisture in the butter creates steam, causing the pastry to puff into flaky layers.

1 (17¼-ounce) package frozen
  puff pastry sheets, thawed
1 (4-ounce) container garlic-and-
  spice-flavored Alouette cheese*
6 skinned and boned chicken
  breast halves

½ teaspoon salt
⅛ teaspoon pepper
1 large egg, beaten
1 tablespoon water
Kale leaves (optional)

Unfold pastry sheets, and roll each into a 14- x 12-inch rectangle on a lightly floured surface. Cut first sheet into 4 (7- x 6-inch) rectangles; cut second sheet into 2 (7- x 6-inch) rectangles and 1 (12- x 7-inch) rectangle. Set large rectangle aside. Shape each small rectangle into an oval by trimming off corners; spread pastry ovals evenly with cheese.

Sprinkle chicken breast halves with salt and pepper; place one in center of each pastry oval. Lightly moisten pastry edges with water. Fold ends over chicken; fold sides over, and pinch to seal. Place bundles, seam side down, on a lightly greased baking sheet.

Cut large pastry rectangle crosswise into 36 strips (about ¼ inch wide). Braid 3 strips together, and place crosswise over 1 chicken bundle, tucking ends under bundle and trimming any excess length. Braid 3 additional strips, and place lengthwise over bundle, tucking ends under. Repeat procedure with remaining strips and chicken bundles. Cover and chill up to 2 hours, if desired.

Combine egg and 1 tablespoon water; stir until well blended. Brush egg mixture over pastry bundles. Bake at 400° on lower oven rack 25 minutes or until golden. Arrange chicken bundles on a kale-lined serving platter, if desired. Yield: 6 servings.

*One-half cup chives-and-onion-flavored cream cheese may be substituted for Alouette cheese, if desired.

VEGETABLES TOSSED IN OLIVE BUTTER

⅓ cup sliced ripe olives
⅓ cup butter, melted
1 tablespoon lemon zest
3 tablespoons lemon juice
1 pound fresh asparagus
4 small red potatoes, unpeeled
  and sliced

1 zucchini, sliced
1 small sweet red pepper, cut into
  very thin 2-inch-long strips
½ pound sliced fresh mushrooms
1 (7-ounce) jar baby corn ears

Combine first 4 ingredients; set aside. Snap off tough ends of asparagus; remove scales from stalks with a knife or vegetable peeler, if desired. Cut asparagus into 2-inch pieces. Set aside.

Arrange potato slices in a vegetable steamer over boiling water in a large Dutch oven; cover and steam 8 minutes. Add asparagus, zucchini, pepper, and mushrooms; cover and steam 5 minutes. Add corn; cover and steam 1 minute. Transfer vegetable mixture to a bowl; toss gently with olive mixture. Yield: 6 servings.

CRANBERRY CONGEALED SALADS

1 (3-ounce) package cherry-flavored gelatin
¾ cup boiling water
1 (16-ounce) can whole-berry cranberry sauce
1 orange, peeled, sectioned, chopped, and drained
½ cup diced apple
½ cup chopped pecans
Lettuce leaves
2 tablespoons sour cream
2 tablespoons mayonnaise or salad dressing

Combine gelatin and boiling water, stirring 2 minutes or until gelatin dissolves. Stir in cranberry sauce. Chill until mixture is the consistency of unbeaten egg white.

Fold in orange, apple, and pecans. Spoon mixture into 6 lightly oiled ⅔-cup molds or custard cups; cover and chill until firm.

Unmold salads onto lettuce leaves. Combine sour cream and mayonnaise; serve with salads, or top each serving with a dollop. Yield: 6 servings.

CHOCOLATE MOUSSE AU GRAND MARNIER

1 (4-ounce) package sweet baking chocolate
4 (1-ounce) squares semisweet chocolate
¼ cup Grand Marnier or other orange-flavored liqueur
2 cups whipping cream
½ cup sifted powdered sugar
Garnishes: orange rind strips, whipped cream

Mousse, a French term meaning "froth" or "foam," is a rich, airy concoction that may be sweet or savory as well as hot or cold. Most mousses get their fluffiness from the addition of a whipped mixture.

Combine first 3 ingredients in top of a double boiler; bring water to a boil. Reduce heat to low; cook until chocolates melt. Remove from heat, and cool to lukewarm. (Mixture will thicken and appear grainy as it cools.)

Beat whipping cream until foamy; gradually add powdered sugar, beating until soft peaks form. Gently fold about one-fourth of whipped cream mixture into chocolate mixture; fold in remaining whipped cream mixture. Spoon into individual dishes; chill until ready to serve. Garnish, if desired. Yield: 6 servings.

Chocolate Mousse au Grand Marnier is proof that sometimes the simplest desserts can also be the most elegant.

Progressive Dinner In Three Parts

Crabmeat Mousse   Mushroom Roll-Ups
Bibb Salad with Raspberry-Maple Dressing
Beef Tenderloin with Peppercorns
Parmesan Scalloped Potatoes
Vegetables with Horseradish Sauce
Commercial Whole Wheat Dinner Rolls
Red Wine   Water
Lemon-Raspberry Cake   Cranberry Tart
Coffee

Serves 12

A progressive dinner presents a unique dining experience for your supper club or neighborhood. This dinner-party-on-the-move allows the group to multiply the merriment and divide the chores by traveling to a different home for each course. Distribute the recipes, and plan at least three stops: appetizers, main course, and dessert.

Clockwise from top: Whole wheat rolls, Vegetables with Horseradish Sauce, Parmesan Scalloped Potatoes, Beef Tenderloin with Peppercorns. (Recipes begin on page 27.)

CRABMEAT MOUSSE

1 envelope unflavored gelatin
¾ cup cold water
½ cup mayonnaise or salad dressing
2 tablespoons minced fresh chives or freeze-dried chives
2 tablespoons minced fresh dillweed or 2 teaspoons dried dillweed

1 tablespoon grated onion
1 tablespoon lemon juice
1 teaspoon salt
¼ teaspoon paprika
Dash of hot sauce
1 pound fresh crabmeat, drained and flaked
1 cup whipping cream, whipped

Sprinkle gelatin over cold water in a small saucepan; let stand 1 minute. Cook over low heat, stirring until gelatin dissolves, about 2 minutes. Let cool. Stir in mayonnaise and next 7 ingredients. Chill until the consistency of unbeaten egg white.

Spoon gelatin mixture into a large bowl; fold in crabmeat and whipped cream. Spoon into a lightly oiled 6-cup mold. Cover and chill until firm. Unmold and serve with assorted crackers. Yield: 12 to 14 appetizer servings.

MUSHROOM ROLL-UPS

To freeze unbaked Mushroom Roll-Ups, don't brush the roll-ups with melted butter. Freeze in an airtight container up to one month. To serve, let thaw in the refrigerator. Brush the roll-ups with melted butter, and cut in half. Bake as directed.

1½ cups finely chopped fresh mushrooms
3 tablespoons butter or margarine, melted
1½ tablespoons all-purpose flour
½ cup half-and-half

1 teaspoon chopped fresh chives or freeze-dried chives
½ teaspoon lemon juice
¼ teaspoon salt
24 slices sandwich bread
¼ cup butter or margarine, melted

Cook mushrooms in 3 tablespoons butter in a small saucepan over medium heat, stirring constantly, until tender. Reduce heat to low; add flour. Cook, stirring constantly, 1 minute. Gradually add half-and-half; cook over medium heat, stirring constantly, until mixture is thickened and bubbly. Stir in chives, lemon juice, and salt. Remove from heat; set aside.

Trim crusts from bread slices. Roll each slice to ¼- to ⅛-inch thickness with a rolling pin. Spread each slice with a rounded teaspoonful of mushroom mixture; roll up tightly. Brush rolls with ¼ cup melted butter. Cut each roll in half, and place on ungreased baking sheets. Bake at 400° for 10 minutes or until lightly browned. Serve warm. Yield: 4 dozen.

BIBB SALAD WITH RASPBERRY-MAPLE DRESSING

⅔ cup vegetable oil
¼ cup raspberry vinegar
2 tablespoons maple syrup
5 heads Bibb lettuce, torn

2 small purple onions, sliced and
    separated into rings
2 cups crumbled blue cheese
½ cup pine nuts, toasted

Combine first 3 ingredients in a jar. Cover tightly, and shake vigorously. Arrange lettuce and onion rings on individual salad plates. Sprinkle evenly with blue cheese and pine nuts, and drizzle evenly with dressing mixture. Yield: 12 servings.

BEEF TENDERLOIN WITH PEPPERCORNS

2 (2½- to 3-pound) trimmed beef
    tenderloins
3 tablespoons Dijon mustard
1 tablespoon dried sage
1½ tablespoons white
    peppercorns, ground and divided
1½ tablespoons green
    peppercorns, ground and divided

1½ tablespoons black
    peppercorns, ground and divided
2 tablespoons butter or margarine,
    softened
Fresh spinach leaves (optional)

Cut each tenderloin lengthwise to within ½ inch of 1 long edge, leaving edge intact. Open tenderloins out flat. Place heavy-duty plastic wrap over tenderloins; pound meat to flatten slightly, using a meat mallet or rolling pin. Remove plastic wrap; spread tenderloins evenly with mustard. Sprinkle tenderloins evenly with sage and 1½ teaspoons of each type of ground peppercorns.

Fold 1 side of each tenderloin back over, and tie each securely with heavy string at 3-inch intervals. Spread butter evenly over outside of tenderloins, and sprinkle evenly with remaining ground peppercorns, gently pressing peppercorns into tenderloins. Place tenderloins, seam side down, on a greased rack in a roasting pan; insert meat thermometer into thickest portion of 1 tenderloin.

Bake at 425° for 30 to 45 minutes or until meat thermometer registers desired degree of doneness (rare 140°, medium-rare 150°, or medium 160°). Let stand 10 minutes before slicing. Arrange slices on fresh spinach leaves, if desired. Yield: 12 to 14 servings.

PARMESAN SCALLOPED POTATOES

¾ cup freshly grated Parmesan
   cheese
3 tablespoons chopped fresh
   marjoram or 1 tablespoon dried
   marjoram
1 teaspoon salt
¾ teaspoon garlic powder
¼ teaspoon ground nutmeg
¼ teaspoon coarsely ground
   pepper

5 large baking potatoes, peeled
   and thinly sliced
3 cups whipping cream
¾ cup water
3 tablespoons freshly grated
   Parmesan cheese
1½ tablespoons chopped fresh
   marjoram or 1½ teaspoons
   dried marjoram
Garnish: fresh marjoram sprigs

Combine first 6 ingredients in a small bowl; set aside.

Arrange one-third of potato slices in a lightly greased shallow 3-quart baking dish; sprinkle with half of cheese mixture. Repeat layers with remaining potato slices and cheese mixture, ending with potato slices.

Combine whipping cream and water; pour over top layer. Sprinkle with 3 tablespoons Parmesan cheese and 1½ tablespoons chopped fresh marjoram. Cover and bake at 350° for 1½ hours. Uncover and bake an additional 30 minutes or until potato is tender. Let stand 10 minutes before serving. Garnish, if desired. Yield: 12 servings.

VEGETABLES WITH HORSERADISH SAUCE

1 cup mayonnaise or salad
   dressing
⅓ cup milk
⅓ cup prepared horseradish
¼ cup minced onion
¼ teaspoon salt

⅛ teaspoon pepper
6 cups fresh broccoli flowerets
1½ pounds carrots, scraped and
   diagonally sliced

Combine first 6 ingredients in a small saucepan; cook over low heat, stirring constantly, until hot. (Do not boil.) Set aside, and keep warm.

Arrange broccoli flowerets and carrot slices in a vegetable steamer over boiling water. Cover and steam 4 to 5 minutes or until crisp-tender. Serve vegetables with sauce. Yield: 12 servings.

LEMON-RASPBERRY CAKE

1 cup shortening
2 cups sugar
4 large eggs
3 cups cake flour, sifted
2½ teaspoons baking powder
½ teaspoon salt
1 cup milk

1 teaspoon almond extract
1 teaspoon vanilla extract
1 (10-ounce) jar seedless
 raspberry preserves
Lemon Buttercream Frosting
Garnish: lemon slice wedges

To make splitting cake layers easy, mark the center of each cake layer with wooden picks, inserting the picks around the circumference of each layer. An electric knife works especially well for splitting the layers.

Grease 3 (9-inch) round cakepans; line with wax paper. Grease and flour wax paper. Set pans aside.

Beat shortening at medium speed of an electric mixer until creamy; gradually add sugar, beating well. Add eggs, one at a time, beating well after each addition. Combine flour, baking powder, and salt; add to shortening mixture alternately with milk, beginning and ending with flour mixture. Mix after each addition. Stir in flavorings.

Pour batter into prepared pans. Bake at 375° for 16 to 18 minutes or until a wooden pick inserted in center comes out clean. Cool in pans on wire racks 10 minutes; remove from pans, and let cool completely on wire racks.

Slice cake layers in half horizontally to make 6 layers. Place 1 layer, cut side up, on a cake plate; spread with 2½ tablespoons preserves. Repeat procedure with remaining 5 layers and preserves, omitting preserves on top of last layer.

Reserve 1 cup Lemon Buttercream Frosting; spread remaining 1¾ cups frosting on top and sides of cake. Using a star tip, pipe reserved frosting on top of cake. Garnish, if desired. Store in an airtight container in refrigerator. Yield: one 6-layer cake.

Lemon Buttercream Frosting

1¼ cups butter or margarine,
 softened
2 teaspoons grated lemon rind

3 tablespoons lemon juice
3 cups sifted powdered sugar

Beat first 3 ingredients at medium speed of an electric mixer until creamy. Gradually add powdered sugar, beating until frosting is spreading consistency. Yield: 2¾ cups.

CRANBERRY TART

1¾ cups plus 2 tablespoons all-
   purpose flour
¾ teaspoon salt
⅔ cup shortening
3 tablespoons cold water
1 (8-ounce) package cream cheese,
   softened

½ cup sugar
2 large eggs
½ teaspoon almond extract
Cranberry Topping
Orange Cream (facing page)
Garnishes: fresh mint sprigs,
   fresh cranberries

Combine flour and salt; cut in shortening with a pastry blender until mixture is crumbly. Sprinkle cold water (1 tablespoon at a time) evenly over surface; stir with a fork until dry ingredients are moistened. Shape dough into a ball; cover and chill.

Roll pastry into a 13½- x 10-inch rectangle on a floured surface. Place in an 11- x 7½- x 1-inch tart pan; roll over top of pan with a rolling pin to trim excess pastry. Bake at 450° for 10 minutes or until lightly browned.

Beat cream cheese at high speed of an electric mixer until creamy; gradually add sugar, beating well. Add eggs, one at a time, beating after each addition. Stir in almond extract. Pour mixture into prepared pastry. Bake at 350° for 20 minutes. Cool completely on a wire rack.

Spread Cranberry Topping evenly over tart. Pipe Orange Cream on top of tart using a decorator bag fitted with tip No. 22. Garnish, if desired. Chill thoroughly. Yield: 10 to 12 servings.

Cranberry Topping

¾ cup sugar
¾ cup water
1½ tablespoons grated orange
   rind
½ teaspoon ground cinnamon

¼ teaspoon ground cloves
1½ cups fresh cranberries
⅓ cup chopped walnuts
3 tablespoons raisins

Combine first 5 ingredients in a saucepan; bring to a boil. Add cranberries; reduce heat, and simmer 7 minutes. Stir in walnuts and raisins; cook, uncovered, 10 minutes, stirring occasionally. Cool. Yield: 1¾ cups.

Cranberry Tart and Lemon-Raspberry Cake (page 29)
offer a stunning finale to the progressive feast.

Orange Cream

**2 (3-ounce) packages cream
   cheese, softened**
**3 tablespoons Grand Marnier or
   other orange-flavored liqueur**

2 tablespoons light corn syrup

Combine all ingredients in a small mixing bowl; beat at medium speed of an
electric mixer until smooth. Yield: ¾ cup.

Feast on Tradition

Holiday Oyster Stew
Fast-and-Savory Turkey
Cornbread Dressing
Orange-Glazed Sweet Potatoes
Steamed Green Beans
Jellied Cranberry Salad
Cranberry-Orange Relish
Extra-Special Rolls
Iced Tea   Water
Ambrosia Cake
Peppermint Candy-Ice Cream Pie
Coffee

Serves 8

When families gather to share Christmas dinner, the highlight often is the attendance of three or more generations. If your family insists on a traditional, old-fashioned feast, yet your recipes need a new twist, try our special variations.

Clockwise from right: Cornbread Dressing, Extra-Special Rolls, and, on plate, Fast-and-Savory Turkey, Cranberry-Orange Relish, Orange-Glazed Sweet Potatoes, steamed green beans. (Recipes begin on following page.)

HOLIDAY OYSTER STEW

4 (12-ounce) containers fresh
    Standard oysters, undrained
2½ cups sliced fresh mushrooms
1 cup chopped celery
1 cup chopped green onions
½ cup butter or margarine,
    melted
½ cup all-purpose flour
2 cups Chablis or other dry white
    wine

1½ tablespoons chicken-flavored
    bouillon granules
1 cup whipping cream
¼ cup grated Parmesan cheese
¼ teaspoon dried thyme
¼ teaspoon ground nutmeg
¼ teaspoon pepper

Drain oysters, reserving 2 cups liquid. Set oysters and reserved liquid aside.

Cook mushrooms, celery, and green onions in butter in a large Dutch oven over medium heat, stirring constantly, until tender. Reduce heat to low; add flour. Cook, stirring constantly, 1 minute. Gradually add oyster liquid, wine, and bouillon granules; cook over medium heat, stirring constantly, until thickened and bubbly. Stir in oysters, whipping cream, and remaining ingredients; cook over low heat until edges of oysters begin to curl and mixture is thoroughly heated. (Do not boil.) Yield: 2½ quarts.

FAST-AND-SAVORY TURKEY

Fast-and-Savory Turkey cooks covered at a higher temperature for a shorter period of time than does traditional roasted turkey. Although the skin of the turkey will not be as golden and crisp with this technique, the meat will be very moist and tender.

Vegetable cooking spray
1 (10- to 12-pound) turkey
2 teaspoons salt
2 teaspoons lemon-pepper
    seasoning
1 medium onion, quartered
Fresh parsley sprigs
2 teaspoons dried rosemary,
    divided
1 large onion, sliced
1 carrot, sliced

1 celery stalk, sliced
1½ cups chicken broth
1 cup Chablis or other dry white
    wine
½ cup brandy or Cognac
½ cup tomato juice
¼ cup cornstarch
⅓ cup whipping cream
1 teaspoon browning-and-
    seasoning sauce

Line a large roasting pan with heavy-duty aluminum foil, leaving a 3-inch overhang on all sides. Spray foil with cooking spray. Set aside. Remove giblets and neck from turkey; set aside. Rinse turkey; pat dry.

Sprinkle cavities with salt and lemon-pepper seasoning. Place onion quarters in neck cavity. Lift wingtips up and over back; tuck under bird. Place several parsley sprigs and 1 teaspoon rosemary in other cavity. Tie ends of legs to tail with cord or tuck them under flap of skin around tail.

Place turkey in prepared pan, breast side up; arrange giblets, sliced onion, carrot, and celery around turkey. Sprinkle giblets and vegetables with remaining 1 teaspoon rosemary. Combine chicken broth and next 3 ingredients in a saucepan; cook until thoroughly heated. Pour mixture over turkey. Cover with a sheet of heavy-duty aluminum foil without letting foil touch turkey. Fold edges of foil together, and crimp to form an airtight seal.

Bake at 425° for 1½ hours on lowest rack in oven. Cut a lengthwise slit in top of foil; fold sides of foil back. Insert meat thermometer into meaty portion of thigh, making sure it does not touch bone. Cut cord or band of skin holding drumstick ends to tail. Reduce heat to 400°, and bake 1 hour or until meat thermometer registers 180°. (Do not baste.) Turkey is done when drumsticks are easy to move up and down.

Pour drippings through a wire-mesh strainer into a medium saucepan, discarding giblets and vegetables. Combine cornstarch and whipping cream; gradually stir into drippings. Bring mixture to a boil, stirring constantly; boil 1 minute. Remove from heat; stir in browning-and-seasoning sauce. Serve gravy with turkey. Yield: 12 to 14 servings.

CORNBREAD DRESSING

2 (6-ounce) packages cornbread
  mix
1 (5.5-ounce) can refrigerated
  buttermilk biscuits
2¼ cups chopped onion
1½ cups chopped celery
¼ cup butter or margarine,
  melted

5½ cups chicken broth
5 large eggs, lightly beaten
1½ teaspoons rubbed sage
1½ teaspoons pepper
¾ teaspoon salt

To make Cornbread Dressing ahead of time, prepare the recipe as directed; do not bake. Cover and refrigerate up to 24 hours. Remove from refrigerator; let stand, covered, 30 minutes. Uncover and bake as directed.

Prepare cornbread mix and biscuits according to package directions; let cool. Crumble cornbread and biscuits in a large bowl. Set aside.

Cook onion and celery in butter in a skillet over medium heat, stirring constantly, until tender. Add vegetables, broth, and remaining ingredients to cornbread mixture; stir well. Spoon into a greased 13- x 9- x 2-inch baking dish; bake at 350° for 55 minutes or until golden. Yield: 8 to 10 servings.

ORANGE-GLAZED SWEET POTATOES

To keep things flowing as smoothly as possible if you have only one oven, put the Cornbread Dressing in to bake after the turkey is done. After the dressing bakes about 30 minutes, put the sweet potatoes in the oven also; both will be ready at the same time.

8 medium-size sweet potatoes (about 4 pounds)
2 tablespoons grated orange rind
1 cup orange juice
⅓ cup sugar

⅓ cup firmly packed brown sugar
3 tablespoons butter or margarine, melted
1 tablespoon cornstarch
¼ teaspoon salt

Place washed sweet potatoes in a large Dutch oven; add water to cover. Bring to a boil; cover, reduce heat to medium, and simmer 25 to 30 minutes or until tender. Let cool to touch; peel potatoes, and cut into ½-inch-thick slices. Arrange slices in a lightly greased 13- x 9- x 2-inch baking dish.

Combine orange rind and remaining ingredients in a small saucepan. Bring to a boil; boil 1 minute. Pour mixture over sweet potato slices. Bake at 350° for 25 minutes or until thoroughly heated. Yield: 8 to 10 servings.

Note: Potatoes may be prepared ahead. Prepare as directed above; do not bake. Cover and refrigerate up to 8 hours. Remove from refrigerator; let stand, covered, 30 minutes. Uncover and bake as directed above.

JELLIED CRANBERRY SALAD

2 (3-ounce) packages raspberry-flavored gelatin
1 cup boiling water
1 cup cold water
2 cups fresh cranberries
1 cup pecan or walnut pieces
2 large oranges, seeded and quartered

1 carrot, scraped and cut into 6 pieces
1 (8-ounce) can crushed pineapple in juice, drained
¾ cup sugar
Lettuce leaves
Garnish: carrot curls

Combine gelatin and boiling water, stirring 2 minutes or until gelatin dissolves. Add cold water, and chill until the consistency of unbeaten egg white.

Position knife blade in food processor bowl; add cranberries and next 3 ingredients. Pulse until mixture is finely chopped. Combine cranberry mixture, pineapple, and sugar, stirring well. Fold cranberry mixture into gelatin mixture. Pour into a lightly oiled 6½-cup mold. Cover and chill until firm. Unmold salad onto a lettuce-lined serving plate, and garnish, if desired. Yield: 8 servings.

CRANBERRY-ORANGE RELISH

4 cups fresh cranberries
2 cups sugar
½ cup water

1 teaspoon grated orange rind
½ cup orange juice
⅓ cup slivered almonds, toasted

Combine first 5 ingredients in a saucepan; bring to a boil. Reduce heat, and simmer 10 minutes or until cranberry skins pop, stirring occasionally. Cool; cover and refrigerate up to 1 week. Stir in almonds just before serving. Yield: 3½ cups.

EXTRA-SPECIAL ROLLS

4½ to 5 cups all-purpose flour,
  divided
½ cup sugar
1¼ teaspoons salt
2 packages active dry yeast

1 cup plus 3 tablespoons milk
½ cup butter or margarine
2 large eggs
¼ cup butter or margarine,
  softened

Combine 2 cups flour, sugar, salt, and yeast in a large mixing bowl; stir well. Combine milk and ½ cup butter in a saucepan; heat until butter melts, stirring occasionally. Cool to 120° to 130°.

Gradually add liquid mixture to flour mixture, beating at low speed of an electric mixer. Beat an additional 2 minutes at medium speed. Add eggs; beat well. Gradually stir in enough remaining flour to make a soft dough.

Turn dough out onto a floured surface; knead until smooth and elastic (about 10 minutes). Place in a greased bowl; turn to grease top. Cover and let rise in a warm place (85°), free from drafts, 1 hour or until doubled in bulk.

Punch dough down; turn out onto a lightly floured surface, and knead lightly 4 or 5 times. Divide dough into fourths; roll each portion into a 12-inch circle on a floured surface. Spread 1 tablespoon softened butter on each circle. Cut each circle into 12 wedges; roll up each wedge, beginning at wide end. Place on lightly greased baking sheets, point side down. Cover and let rise in a warm place, free from drafts, 35 minutes or until doubled in bulk. Bake at 350° for 12 minutes or until golden. Yield: 4 dozen.

Note: Rolls may be prepared ahead and frozen. Bake at 350° for 5 minutes; let cool. Cover and freeze up to 1 month. Let rolls thaw, covered, at room temperature. Uncover and bake at 350° for 6 to 8 minutes or until golden.

AMBROSIA CAKE

1 cup butter or margarine,
  softened
2 cups sugar
4 large eggs
3 cups sifted cake flour
2½ teaspoons baking powder
½ teaspoon salt

1 cup milk
1 teaspoon vanilla extract
1 teaspoon butter flavoring
Orange Filling
Divinity Frosting (facing page)
½ cup flaked coconut

Beat butter at medium speed of an electric mixer until creamy; gradually add sugar, beating well. Add eggs, one at a time, beating after each addition. Combine flour, baking powder, and salt; add to butter mixture alternately with milk, beginning and ending with flour mixture. Mix after each addition. Stir in flavorings.

Pour batter into 3 greased and floured 9-inch round cakepans. Bake at 350° for 20 to 25 minutes or until a wooden pick inserted in center comes out clean. Cool in pans on wire racks 10 minutes; remove from pans, and let cool completely on wire racks.

Spread Orange Filling between layers. Spread top and sides of cake with Divinity Frosting; sprinkle with coconut. Yield: one 3-layer cake.

Orange Filling

1 cup sugar
3 tablespoons cornstarch
¼ teaspoon salt
¾ cup orange juice

⅓ cup water
¼ cup lemon juice
3 egg yolks, lightly beaten
1 tablespoon grated orange rind

Combine first 3 ingredients in a small saucepan. Combine orange juice, water, and lemon juice; gradually add orange juice mixture to sugar mixture. Cook over medium heat, stirring constantly, until mixture comes to a boil; boil 1 minute.

Gradually stir about one-fourth of hot mixture into yolks; add to remaining hot mixture, stirring constantly. Cook, stirring constantly, 1 minute. Remove from heat, and stir in grated orange rind. Cool to room temperature. Yield: about 2 cups.

Divinity Frosting

1½ cups sugar
½ cup water
½ teaspoon cream of tartar

3 egg whites
½ teaspoon vanilla extract

Combine first 3 ingredients in a heavy saucepan. Cook over medium heat, stirring constantly, until mixture is clear. Cook, without stirring, until mixture reaches soft ball stage or candy thermometer registers 240°.

Beat egg whites at high speed of an electric mixer until soft peaks form; continue to beat, slowly adding hot syrup mixture. Add vanilla. Beat until stiff peaks form and frosting is spreading consistency. Yield: enough for one 3-layer cake.

Divinity Frosting, often called boiled frosting, is easy to make if you use a candy thermometer.

PEPPERMINT CANDY-ICE CREAM PIE

1¼ cups chocolate wafer crumbs
⅓ cup butter or margarine, melted
1 pint peppermint ice cream, softened
1 (8-ounce) container frozen whipped topping, partially thawed

Frozen whipped topping, thawed (optional)
3 tablespoons finely crushed peppermint candy (optional)

Combine chocolate wafer crumbs and butter, stirring well. Press mixture firmly into a 9-inch pieplate. Bake at 350° for 8 minutes. Cool.

Combine softened ice cream and partially thawed whipped topping; spoon mixture into prepared crust. Freeze until firm. If desired, top each serving with a dollop of whipped topping, and sprinkle with crushed peppermint candy. Yield: one 9-inch pie.

Note: One (6-ounce) chocolate-flavored crumb crust may be substituted for chocolate wafer crumb crust.

Make-Ahead Dessert Party

White Chocolate Charlotte Russe
Crème de Menthe Cheesecake
Lemon Bars
Cranberry Relish over Cream Cheese
Orange Shortbread
Mixed Nuts
Strawberry Champagne Punch
Cranberry Punch
Coffee Bar

Serves 20 to 25

If the guest list for your holiday party includes more people than can fit around your dinner table, host a dessert party. Plan this evening celebration for eight or nine o'clock, and serve our rich make-ahead selections for the grandest party of the season.

Clockwise from center: Crème de Menthe Cheesecake, Cranberry Punch, Cranberry Relish over Cream Cheese with Orange Shortbread, White Chocolate Charlotte Russe. (Recipes begin on following page.)

WHITE CHOCOLATE CHARLOTTE RUSSE

1 envelope unflavored gelatin
⅔ cup cold water
2 (6-ounce) packages white chocolate-flavored baking bars, grated
½ cup whipping cream
¼ cup sugar
2 egg yolks, lightly beaten

1 teaspoon vanilla extract
2 tablespoons sugar
1½ tablespoons meringue powder
¾ cup water
1½ cups whipping cream, whipped
10 ladyfingers, split
Garnish: fresh strawberry fans
Raspberry-Strawberry Sauce

Sprinkle gelatin over cold water in a small saucepan; let stand 1 minute. Cook over low heat, stirring until gelatin dissolves, about 2 minutes. Add white chocolate, stirring until chocolate melts. Remove from heat, and let cool slightly.

Combine ½ cup whipping cream, ¼ cup sugar, and egg yolks in a medium saucepan. Cook over medium heat, stirring constantly, 3 to 4 minutes or until mixture thickens. Remove from heat; stir in gelatin mixture and vanilla. Transfer white chocolate mixture to a large bowl; cool to room temperature, stirring occasionally.

Combine 2 tablespoons sugar, meringue powder, and ¾ cup water in a mixing bowl; beat at high speed of an electric mixer 8 to 10 minutes or until stiff peaks form. Gently fold meringue mixture and whipped cream into egg yolk mixture.

Line sides of a 2-quart trifle bowl with ladyfingers; spoon in filling mixture. Cover and chill at least 8 hours. Garnish, if desired. Serve with Raspberry-Strawberry Sauce. Yield: 8 to 10 servings.

Raspberry-Strawberry Sauce

1 (10-ounce) package frozen raspberries in light syrup, thawed and undrained
1 (10-ounce) package frozen strawberries in light syrup, thawed and undrained

3 tablespoons cornstarch
2 teaspoons sugar
3 tablespoons Chambord or other raspberry-flavored liqueur
2 tablespoons lemon juice

Combine raspberries and strawberries in container of an electric blender; process until smooth. Pour mixture through a wire-mesh strainer into a heavy saucepan, discarding seeds. Add cornstarch and sugar to strained mixture, stirring until smooth. Cook over low heat, stirring constantly, until thickened. Remove from heat; stir in liqueur and lemon juice. Cover and chill thoroughly. Stir before serving. Yield: 2 cups.

CRÈME DE MENTHE CHEESECAKE

5 (8-ounce) packages cream
  cheese, softened
1½ cups sugar
3 large eggs
1 (16-ounce) carton sour cream
¼ cup white crème de cacao

¼ cup green crème de menthe
2½ teaspoons vanilla extract
Chocolate Crust
½ cup whipping cream, whipped
Garnish: chocolate-covered mint
  wafer candy shavings

Beat cream cheese at medium speed of an electric mixer until creamy; gradually add sugar, beating well. Add eggs, one at a time, beating after each addition. Stir in sour cream and next 3 ingredients. Pour mixture into Chocolate Crust.

  Bake at 350° for 40 minutes. Turn oven off, leaving cheesecake in oven with oven door closed 30 minutes. Open oven door; leave cheesecake in oven an additional 30 minutes. Remove from oven, and run a knife around edge of cheesecake. Cool completely on a wire rack. Cover and refrigerate at least 8 hours. Pipe whipped cream around outer edge of cheesecake, and garnish, if desired. Yield: 16 to 18 servings.

Chocolate Crust

1 (9-ounce) package chocolate
  wafer cookies, crushed (about
  2 cups)

⅓ cup butter or margarine,
  melted

Combine chocolate wafer crumbs and butter; firmly press mixture evenly onto bottom and 1 inch up sides of a 10-inch springform pan. Bake at 350° for 8 minutes. Yield: one 10-inch crust.

You can wrap a cheesecake in heavy-duty plastic wrap or place it in an airtight container and freeze up to one month. Freezing will not harm the flavor or texture. For an impressive garnish, use a vegetable peeler to shave tiny stripes of color from the narrow edge of chocolate-covered mint wafer candies.

LEMON BARS

2½ cups all-purpose flour, divided
½ cup sifted powdered sugar
¾ cup butter or margarine
½ teaspoon baking powder
4 large eggs, lightly beaten
2 cups sugar
½ teaspoon grated lemon rind
   (optional)
⅓ cup fresh lemon juice
Powdered sugar

Combine 2 cups flour and ½ cup powdered sugar; cut in butter with a pastry blender until mixture is crumbly. Spoon mixture into a greased 13- x 9- x 2-inch pan; press firmly and evenly into pan using fingertips. Bake at 350° for 20 to 25 minutes or until crust is lightly browned.

Combine remaining ½ cup flour and baking powder in a small bowl; stir well. Combine eggs, 2 cups sugar, lemon rind, if desired, and lemon juice in a large bowl; stir in flour mixture. Pour mixture over prepared crust. Bake at 350° for 25 minutes or until lightly browned and set. Cool completely on a wire rack. Dust with powdered sugar; cut into bars. Yield: 2 dozen.

Lime Bars: Substitute lime rind and fresh lime juice for lemon rind and lemon juice.

CRANBERRY RELISH OVER CREAM CHEESE

2 (8-ounce) packages cream
   cheese, softened
2 cups fresh cranberries
¾ cup sugar
¾ teaspoon grated orange rind
⅓ cup orange juice
½ teaspoon grated lemon rind
1½ tablespoons lemon juice
Garnishes: lemon rind strips,
   orange rind strips

Beat cream cheese at medium speed of an electric mixer until creamy; spread into bottom of a 2-cup mold lined with plastic wrap. Cover and chill at least 8 hours.

Combine cranberries and next 5 ingredients in a saucepan; bring to a boil over medium-high heat. Cook 3 to 5 minutes or until cranberry skins pop; cool. Cover and chill at least 8 hours.

To serve, unmold cream cheese onto a serving plate. Stir cranberry relish mixture, and spoon over cream cheese. Garnish, if desired. Serve with Orange Shortbread or other assorted shortbread cookies. Yield: 20 to 25 appetizer servings.

ORANGE SHORTBREAD

1 cup butter, softened
¾ cup sifted powdered sugar
1¾ cups all-purpose flour
1 teaspoon grated orange rind

2 teaspoons frozen orange juice concentrate, thawed and undiluted

Beat butter at medium speed of an electric mixer until creamy; gradually add powdered sugar, beating well. Add flour, orange rind, and orange juice concentrate, mixing well.

Spread dough evenly into a lightly greased 15- x 10- x 1-inch jellyroll pan. Bake at 300° for 28 to 30 minutes or until lightly browned. Remove pan from oven, and cut shortbread into rectangles. Cool in pan on a wire rack. Remove rectangles from pan, and store in an airtight container up to 1 week. Yield: 4 dozen.

Shortbread is a tender-crisp, buttery cookie that once was associated mainly with the Christmas holidays but is now enjoyed year-round.

STRAWBERRY CHAMPAGNE PUNCH

5 cups water
3 (6-ounce) cans frozen lemonade concentrate, thawed and undiluted
1 pint fresh strawberries, sliced

2 (750-milliliter) bottles dry champagne, chilled
1 (1-liter) bottle ginger ale, chilled

Combine first 3 ingredients; cover and chill at least 4 hours. To serve, pour lemonade mixture into a punch bowl; gently stir in champagne and ginger ale. Yield: 4½ quarts.

CRANBERRY PUNCH

1 quart cranberry juice cocktail
1 quart pineapple juice
¼ cup sugar

2 teaspoons almond extract
1 (2-liter) bottle ginger ale, chilled

Combine first 4 ingredients, stirring until sugar dissolves; cover and chill at least 4 hours. To serve, pour juice mixture into a punch bowl; gently stir in ginger ale. Yield: 1 gallon.

Instead of serving plain coffee with this dessert menu, set up a coffee bar.
•Brew coffee with strips of orange peel for flavor.
•Set out brandy or liqueurs such as amaretto, Galliano, or Kahlúa.
•Offer sugar cubes, whipped cream, and grated chocolate along with cinnamon-stick stirrers.

Casual Christmas Cheer

Think back to your most vivid recollection of the holidays. Perhaps it was chopping down the perfect Christmas tree, or maybe it was an evening of caroling with friends. It may even have been a neighborhood open house. Casual gatherings such as these are fondly thought of as the essence of good times and warm fellowship. And one of the best ways to make happy holiday memories is by sharing your traditions and festivities with family and friends. However you choose to celebrate the season, these menus will suit any casual style of entertaining.

"Welcome the Carolers" menu features Chicken-and-Sausage Gumbo (page 62).

Tree-Trimming Supper

Spiced White Grape Juice
Bite-Size Cheese Balls
Sweet-and-Spicy Pecans
White Lightning Texas Chili
Mexican Salad with Avocado Dressing
Chocolate-Peanut Butter Drops
Cranberry-Peach Cobbler
Soft Drinks   Beer

Serves 8

*C*hances are that one of your family's favorite holiday activities is trimming the Christmas tree. Memories of holidays past are shared as each ornament is unwrapped. As the family members hang the ornaments, let them sip Spiced White Grape Juice and snack on Bite-Size Cheese Balls and Sweet-and-Spicy Pecans. After the last strands of tinsel are hung, ladle bowls of White Lightning Texas Chili for a satisfying meal.

White Lightning Texas Chili (page 51), Mexican Salad with Avocado Dressing (page 52).

SPICED WHITE GRAPE JUICE

2 (24-ounce) bottles white grape
  juice
6 cups water
1 tablespoon whole cloves
3 (3-inch) sticks cinnamon

2 whole nutmegs, halved
1/3 cup lemon juice
1/4 cup sugar
Cinnamon sticks (optional)

Combine first 5 ingredients in a Dutch oven. Bring to a boil; reduce heat, and simmer, uncovered, 20 minutes. Remove spices; stir in lemon juice and sugar. Serve hot with cinnamon-stick stirrers, if desired. Yield: 11 cups.

BITE-SIZE CHEESE BALLS

1 (3-ounce) package cream cheese,
  softened
1 cup (4 ounces) finely shredded
  Cheddar cheese

3/4 cup finely shredded carrot
1 teaspoon honey
1/2 cup finely chopped pecans
24 pretzel sticks

Combine first 4 ingredients; cover and chill 1 hour. Shape mixture into 1-inch balls; roll in chopped pecans. Cover and chill up to 24 hours. Just before serving, insert a pretzel stick into each cheese ball. Yield: 2 dozen.

SWEET-AND-SPICY PECANS

Sweet-and-Spicy Pecans will keep for at least a week in an airtight container. Be sure to make enough to give as gifts.

2 cups pecan halves
2 tablespoons butter or
  margarine, melted
1 tablespoon sugar
1 teaspoon ground cumin

1 teaspoon chili powder
1/2 teaspoon dried crushed
  red pepper
1/4 teaspoon salt

Toss pecans in butter. Combine sugar and remaining ingredients. Sprinkle over pecans; toss. Spread on a baking sheet; bake at 325° for 15 minutes, stirring every 5 minutes. Cool. Store in an airtight container. Yield: 2 cups.

Hearty appetites will appreciate the way White Lightning Texas Chili satisfies. A bit of jalapeño pepper adds fiery flavor.

WHITE LIGHTNING TEXAS CHILI

1 pound dried navy beans
4 (14½-ounce) cans ready-to-
   serve chicken broth, divided
1 large onion, chopped
2 cloves garlic, minced
1 tablespoon ground white pepper
1 tablespoon dried oregano
1 tablespoon ground cumin
½ teaspoon ground cloves
5 cups chopped cooked chicken

2 (4-ounce) cans chopped green
   chiles, undrained
1 cup water
1 teaspoon salt
1 jalapeño pepper, seeded and
   chopped
Shredded Monterey Jack cheese
Commercial salsa
Sour cream
Sliced green onions

Sort and wash beans; place in a large Dutch oven. Cover with water 2 inches above beans; let soak 8 hours. Drain beans, and return to pan. Add 3 cans chicken broth, chopped onion, and next 5 ingredients. Bring to a boil; cover, reduce heat, and simmer 2 hours or until beans are tender.

    Add remaining can of chicken broth, chicken, and next 4 ingredients. Bring to a boil; cover, reduce heat, and simmer 1 hour, stirring occasionally. Serve with cheese, salsa, sour cream, and green onions. Yield: 11 cups.

MEXICAN SALAD WITH AVOCADO DRESSING

Cilantro is a pungent herb that closely resembles flat-leaf parsley. You'll find cilantro widely used in Mexican and Caribbean cuisines.

6 cups shredded iceberg lettuce
3 tomatoes, cut into wedges
½ cup sliced ripe olives
1 small purple onion, sliced and separated into rings

2 tablespoons chopped fresh cilantro or parsley
Avocado Dressing

Place shredded lettuce on a large serving plate. Arrange tomato wedges, sliced olives, and onion rings on lettuce; sprinkle with cilantro. Serve with Avocado Dressing. Yield: 8 to 10 servings.

Avocado Dressing

1 ripe avocado, peeled and mashed
¾ cup sour cream
1½ tablespoons lime juice
½ teaspoon ground cumin

¼ teaspoon salt
¼ teaspoon ground red pepper
2 cloves garlic, crushed
2 tablespoons vegetable oil

Combine first 7 ingredients in a mixing bowl; beat at medium speed of an electric mixer until smooth. Add oil, 1 tablespoon at a time, beating until well blended. Cover and chill up to 24 hours. Yield: 1½ cups.

CHOCOLATE-PEANUT BUTTER DROPS

1 cup sugar
½ cup light corn syrup
¼ cup honey
1 (12-ounce) jar chunky peanut butter

4 cups chocolate-flavored frosted puffed corn cereal

Combine first 3 ingredients in a Dutch oven; bring to a boil, stirring constantly. Remove from heat; add peanut butter, stirring until blended. Stir in cereal. Working quickly, drop mixture by tablespoonfuls onto wax paper. Let cool. Store in an airtight container up to 24 hours. Yield: 4 dozen.

Cranberry-Peach Cobbler is quick to fix—it uses cake mix for the crunchy topping.
A scoop of ice cream is the perfect accompaniment to the warm cobbler.

CRANBERRY-PEACH COBBLER

1 (21-ounce) can peach pie filling
1 (16-ounce) can whole-berry
  cranberry sauce
1 (18.25-ounce) package yellow
  cake mix without pudding

½ teaspoon ground cinnamon
¼ teaspoon ground nutmeg
½ cup butter or margarine
½ cup chopped pecans
Vanilla ice cream (optional)

Combine pie filling and cranberry sauce; spoon mixture into a lightly greased 13- x 9- x 2-inch baking dish. Set aside.

Combine cake mix, cinnamon, and nutmeg; cut in butter with a pastry blender until mixture is crumbly. Stir in pecans. Sprinkle crumb mixture evenly over fruit mixture. Bake at 350° for 45 minutes or until golden and bubbly. Serve warm with vanilla ice cream, if desired. Yield: 8 servings.

Holiday Open House

Marinated Pork Party Sandwiches
Cajun Shrimp
Spinach-Stuffed Mushrooms
Chunky Onion Dip
Assorted Fresh Vegetables
Fruit and Cheese Buffet
Chocolate-Peppermint Brownies
Crescents
Blushing Champagne Punch
Coffee

Serves 25

One of the nicest things about the holiday season is opening your home to family and friends. The relaxed atmosphere of a casual open house is a fun way to entertain several people at one time. Many of the recipes in this buffet-style menu can be prepared ahead or purchased, making party-hosting less hectic.

Clockwise from top left: Spinach-Stuffed Mushrooms, Cajun Shrimp, items for assembling Marinated Pork Party Sandwiches, Chunky Onion Dip with assorted fresh vegetables. (Recipes begin on following page.)

MARINATED PORK PARTY SANDWICHES

2 cups mayonnaise
2 tablespoons minced fresh chives
1½ tablespoons white wine
 vinegar
1¼ teaspoons ground ginger
¼ teaspoon salt
Pinch of paprika
3 (¾-pound) pork tenderloins
½ cup olive oil

3 tablespoons grated onion
3 tablespoons white wine vinegar
¾ teaspoon garlic powder
½ teaspoon salt
½ teaspoon chili powder
½ teaspoon dried oregano
Kale leaves (optional)
Cocktail rolls

Combine first 6 ingredients; cover and chill at least 8 hours. Trim fat from tenderloins. Place tenderloins in a large heavy-duty, zip-top plastic bag. Combine oil and next 6 ingredients; pour over tenderloins. Seal bag; marinate in refrigerator 8 hours, turning bag occasionally.

Remove tenderloins from marinade, reserving marinade. Place tenderloins on a rack in a shallow roasting pan. Insert meat thermometer into thickest portion of 1 tenderloin. Bake at 425° for 10 minutes. Reduce heat to 350°, and bake an additional 30 minutes or until meat thermometer registers 160°, basting occasionally with marinade. Let stand 10 minutes.

Cut tenderloins into ¼-inch slices, and arrange on a serving platter lined with kale leaves, if desired. Serve with mayonnaise mixture and cocktail rolls. Yield: 25 appetizer servings.

CAJUN SHRIMP

3 quarts water
1 large lemon, sliced
4 pounds unpeeled large fresh
 shrimp
2 cups vegetable oil
¼ cup hot sauce
1 tablespoon minced garlic
1 tablespoon olive oil

1½ teaspoons salt
1½ teaspoons seafood seasoning
1½ teaspoons dried basil
1½ teaspoons dried oregano
1½ teaspoons dried thyme
1½ teaspoons minced fresh
 parsley

Bring water and lemon to a boil; add shrimp, and cook 3 to 5 minutes or until shrimp turn pink. Drain well; rinse with cold water. Chill. Peel and devein shrimp. Place shrimp in a large heavy-duty, zip-top plastic bag.

Combine vegetable oil and remaining ingredients; stir well, and pour over shrimp. Seal bag; marinate in refrigerator 8 hours. Drain before serving. Yield: 25 appetizer servings.

SPINACH-STUFFED MUSHROOMS

1 (12-ounce) package frozen
  spinach soufflé
1 cup soft breadcrumbs, toasted
2 tablespoons grated Parmesan
  cheese
1 teaspoon dried minced onion
2 teaspoons lemon juice

¼ teaspoon salt
25 large fresh mushrooms
1 tablespoon butter or margarine,
  melted
Grated Parmesan cheese
Fresh spinach leaves (optional)
Garnish: pimiento strips

Bake frozen soufflé, uncovered, at 350° for 15 minutes or until slightly warm. Combine soufflé, breadcrumbs, and next 4 ingredients; set aside.

Clean mushrooms with damp paper towels. Remove stems; reserve for another use. Cook mushroom caps in butter in a large skillet over medium-high heat, stirring constantly, 5 minutes. Drain. Place caps on rack of a broiler pan, stem side up. Spoon spinach mixture evenly into mushroom caps; sprinkle with Parmesan cheese. Broil 5½ inches from heat (with electric oven door partially opened) 2 minutes or until thoroughly heated.

Arrange mushrooms on a large serving platter lined with fresh spinach leaves, if desired. Garnish, if desired. Yield: 25 appetizers.

Stuffed mushrooms aren't ideal for advance preparation, but you don't have to wait until the last minute either. Prepare the stuffing a few hours ahead; cover and chill. At the same time, clean the mushrooms and remove the stems; cover and chill. Just before the party, sauté the mushroom caps; then stuff and broil them.

CHUNKY ONION DIP

2 (8-ounce) packages cream
  cheese, softened
⅔ cup chili sauce
⅓ cup mayonnaise

½ teaspoon Worcestershire sauce
⅔ cup finely chopped onion
1 large cabbage (optional)

Combine first 4 ingredients; beat at medium speed of an electric mixer until smooth. Stir in onion. Cover and chill at least 2 hours.

If using a cabbage as a serving bowl, trim core end to form a flat base; fold back several outer leaves. Cut a crosswise slice from top of cabbage, removing about one-fourth of the head; lift out enough inner leaves to form a shell. Spoon dip into cabbage; serve with fresh vegetables. Yield: 3½ cups.

CHOCOLATE-PEPPERMINT BROWNIES

½ cup butter or margarine
2 (1-ounce) squares unsweetened
   chocolate
1 cup sugar
2 large eggs, lightly beaten
½ cup all-purpose flour
¼ teaspoon baking powder

¼ teaspoon salt
1 teaspoon vanilla extract
½ cup chopped pecans
Peppermint Frosting
1 tablespoon butter or margarine
1 (1-ounce) square unsweetened
   chocolate

Melt ½ cup butter and 2 chocolate squares in a large saucepan over low heat. Remove from heat, and let cool 10 minutes. Add sugar and eggs, stirring well. Combine flour, baking powder, and salt; add to chocolate mixture, stirring well. Stir in vanilla and pecans.

Spoon batter into a greased and floured 13- x 9- x 2-inch pan. Bake at 350° for 20 minutes or until a wooden pick inserted in center comes out clean. Cool brownies completely on a wire rack. Spread with Peppermint Frosting.

Melt 1 tablespoon butter and 1 chocolate square in a small saucepan over low heat. Remove from heat, and let cool. Spoon chocolate mixture into a small heavy-duty, zip-top plastic bag or a decorating bag fitted with tip No. 2; seal bag. Snip a tiny hole in one corner of zip-top bag, using scissors; pipe chocolate mixture in a decorative design over Peppermint Frosting. Cover and chill thoroughly. Cut into 2- x 1-inch bars. Store brownies in an airtight container in refrigerator. Yield: 4½ dozen.

Peppermint Frosting

¼ cup butter or margarine,
   softened
2 cups sifted powdered sugar
2 tablespoons whipping cream

1½ teaspoons peppermint
   flavoring
2 drops red food coloring

Beat butter at medium speed of an electric mixer until creamy; gradually add powdered sugar, beating well. Add whipping cream, flavoring, and food coloring; beat until frosting is spreading consistency. Yield: 1 cup.

CRESCENTS

1 cup butter or margarine,
softened
3 cups sifted powdered sugar,
divided

2 cups all-purpose flour
¼ teaspoon salt
2 teaspoons vanilla extract
2 cups finely chopped pecans

Beat butter at medium speed of an electric mixer until creamy. Add ½ cup powdered sugar; beat well. Combine flour and salt; gradually add flour mixture to butter mixture, beating at low speed just until blended after each addition. Stir in vanilla and pecans. Divide dough into fourths; cover and chill at least 2 hours.

Work with 1 portion of dough at a time, storing remainder in refrigerator. Divide each portion into 12 equal pieces. Roll each piece into a 2½-inch log; curve ends of each log to form a crescent. Place crescents 2 inches apart on lightly greased cookie sheets. Bake at 350° for 12 to 14 minutes or until very lightly browned. Cool on cookie sheets 1 minute.

Carefully roll warm cookies in 1½ cups powdered sugar; cool completely on a wire rack. Roll cooled cookies in remaining 1 cup powdered sugar. Store up to 1 week in an airtight container. Yield: 4 dozen.

BLUSHING CHAMPAGNE PUNCH

1 (12-ounce) can frozen cranberry
juice concentrate, thawed and
diluted
1 (7.5-ounce) bottle frozen lemon
juice, thawed
½ (12-ounce) can frozen
pineapple juice concentrate,
thawed and diluted

1 (6-ounce) can frozen orange
juice concentrate, thawed and
diluted
2 cups brandy
2 (750-milliliter) bottles
champagne, chilled

Combine first 5 ingredients in a large container, stirring well. Cover and chill.

Pour mixture into a large punch bowl; add champagne, stirring gently. Add ice cubes or an ice ring, if desired. Yield: about 6 quarts.

Welcome the Carolers

Shrimp Rémoulade
Chicken-and-Sausage Gumbo
Commercial French Bread
Iced Tea   White Wine
Pecan Tart with Praline Cream
Coffee

Serves 8

For a memorable holiday event, bundle up for an evening of caroling with friends. After countless rounds of "We Wish You a Merry Christmas" and "Jingle Bells," invite the gang for gumbo and other Cajun goodies. While the gumbo heats, have guests sample a truly delectable shrimp rémoulade. Then let everyone ladle bowls of the steaming gumbo to enjoy around the fireplace. After dinner, savor the pecan tart with a cup of robust coffee.

Pecan Tart with Praline Cream (page 63)

SHRIMP RÉMOULADE

¼ cup mayonnaise or salad
   dressing
¼ cup vegetable oil
3 tablespoons Dijon mustard
1 to 2 tablespoons prepared
   horseradish
1 tablespoon lemon juice
2 teaspoons chopped fresh parsley
1 teaspoon red wine vinegar
½ teaspoon paprika

2 cloves garlic, crushed
4½ cups water
1 tablespoon salt
1½ teaspoons liquid shrimp-
   and-crab boil seasoning
1½ pounds unpeeled medium-size
   fresh shrimp
6 cups shredded lettuce
Lettuce leaves

Combine first 9 ingredients in container of an electric blender. Process until smooth, stopping once to scrape down sides. Cover and chill thoroughly.

Combine water, salt, and seasoning in a Dutch oven; bring to a boil. Add shrimp, and cook 3 to 5 minutes or until shrimp turn pink. Drain well; rinse with cold water. Chill. Peel and devein shrimp.

Combine mayonnaise mixture, shrimp, and shredded lettuce, tossing to coat. Serve on lettuce leaves. Yield: 8 appetizer servings.

CHICKEN-AND-SAUSAGE GUMBO

Gumbo filé is a seasoning commonly used to thicken and flavor gumbos and other Creole dishes. It's made from the ground dried leaves of the sassafras tree and can be found in the spice section of most supermarkets. Stir filé into a dish after it's removed from the heat—cooking makes filé stringy and tough.

1 pound hot smoked link sausage,
   cut into ¼-inch slices
4 skinned chicken breast halves
¼ to ⅓ cup vegetable oil
¾ cup all-purpose flour
1 cup chopped onion
½ cup chopped green pepper
½ cup sliced celery
3 cloves garlic, minced

2 quarts hot water
2 teaspoons Creole seasoning
1 tablespoon Worcestershire sauce
½ teaspoon dried thyme
½ to 1 teaspoon hot sauce
2 bay leaves
½ cup sliced green onions
Hot cooked rice
Gumbo filé (optional)

Cook sausage in a Dutch oven over medium heat until browned. Remove sausage, reserving drippings. Set sausage aside. Cook chicken in drippings until browned. Remove chicken, reserving drippings.

Measure drippings, adding enough oil to measure ½ cup. Add oil mixture to Dutch oven; place over medium heat until hot. Add flour, and cook, stirring constantly, until roux is chocolate-colored (about 20 minutes).

Add chopped onion, green pepper, celery, and garlic to roux; cook until vegetables are tender, stirring often. Gradually stir in hot water; bring to a boil. Add chicken, Creole seasoning, and next 4 ingredients to Dutch oven; reduce heat, and simmer, uncovered, 1 hour, stirring occasionally.

Remove chicken from Dutch oven; set aside to cool. Add sausage to Dutch oven; cook, uncovered, 30 minutes. Stir in green onions; cook, uncovered, an additional 30 minutes. Bone chicken; coarsely shred. Add chicken to gumbo; cook until thoroughly heated. Remove and discard bay leaves. Serve gumbo over hot rice with gumbo filé, if desired. Yield: 8 servings.

PECAN TART WITH PRALINE CREAM

1 (9-inch) refrigerated piecrust
1 cup sugar
1 cup light corn syrup
⅓ cup butter or margarine
4 large eggs, lightly beaten
1 teaspoon vanilla extract
¼ teaspoon salt
1 cup pecan halves

¼ cup semisweet chocolate morsels
1 cup whipping cream
2 teaspoons praline liqueur
1 teaspoon vanilla extract
¼ cup sifted powdered sugar
Garnish: chocolate-dipped pecan halves

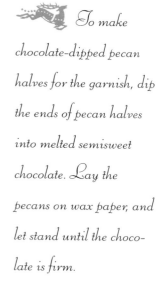 To make chocolate-dipped pecan halves for the garnish, dip the ends of pecan halves into melted semisweet chocolate. Lay the pecans on wax paper, and let stand until the chocolate is firm.

Roll piecrust into a 12-inch circle on a lightly floured surface. Place in a 9-inch round tart pan with removable bottom; roll over top of tart pan with a rolling pin to trim excess pastry. Prick bottom of piecrust with a fork. Line bottom of piecrust with parchment paper; fill with dried beans or pie weights. Bake at 450° for 5 minutes. Carefully remove beans and paper; bake an additional 2 minutes. Set aside.

Combine 1 cup sugar, corn syrup, and butter in a saucepan; cook over medium heat, stirring constantly, until sugar dissolves and butter melts. Cool slightly. Add eggs, 1 teaspoon vanilla, and salt; stir well. Pour into prepared piecrust; top with pecan halves. Bake at 325° for 55 minutes or until set.

Place chocolate morsels in a small heavy-duty, zip-top plastic bag; seal bag. Submerge bag in hot water until chocolate melts. Snip a tiny hole in 1 corner of bag using scissors; pipe chocolate in a decorative design over top of tart. Combine whipping cream, praline liqueur, and 1 teaspoon vanilla in a small mixing bowl; beat at medium speed of an electric mixer until mixture is foamy. Add powdered sugar, 1 tablespoon at a time, beating until soft peaks form. Serve whipped cream mixture with tart. Garnish, if desired. Yield: one 9-inch tart.

I'll Be Home for Christmas

Roast Pork with Creamy Mushroom Gravy
Holiday Potato Casserole
Broccoli with Bacon   Gingered Carrots
Frozen Yogurt Salad
Velvet Cream Biscuits or Commercial Rolls
Cran-Apple Pie

Iced Tea   Coffee

Serves 8

More than any other holiday, Christmas is a family time. And if you're hosting the holiday feast, you won't want to spend the day in the kitchen. This menu offers several recipes with make-ahead hints. The roast pork is a nice departure from turkey or ham, and it's a no-fuss recipe with down-home flavor. It's accompanied by side dishes that are sure to please.

Clockwise from top: Broccoli with Bacon, Gingered Carrots, Holiday Potato Casserole, Roast Pork with Creamy Mushroom Gravy. (Recipes begin on following page.)

65

ROAST PORK WITH CREAMY MUSHROOM GRAVY

4 to 5 cloves garlic
1½ teaspoons salt, divided
1 (3- to 3½-pound) boneless
   double pork loin roast, tied
2 tablespoons lemon juice

½ teaspoon freshly ground
   pepper
Garnishes: fresh baby pears,
   fresh rosemary sprigs
Creamy Mushroom Gravy

Cut garlic into ⅛-inch slices; sprinkle with ¼ teaspoon salt. Place roast, fat side up, on a greased rack in a shallow roasting pan. Cut ½-inch slits at 1-inch intervals in diagonal rows on top of roast; insert garlic slices deep into slits. Brush lemon juice evenly over roast; sprinkle with pepper and remaining 1¼ teaspoons salt.

Insert meat thermometer, making sure it does not touch fat. Bake, uncovered, at 325° for 1½ hours (30 minutes per pound) or until meat thermometer registers 160°. Transfer roast to a serving platter; let stand 10 minutes before slicing. Garnish, if desired. Serve with Creamy Mushroom Gravy. Yield: 8 servings.

Creamy Mushroom Gravy

1½ cups sliced fresh mushrooms
2 tablespoons butter or margarine,
   melted
1 tablespoon all-purpose flour
1 (8-ounce) carton sour cream

2 tablespoons milk
¼ teaspoon salt
¼ teaspoon freshly ground
   pepper

Cook mushrooms in butter in a small saucepan over medium-high heat, stirring constantly, until tender. Add flour, stirring well. Cook, stirring constantly, 1 minute. Combine sour cream and remaining ingredients; gradually add sour cream mixture to mushroom mixture, stirring constantly. Cook over medium-low heat, stirring constantly, just until mixture is thickened and thoroughly heated. (Do not boil.) Yield: 1½ cups.

HOLIDAY POTATO CASSEROLE

3 pounds baking potatoes, peeled
  and quartered
½ cup butter or margarine
2 (3-ounce) packages cream
  cheese, softened
1 cup (4 ounces) shredded
  Cheddar cheese, divided
¾ cup finely chopped green
  pepper

¾ cup finely chopped green
  onions
1 (2-ounce) jar diced pimiento,
  drained
½ cup grated Parmesan cheese
½ cup milk
1 teaspoon salt

Cook potato in boiling water to cover 15 minutes or until tender; drain and
mash. Add butter and cream cheese; beat at medium speed of an electric
mixer until smooth. Stir in ½ cup Cheddar cheese, green pepper, and remaining ingredients.

Spoon mixture into a lightly greased 11- x 7- x 1½-inch baking dish.
Bake, uncovered, at 350° for 25 to 30 minutes or until thoroughly heated.
Sprinkle with remaining ½ cup Cheddar cheese; bake an additional 5 min-
utes or until cheese melts. Yield: 8 servings.

Note: Casserole may be prepared ahead. Prepare as directed above; do not
bake. Cover and refrigerate up to 24 hours. Remove from refrigerator; let
stand, covered, 30 minutes. Uncover and bake as directed above.

BROCCOLI WITH BACON

2 pounds fresh broccoli
6 slices bacon

¾ cup coarsely chopped walnuts
½ cup chopped green onions

Remove broccoli leaves, and cut off tough ends of stalks; discard. Wash
broccoli thoroughly, and cut into spears. Cook broccoli spears in a small
amount of boiling water 6 to 8 minutes or just until tender; drain. Set aside,
and keep warm.

Cook bacon in a large skillet over medium heat until crisp; remove bacon,
reserving 3 tablespoons drippings in skillet. Crumble bacon, and set aside.
Cook walnuts and green onions in drippings, stirring constantly, until green
onions are tender. Add broccoli, and cook 1 minute, tossing gently. Transfer
mixture to a serving dish; sprinkle with bacon. Yield: 8 servings.

*Pecans may
be substituted for the
walnuts in Broccoli
with Bacon.*

GINGERED CARROTS

2 pounds carrots, scraped
2 tablespoons sugar
2 teaspoons cornstarch
½ teaspoon salt

½ teaspoon ground ginger
½ cup orange juice
2 tablespoons butter or margarine
Chopped fresh parsley (optional)

Cut carrots diagonally into ¼-inch slices. Cook carrot slices, covered, in a large saucepan in boiling water to cover 10 minutes or until tender. Drain. Set aside, and keep warm.

Combine sugar and next 3 ingredients in a small saucepan; gradually stir in orange juice. Bring to a boil over medium heat, stirring constantly; cook, stirring constantly, 1 minute. Remove from heat; add butter, stirring until butter melts. Pour mixture over carrot slices, tossing to coat. Transfer mixture to a serving dish, and sprinkle with chopped fresh parsley, if desired. Yield: 8 servings.

FROZEN YOGURT SALAD

 *After 10 to 15 minutes at room temperature, the frozen salads should release easily from the molds. It's best not to dip the molds in hot water to loosen the salads. This will quickly melt the surface of the salads.*

1 cup whipping cream
2 tablespoons honey
1 (15¼-ounce) can pineapple tidbits, drained
1 (10-ounce) package frozen sliced strawberries, thawed and undrained

1 (8-ounce) carton strawberry yogurt
Lettuce leaves

Beat whipping cream at medium speed of an electric mixer until soft peaks form; gradually add honey, beating until stiff peaks form. Fold in pineapple, strawberries, and yogurt. Spoon mixture into 8 lightly oiled ½-cup molds. Cover and freeze at least 8 hours.

Remove from refrigerator; let stand 10 to 15 minutes. Run a knife blade around edges to release salads from molds. Serve on lettuce leaves. Yield: 8 servings.

VELVET CREAM BISCUITS

4 cups all-purpose flour
2 tablespoons baking powder
1 teaspoon salt
2 tablespoons sugar

2½ cups whipping cream
2 tablespoons butter or
   margarine, melted

Combine first 4 ingredients in a large bowl; add whipping cream, stirring with a fork just until dry ingredients are moistened. Turn dough out onto a floured surface, and knead lightly 10 to 12 times.

Roll dough to ½-inch thickness; cut with a 2-inch biscuit cutter. Place biscuits on lightly greased baking sheets; bake at 425° for 12 minutes or until golden. Brush biscuits with melted butter. Yield: 2½ dozen.

Velvet Cream Biscuits offer a twist on the traditional biscuit made with shortening. Stirring in whipping cream is easier and quicker than cutting in shortening, and the result is a velvety smooth-textured biscuit.

CRAN-APPLE PIE

3 tablespoons butter or margarine
2 cups peeled, sliced cooking
   apple
⅔ cup sugar
⅓ cup firmly packed brown sugar
3 tablespoons cornstarch

1 tablespoon apple jelly
½ teaspoon ground cinnamon
2 cups fresh cranberries
1 unbaked 9-inch pastry shell
⅓ cup chopped pecans

Melt butter in a large heavy saucepan over medium heat. Add apple and next 5 ingredients; bring to a boil, stirring constantly. Cook, stirring constantly, 1 minute. Remove from heat; stir in cranberries.

Pour mixture into pastry shell; sprinkle with pecans. Bake at 400° for 20 minutes. Shield edges of pastry with aluminum foil; bake an additional 15 to 20 minutes or until set. Cool on a wire rack. Yield: one 9-inch pie.

New Year's Eve Dinner

Honey Spinach Salad
Roast Duckling with Tangerine Stuffing
Asparagus with Curry Sauce
Dilled Carrots
Sour Cream Yeast Rolls
Red Wine   Water
Lemon Cheesecake
Champagne   Coffee

Serves 4

Usher in the New Year with this cozy dinner for four. To help ease your busy holiday schedule, make the cheesecake a day or two ahead, and bake and freeze the rolls. Much of the vegetable preparation can be done in advance, leaving the entrée as your main project on the day of the party. As midnight approaches, offer a champagne toast to the memories of the past year and a salute to the surprises of the new.

Roast Duckling with Tangerine Stuffing (following page)

HONEY SPINACH SALAD

¼ teaspoon salt
1 clove garlic, crushed
⅓ cup honey
⅓ cup olive oil
1 tablespoon lemon juice

¾ pound fresh spinach
1 (11-ounce) can mandarin
 oranges, drained
¾ cup coarsely chopped walnuts,
 toasted

Sprinkle salt in a large bowl; add garlic. Mash garlic to a paste, using the back of a spoon. Combine honey, olive oil, and lemon juice in a jar. Cover tightly, and shake vigorously. Add honey mixture to garlic mixture; stir well. Cover and chill at least 2 hours.

Remove stems from spinach; wash leaves thoroughly, and pat dry. Tear leaves into bite-size pieces. Combine spinach, oranges, and walnuts in a large bowl; toss well. Pour honey mixture over salad, tossing to coat. Serve immediately. Yield: 4 to 6 servings.

ROAST DUCKLING WITH TANGERINE STUFFING

1 (5-pound) dressed duckling
¼ teaspoon salt
⅛ teaspoon pepper
½ lemon
Tangerine Stuffing (facing page)

¼ teaspoon lemon-pepper
 seasoning
Garnishes: red grapes, orange
 wedges, lemon wedges, lime
 wedges, celery leaves

Remove giblets and neck from duckling; reserve for another use. Rinse duckling with cold water; pat dry. Sprinkle cavity with salt and pepper. Rub duckling with lemon half, squeezing juice over duckling.

Spoon Tangerine Stuffing into cavity of duckling; close cavity with skewers, and truss. Place duckling on a rack in a shallow roasting pan, breast side up. Insert meat thermometer into meaty portion of thigh, making sure it does not touch bone. Bake, uncovered, at 325° for 1½ hours. Sprinkle duckling with lemon-pepper seasoning, and bake an additional 20 to 30 minutes or until meat thermometer registers 180°. Cover loosely with aluminum foil to prevent excessive browning, if necessary. Transfer duckling to a serving platter; let stand 10 minutes before carving. Garnish, if desired. Yield: 4 servings.

Tangerine Stuffing

⅓ cup chopped celery
3 tablespoons butter or
 margarine, melted
2⅔ cups herb-seasoned
 stuffing mix
2 cups cooked wild rice

2 tangerines, peeled, sectioned,
 and chopped
⅓ cup fresh cranberries
⅓ cup chicken broth
¼ teaspoon poultry seasoning

Cook celery in butter in a small skillet over medium-high heat, stirring constantly, until tender. Combine celery mixture, stuffing mix, and remaining ingredients in a large bowl; stir well. Yield: 5½ cups.

ASPARAGUS WITH CURRY SAUCE

½ cup mayonnaise or salad
 dressing
2½ teaspoons curry powder

1½ teaspoons lemon juice
1 pound fresh asparagus
2 tablespoons capers

Combine first 3 ingredients; stir well. Cover and chill.
 Snap off tough ends of asparagus. Remove scales from stalks with a knife or vegetable peeler, if desired. Cook asparagus, covered, in a small amount of boiling water 6 to 8 minutes or until crisp-tender; drain. Arrange asparagus on a serving platter; top with curry mixture, and sprinkle with capers. Yield: 4 servings.

Note: Two (10-ounce) packages frozen asparagus spears, thawed, may be substituted for fresh asparagus.

Capers are the flower buds of a Mediterranean bush. The buds are picked, sun-dried, and then pickled in a vinegar brine. They lend a tangy flavor to many sauces and condiments.

DILLED CARROTS

1 (16-ounce) package frozen
 whole baby carrots
1 teaspoon sugar

1 tablespoon butter or margarine
1 teaspoon dried dillweed

Cook carrots according to package directions, adding sugar to water; drain well. Add butter and dillweed, tossing gently until butter melts and carrots are evenly coated. Yield: 4 servings.

SOUR CREAM YEAST ROLLS

2 cups all-purpose flour
¼ cup sugar
½ teaspoon salt
1 package active dry yeast
½ cup sour cream

¼ cup water
¼ cup butter or margarine
1 large egg
2 egg whites, lightly beaten

Combine first 4 ingredients in a large mixing bowl; stir well. Combine sour cream, water, and butter in a saucepan; heat until butter melts, stirring occasionally. Cool to 120° to 130°.

Gradually add liquid mixture to flour mixture, beating well at low speed of an electric mixer. Beat an additional 2 minutes at medium speed. Add 1 egg; beat well. Cover and refrigerate 8 hours.

Punch dough down, and divide in half. Roll 1 portion of dough into a 12-inch circle on a floured surface; cut into 12 wedges. Roll up each wedge, beginning at wide end. Seal points, and place on greased baking sheets, point side down. Repeat procedure with remaining portion of dough.

Cover and let rise in a warm place (85°), free from drafts, 45 minutes or until doubled in bulk. Gently brush with egg whites. Bake at 375° for 10 minutes or until golden. Yield: 2 dozen.

LEMON CHEESECAKE

¾ cup graham cracker crumbs
2 tablespoons sugar
1 tablespoon ground cinnamon
1 tablespoon butter or margarine, melted
5 (8-ounce) packages cream cheese, softened
1⅔ cups sugar

5 large eggs
1 teaspoon grated lemon rind
¼ cup lemon juice
1½ teaspoons vanilla extract
⅛ teaspoon salt
Garnishes: lemon twists, fresh mint sprigs

Combine first 3 ingredients; stir well. Brush bottom and sides of a 10-inch springform pan with melted butter. Add crumb mixture, tilting pan to coat sides and bottom. Chill.

Beat cream cheese at medium speed of an electric mixer until creamy; gradually add 1⅔ cups sugar, beating well. Add eggs, one at a time, beating after each addition. Stir in lemon rind, lemon juice, vanilla, and salt. Pour mixture into prepared pan. Bake at 300° for 1 hour and 20 minutes. (Center may be soft but will set when chilled.) Cool on a wire rack; cover and chill at least 8 hours. Garnish, if desired. Yield: 10 to 12 servings.

Toast the old year and welcome the new with a glass of bubbly champagne and a slice of rich Lemon Cheesecake. Lemon twists and mint sprigs add a pretty touch.

In the Nick of Time

Along with Christmas comes a festive spirit that makes a party of every gathering, no matter how planned or spontaneous. It's a time for family and friends, for children, teens, and grown-ups to enjoy each other's company in groups both large and small. But with gifts to wrap, confections to make, and parties to attend, there is little time to prepare for these occasions. With make-ahead menus and quick recipes, you'll be ready to host a spur-of-the-moment event and still feel relaxed enough to enjoy it along with your guests.

"Teen Fiesta Italiano" menu. *Clockwise from top left:* Marinated Vegetables, Mexican Slush, Blender Chile Dip with tortilla chips, Stromboli. (Recipes begin on page 92.)

Early Start on Brunch

Overnight Bloody Marys
Country Grits-and-Sausage Casserole
Hot Fruit Bake
Sour Cream Coffee Cake
Orange Juice   Coffee

Serves 8

If you'd rather be involved in the excitement of opening gifts instead of cooking in the kitchen on Christmas morning, you'll welcome this menu. Our midmorning brunch is festive enough to suit the occasion and hearty enough to satisfy any appetite. While grown-ups toast the day with Overnight Bloody Marys, the younger set can enjoy a refreshing glass of orange juice. Best of all, the recipes can be prepared the day before.

Country Grits-and-Sausage Casserole, Overnight Bloody Marys. (Recipes begin on following page.)

OVERNIGHT BLOODY MARYS

1 (46-ounce) can tomato juice
1 (46-ounce) can vegetable juice
1 cup lemon juice
½ cup water
2 tablespoons Worcestershire sauce

1 teaspoon salt
½ teaspoon seasoned salt
3 cups vodka
Garnish: celery stalks

Combine first 7 ingredients in a large container; stir well. Cover and chill at least 8 hours. Stir in vodka just before serving. Serve over ice. Garnish, if desired. Yield: 1 gallon.

COUNTRY GRITS-AND-SAUSAGE CASSEROLE

To punch up the flavor, use one pound of mild sausage and one pound of hot in Country Grits-and-Sausage Casserole. Or if you're really brave, use hot sausage exclusively— but beware!

2 pounds mild ground pork
  sausage
4 cups water
1¼ cups quick-cooking grits,
  uncooked
4 cups (1 pound) shredded sharp
  Cheddar cheese

1 cup milk
½ teaspoon dried thyme
⅛ teaspoon garlic powder
4 large eggs, lightly beaten
Paprika
Garnishes: tomato wedges, fresh
  parsley sprigs

Brown sausage in a large skillet, stirring until it crumbles. Drain well, and set aside.

Bring water to a boil in a large saucepan; stir in grits. Return to a boil; cover, reduce heat, and simmer 5 minutes, stirring occasionally. Remove from heat; add cheese and next 3 ingredients, stirring until cheese melts. Stir in sausage and eggs.

Spoon mixture into a lightly greased 13- x 9- x 2-inch baking dish, and sprinkle with paprika. Bake at 350° for 1 hour or until golden and thoroughly heated. Let stand 5 minutes before serving. Garnish, if desired. Yield: 8 to 10 servings.

Note: Casserole may be prepared ahead. Prepare grits mixture as directed above; do not bake. Cover and refrigerate overnight. Remove from refrigerator; let stand, covered, 30 minutes. Uncover and bake as directed above.

HOT FRUIT BAKE

1 (20-ounce) can sliced pineapple
1 (17-ounce) can apricot halves
1 (16-ounce) can peach halves
1 (16-ounce) can pear halves
1 (14½-ounce) jar spiced apple
  rings

⅓ cup butter or margarine
½ cup sugar
1 tablespoon cornstarch
1 cup dry sherry

Drain first 5 ingredients, reserving juices for another use. Combine fruit in a 2-quart casserole; set aside.

Melt butter in a small saucepan over medium-low heat. Combine sugar and cornstarch; add to butter, stirring constantly. Stir in sherry. Cook, stirring constantly, until mixture is slightly thickened; pour over fruit mixture. Bake at 350° for 35 to 40 minutes or until bubbly. Yield: 8 servings.

To prepare Hot Fruit Bake ahead of time, assemble the fruit and sherry mixture as directed; do not bake. Cover and refrigerate overnight. Remove from refrigerator; let stand, covered, 30 minutes. Uncover and bake as directed.

SOUR CREAM COFFEE CAKE

½ cup chopped pecans
2 tablespoons brown sugar
2 teaspoons ground cinnamon
1 cup butter or margarine,
  softened
1 cup sugar
2 large eggs
2 cups all-purpose flour

1 teaspoon baking powder
1 teaspoon baking soda
1 (8-ounce) carton sour cream
1 teaspoon vanilla extract
1¼ cups sifted powdered sugar
1½ tablespoons water
¾ teaspoon vanilla extract

Combine first 3 ingredients in a small bowl; set aside. Beat butter at medium speed of an electric mixer until creamy; gradually add 1 cup sugar, beating well. Add eggs; beat well. Combine flour, baking powder, and soda in a medium bowl; add to butter mixture alternately with sour cream, beginning and ending with flour mixture. Mix after each addition. Stir in 1 teaspoon vanilla.

Pour half of batter into a greased and floured 12-cup Bundt pan; sprinkle half of pecan mixture over batter. Repeat layers. Bake at 375° for 30 to 35 minutes or until a wooden pick inserted in center comes out clean. Cool in pan on a wire rack 10 minutes; remove from pan, and let cool completely on wire rack. Combine powdered sugar, water, and ¾ teaspoon vanilla; drizzle over cake. Yield: one 10-inch coffee cake.

An After-Shopping Feast

Creamy Clam Spread
Assorted Crackers
Kielbasa-Vegetable Dinner
Spoon Rolls
Tart Lemon Pie
Iced Tea   Coffee

Serves 6

It's time for the annual Christmas shopping expedition with your friends, and you've invited them for supper afterward. With this easy-to-manage menu and an hour of prep time before heading out to the mall, you can return home to host a relaxing meal. The clam spread and pie, as well as the batter for the rolls, may be prepared in the morning. You can also go ahead and slice the sausage and cut up the vegetables. (Cover the potato slices with water to prevent their turning brown.) All that will be left to do is bake the rolls and finish preparing the main course.

Kielbasa-Vegetable Dinner, Spoon Rolls. (Recipes begin on following page.)

CREAMY CLAM SPREAD

2 (3-ounce) packages cream
  cheese, softened
1 (6½-ounce) can minced clams,
  drained

2 green onions, finely chopped
1 tablespoon honey mustard
1 tablespoon milk

Combine all ingredients; stir well. Spoon into a serving bowl; cover and chill up to 24 hours. Serve with assorted crackers. Yield: 1 cup.

KIELBASA-VEGETABLE DINNER

To save time, use packaged fresh broccoli flowerets from the produce section and frozen chopped onion to make Kielbasa-Vegetable Dinner.

1½ pounds fresh broccoli
3 slices bacon
1½ pounds small red potatoes,
  thinly sliced
1 cup chopped onion

½ teaspoon dried marjoram
1½ pounds kielbasa, cut into
  ½-inch slices
1½ cups thinly sliced carrot
1 cup water

Remove broccoli leaves, and cut off tough ends of stalks; discard. Wash broccoli thoroughly, and break into flowerets. Set aside.

Cook bacon in a large Dutch oven until crisp; remove bacon, reserving drippings. Crumble bacon, and set aside. Cook potato slices, onion, and marjoram in reserved drippings in Dutch oven over medium heat 7 minutes, stirring frequently.

Add broccoli, kielbasa, carrot, and water to vegetable mixture; bring mixture to a boil. Cover, reduce heat, and simmer 20 to 25 minutes or until potato is tender, stirring occasionally. Spoon into soup bowls; sprinkle with bacon. Yield: 6 servings.

SPOON ROLLS

The yeast flavor in Spoon Rolls will intensify the longer the batter stands after preparation.

1 package active dry yeast
2 cups plus 2 tablespoons warm
  water (105° to 115°), divided
½ cup vegetable oil

¼ cup sugar
1 large egg, lightly beaten
4 cups self-rising flour

Combine yeast and 2 tablespoons warm water in a 1-cup liquid measuring cup; let stand 5 minutes. Combine yeast mixture, remaining 2 cups water, oil, and remaining ingredients in a large mixing bowl; stir until smooth. Cover and refrigerate batter at least 4 hours or up to 3 days.

Stir batter, and spoon into greased muffin pans, filling two-thirds full. Bake at 400° for 20 to 25 minutes or until golden. Remove rolls from pans immediately. Yield: 1½ dozen.

TART LEMON PIE

2 medium lemons	**½ cup butter or margarine, melted**
6 large eggs, lightly beaten	**1 unbaked 9-inch pastry shell**
2½ cups sugar	**Frozen whipped topping, thawed**
¼ cup fresh lemon juice	**Garnish: thin lemon wedges**

Grate rind from lemons; set grated rind aside. Remove and discard pith from lemons. Quarter and seed lemons.

Combine lemon, grated rind, eggs, sugar, and lemon juice in container of an electric blender; process 1 minute or until smooth, stopping once to scrape down sides. Add butter; process 30 seconds. Pour mixture into pastry shell. Bake at 350° for 40 to 45 minutes or until set. Cool on a wire rack. Serve with whipped topping. Garnish, if desired. Yield: one 9-inch pie.

Tart Lemon Pie is equally delicious served at room temperature or chilled.

Saint Nick Party

Easy Cheesy Bobolis
Christmas Confetti Dip
Assorted Fresh Vegetables
Reindeer Nibbles
Santa's Hats
Frosted Pretzels
Commercial Fruit Punch

Serves 8

*A*dd a little excitement to the holidays with a children's party, and make Saint Nick the honored guest. After the children spend a few minutes on Santa's knee, let them help assemble the Easy Cheesy Bobolis. For dessert, the little ones will enjoy adding the "hat" to Santa's Hats by squirting on the canned whipped cream. To extend the Christmas spirit, have the youngsters fill small bags with any extra Reindeer Nibbles for a take-home treat.

From top left: Reindeer Nibbles, Easy Cheesy Bobolis, Christmas Confetti Dip with assorted fresh vegetables. (Recipes begin on following page.)

EASY CHEESY BOBOLIS

Bobolis are baked pizza crusts available in the deli section of many grocery stores. Eight (six-inch) pita bread rounds may be substituted.

8 (6-inch) Bobolis
1 (14-ounce) jar pizza sauce
1 (3½-ounce) package pepperoni
   slices

1 (8-ounce) package shredded
   mozzarella cheese

Place Bobolis on ungreased baking sheets. Spread pizza sauce evenly over Bobolis. Top evenly with pepperoni slices, and sprinkle evenly with cheese. Bake at 350° for 15 minutes or until cheese melts and Bobolis are thoroughly heated. Yield: 8 servings.

CHRISTMAS CONFETTI DIP

⅔ cup sour cream
⅓ cup mayonnaise or salad
   dressing
1 (2-ounce) jar diced pimiento,
   drained

2 tablespoons finely chopped
   fresh chives
1 tablespoon finely chopped onion
⅛ teaspoon garlic salt

Combine all ingredients; cover and chill up to 2 days. Serve with assorted fresh vegetables. Yield: 1 cup.

REINDEER NIBBLES

⅔ cup honey
⅔ cup creamy peanut butter
½ teaspoon ground cinnamon
1 teaspoon vanilla extract

4 cups regular oats, uncooked
1 cup unsalted peanuts
1½ cups raisins

Combine first 3 ingredients in a small saucepan; cook over medium heat, stirring constantly, until mixture is thoroughly heated. (Do not boil.) Remove from heat; stir in vanilla.

Spread oats in a lightly greased 15- x 10- x 1-inch jellyroll pan. Pour peanut butter mixture over oats; stir to coat evenly. Bake at 300° for 25 minutes, stirring occasionally. Stir in peanuts. Turn oven off; let cool in oven 1½ hours with oven door closed, stirring occasionally. Remove from oven; stir in raisins. Store in an airtight container. Yield: 8½ cups.

The children can help assemble Santa's Hats for dessert. Serve them with Frosted Pretzels, which can be prepared ahead of time.

SANTA'S HATS

½ gallon cherry-vanilla ice cream
1 (1-liter) bottle ginger ale, chilled
1 (8.75-ounce) can refrigerated
   instant whipped cream
Red decorator sugar crystals
8 maraschino cherries with stems

Divide ice cream evenly among 8 glasses; pour ½ cup ginger ale over each. Top each with whipped cream, sugar crystals, and a cherry. Yield: 8 servings.

FROSTED PRETZELS

1 cup ready-to-spread vanilla
   frosting
24 large thin pretzel twists

Place frosting in a glass bowl; microwave at HIGH 30 to 45 seconds or until frosting melts, stirring once. Dip half of each pretzel into frosting. Place on wax paper; let dry at least 2 hours. Serve same day. Yield: 2 dozen.

Teen Fiesta Italiano

Stromboli

Marinated Vegetables

Blender Chile Dip
Tortilla Chips

Mexican Slush

Vanilla Ice Cream
Commercial Caramel or Hot Fudge Topping

Serves 8

When school bells ring to signal the beginning of Christmas break, the teenagers at your house will be ready for fun. Encourage them to plan a community project with their friends. Then help them host a casual party with a menu that features international flavors and offers good reason to celebrate — it can be made ahead! To add excitement, hang a candy-filled piñata for a fun finale to the day.

Mexican Slush, Blender Chile Dip with tortilla chips, and, on plate, Stromboli, Marinated Vegetables. (Recipes begin on following page.)

STROMBOLI

To make Stromboli ahead of time, assemble the loaves as directed; do not bake. Cover and refrigerate up to eight hours. (The dough may rise slightly.) Uncover and bake as directed.

½ pound ground beef
½ cup chopped onion
1 (32-ounce) package frozen bread dough, thawed and divided
2 tablespoons prepared mustard, divided
12 (¾-ounce) slices American cheese, divided

2 cups (8 ounces) shredded mozzarella cheese, divided
2 (3½-ounce) packages sliced pepperoni, divided
2 teaspoons dried Italian seasoning, divided
Vegetable oil

Brown ground beef and onion in a large skillet, stirring until meat crumbles. Drain well, and set aside.

For each stromboli, place 1 loaf bread dough on a lightly floured surface; roll dough into a 12-inch square. Spread 1 tablespoon mustard over dough to within ½ inch of edges. Layer 3 slices American cheese, ½ cup mozzarella cheese, half of pepperoni, and half of beef mixture lengthwise down center third of dough, leaving a ½-inch border at top and bottom of dough; sprinkle with 1 teaspoon Italian seasoning. Top with ½ cup mozzarella cheese and 3 slices American cheese. Fold each side of dough over filling; pinch seam and ends to seal.

Transfer loaves to greased baking sheets; brush loaves with oil. Bake at 350° for 25 minutes or until lightly browned. Cut each loaf into 8 slices. Yield: 8 servings.

MARINATED VEGETABLES

2 small green peppers
1 small cauliflower, broken into flowerets
1 pound carrots, scraped and cut into very thin strips
5 stalks celery, cut into very thin strips
1½ cups tarragon vinegar

¾ cup vegetable oil
¼ cup sugar
1½ teaspoons prepared mustard
1 teaspoon dried tarragon
½ teaspoon salt
¼ teaspoon pepper
2 cloves garlic, minced

Cut green peppers crosswise into ¼-inch rings; cut pepper rings in half. Combine green pepper, cauliflower, carrot, and celery in a large bowl.

Combine vinegar and remaining ingredients in a jar. Cover tightly, and shake vigorously. Pour over vegetable mixture, tossing gently to combine. Cover and marinate in refrigerator at least 8 hours, tossing occasionally. Serve with a slotted spoon. Yield: 10 servings.

BLENDER CHILE DIP

1 small onion, quartered
1 dried hot red chile
1 clove garlic
1 (16-ounce) can whole tomatoes,
  drained

½ teaspoon salt
¼ teaspoon ground oregano
⅛ teaspoon ground cumin

Combine first 3 ingredients in container of an electric blender. Process 30 seconds or until chile is minced, stopping twice to scrape down sides. Add tomatoes and remaining ingredients; pulse until tomatoes are chopped. Transfer mixture to a bowl; cover and chill at least 8 hours. Serve with tortilla or corn chips. Yield: 1½ cups.

MEXICAN SLUSH

1 (12-ounce) can frozen lemonade
  concentrate
2 (6-ounce) cans frozen limeade
  concentrate

½ cup sifted powdered sugar
6 cups crushed ice
3 cups club soda, chilled
Garnish: lime slices

Combine half of each of the first 4 ingredients in container of an electric blender. Process until mixture is smooth. Pour mixture into a large freezer container. Repeat procedure with remaining half of first 4 ingredients. Cover and freeze until firm.

Remove mixture from freezer; let stand 10 minutes. Add club soda, stirring until mixture is desired consistency. Pour into glasses, and garnish, if desired. Yield: 2½ quarts.

Easy Entertaining

Parsley-Dill Dip
Assorted Fresh Vegetables
Shrimp au Gratin
Brussels Sprouts Polonaise
Ruby-and-Emerald Salad
Commercial French Bread
White Wine   Water
Commercial Cheesecake
Coffee

Serves 6

Take a much-needed break from the hustle and bustle of the holidays with an evening of relaxed dining. This menu features Shrimp au Gratin, an elegant dish that's assembled one day and baked the next. Welcome your guests with a glass of wine and Parsley-Dill Dip with fresh vegetable dippers. Make the dip the night before, but prepare the vegetables the day of the party.

Shrimp au Gratin, Brussels Sprouts Polonaise, Ruby-and-Emerald Salad. (Recipes begin on following page.)

PARSLEY-DILL DIP

Parsley-Dill Dip develops more flavor the longer it chills, so prepare it at least six hours or up to two days ahead.

½ cup mayonnaise
½ cup sour cream
1 tablespoon chopped fresh
  parsley or 1 teaspoon dried
  parsley flakes

1 teaspoon dried dillweed
1 teaspoon minced onion
1 to 1½ teaspoons hot sauce
½ to ¾ teaspoon seasoned salt

Combine all ingredients in a small bowl; cover and chill at least 6 hours. Serve with assorted fresh vegetables. Yield: 1 cup.

SHRIMP AU GRATIN

2½ quarts water
3 pounds unpeeled medium-size
  fresh shrimp
⅓ cup butter or margarine
⅓ cup all-purpose flour
1 cup chicken broth
1 cup whipping cream
1 cup (4 ounces) shredded
  Swiss cheese

2½ tablespoons dry sherry
1 teaspoon Worcestershire sauce
¼ teaspoon salt
⅛ teaspoon ground white pepper
⅛ teaspoon hot sauce
3 tablespoons grated Parmesan
  cheese
Hot cooked angel hair pasta

Bring water to a boil; add shrimp, and cook 3 to 5 minutes or until shrimp turn pink. Drain well; rinse with cold water. Chill. Peel and devein shrimp. Set aside.

Melt butter in a heavy saucepan over low heat; add flour, stirring until smooth. Cook, stirring constantly, 1 minute. Gradually add chicken broth and whipping cream; cook over medium heat, stirring constantly, until mixture is thickened and bubbly. Add Swiss cheese and next 5 ingredients, stirring until cheese melts. Stir in shrimp.

Spoon shrimp mixture into a lightly greased 2-quart baking dish; sprinkle evenly with Parmesan cheese. Bake at 350° for 40 minutes or until mixture is thoroughly heated and bubbly. Serve shrimp mixture over hot pasta. Yield: 6 servings.

Note: Shrimp au Gratin may be prepared ahead. Prepare shrimp mixture as directed above; do not bake. Cover and refrigerate up to 8 hours. Remove from refrigerator; let stand, covered, 30 minutes. Uncover and bake as directed above.

BRUSSELS SPROUTS POLONAISE

1½ pounds fresh brussels sprouts
2¼ cups water
¼ cup fine, dry breadcrumbs
1 hard-cooked large egg, sieved

2 tablespoons chopped fresh
 parsley
1 tablespoon butter or margarine,
 melted

Wash brussels sprouts thoroughly, and remove discolored leaves. Cut off stem ends, and slash bottom of each sprout with a shallow X.

Combine brussels sprouts and water in a saucepan; bring to a boil. Cover, reduce heat, and simmer 12 to 15 minutes or until tender. Drain; transfer to a serving bowl, and keep warm.

Combine breadcrumbs and remaining ingredients; sprinkle over brussels sprouts, and toss lightly. Yield: 6 servings.

RUBY-AND-EMERALD SALAD

1½ cups tomato juice, divided
1 (3-ounce) package lemon-
 flavored gelatin
½ cup beer
1 tablespoon white vinegar
½ cup finely chopped celery
¼ cup finely chopped green
 pepper

2 green onions, chopped
1 (2-ounce) jar diced pimiento,
 drained
Lettuce leaves
Garnishes: green pepper cutouts,
 green onion curls

Use tiny canapé cutters to make the green pepper cutouts that garnish Ruby-and-Emerald Salad.

Bring 1 cup tomato juice to a boil; remove from heat. Add gelatin, stirring 2 minutes or until gelatin dissolves. Add remaining ½ cup tomato juice, beer, and vinegar. Chill until the consistency of unbeaten egg white.

Fold in finely chopped celery and next 3 ingredients. Spoon mixture into 6 lightly oiled ⅔-cup molds or a lightly oiled 4-cup mold. Cover and chill until firm. Unmold onto a lettuce-lined serving platter, and garnish, if desired. Yield: 6 to 8 servings.

Christmas Recipes

Merry Party Starters

Parties make the holidays memorable, and appetizers and beverages make the parties. Get your festivities off to the right start with an irresistible display of food shared in the spirit of the season. A busy hostess will welcome these recipes because many can be prepared ahead. In fact, we've found that appetizers such as Holiday Cheese Spread and Antipasto Spread with Toast Rounds (page 104) actually improve in flavor when stored a couple of days in the refrigerator. Plenty of tempting hors d'oeuvres go a long way toward making a party outstanding. And whether you welcome guests with cups of spiced wassail or spiked eggnog, pour our best for your holiday guests to toast the season.

Clockwise from top: Roasted Pepper Strips and Endive (page 109), Mushroom Pâté (page 107), Holiday Pastry Swirls (page 108).

GRAND MARNIER DIP FOR FRUIT

3 egg yolks, lightly beaten
⅓ cup sugar
¼ teaspoon salt

¼ cup Grand Marnier or other orange-flavored liqueur
2 cups whipping cream, whipped

Combine first 3 ingredients in a small saucepan; cook over medium heat, stirring constantly, until temperature reaches 160°. Stir in liqueur; let cool.

Fold whipped cream into liqueur mixture. Cover and chill up to 4 hours. Serve with assorted fresh fruit. Yield: 4¾ cups.

MEXICAN ARTICHOKE DIP

1 (14-ounce) can artichoke hearts, drained and chopped
1 cup grated Parmesan cheese

¾ cup mayonnaise
1 (4-ounce) can chopped green chiles, undrained

Combine all ingredients; stir well. Spoon mixture into a lightly greased 1-quart baking dish. Bake, uncovered, at 350° for 20 minutes or until lightly browned. Serve warm with tortilla chips or Melba rounds. Yield: 2¾ cups.

LAYERED NACHO DIP

Homemade guacamole may be substituted for the frozen avocado dip in Layered Nacho Dip.

2 (16-ounce) cans refried beans
1 (4-ounce) can chopped green chiles, drained
1 (1.25-ounce) package taco seasoning
2 cups (8 ounces) shredded Monterey Jack cheese with jalapeño peppers

1 (6-ounce) can frozen avocado dip, thawed
1 (8-ounce) carton sour cream
1 cup seeded and chopped tomato
¾ cup thinly sliced green onions
1 (4½-ounce) can sliced ripe olives, drained

Combine first 3 ingredients; spread mixture in an 11- x 7- x 1½-inch baking dish. Bake, uncovered, at 350° for 20 minutes or until thoroughly heated. Sprinkle with cheese; bake an additional 5 minutes or until cheese melts.

Spread avocado dip over warm bean mixture; spread sour cream over avocado dip. Top evenly with tomato, green onions, and olives. Serve warm with tortilla chips or corn chips. Yield: 10 to 12 appetizer servings.

ALMOND CHEESE

1 (8-ounce) package cream cheese, softened
1 (3-ounce) package cream cheese, softened
¼ cup butter or margarine, softened
½ cup sour cream
2 tablespoons sugar

1 envelope unflavored gelatin
¼ cup cold water
1 cup slivered almonds, toasted and coarsely chopped
½ cup golden raisins
1 teaspoon grated lemon rind
½ teaspoon almond extract
Garnish: fresh strawberry halves

Combine cream cheese and butter in a large mixing bowl; beat at medium speed of an electric mixer until soft and creamy. Add sour cream and sugar, beating until well blended.

Sprinkle gelatin over cold water in a small saucepan; let stand 1 minute. Cook over low heat, stirring until gelatin dissolves, about 2 minutes. Add to cream cheese mixture, beating well. Stir in almonds and next 3 ingredients. Spoon mixture into a lightly oiled 1-quart mold. Cover and chill until firm or up to 2 days.

Unmold cheese onto a serving platter, and garnish, if desired. Serve with gingersnaps or lightly sweetened crackers. Yield: 3½ cups.

APRICOT BRIE SPREAD

½ cup water
¼ cup chopped dried apricots
2 teaspoons brandy

1 (15-ounce) round Brie cheese
2 tablespoons chopped pecans
Garnish: dried apricot rose

Combine first 3 ingredients in a small saucepan; bring to a boil over medium heat. Cook, stirring constantly, 5 minutes or until apricots are soft.

Remove rind from top of cheese, cutting to within ¼ inch of outside edge. Place cheese on a baking sheet; top evenly with warm apricot mixture and chopped pecans. Broil 8 inches from heat (with electric oven door partially opened) 2 to 4 minutes or until cheese softens slightly. Carefully transfer cheese to a serving platter, and garnish, if desired. Serve with gingersnaps or lightly sweetened crackers. Yield: 8 to 10 appetizer servings.

Brie cheese is characterized by an edible, soft white rind and a cream-colored, buttery interior that should ooze when the cheese is at the peak of ripeness.

ANTIPASTO SPREAD WITH TOAST ROUNDS

An Italian term meaning "before the pasta," antipasto is an hors d'oeuvre that includes an assortment of such items as marinated vegetables, olives, cheeses, smoked meats, and fish. Antipasto Spread with Toast Rounds is an easy, make-ahead medley of many of these foods.

1 (13-ounce) package French baguettes
⅓ cup olive oil
1 (14-ounce) can artichoke hearts, drained and finely chopped
1 (4¼-ounce) can chopped ripe olives, drained
1 (4-ounce) can sliced mushrooms, drained and finely chopped
1 (2-ounce) jar diced pimiento, drained

¼ cup chopped green pepper
¼ cup chopped celery
¾ cup olive oil
¼ cup white wine vinegar
1 tablespoon dried Italian seasoning
2 tablespoons water
¼ teaspoon pepper
⅛ teaspoon salt
1 clove garlic, crushed

Cut baguettes into ⅜-inch-thick slices; lightly brush 1 side of baguette slices with ⅓ cup olive oil; place slices, oil side up, on baking sheets. Bake at 400° for 8 to 10 minutes or until crisp and golden. Set aside.

Combine artichoke hearts and next 5 ingredients, tossing gently to combine. Combine ¾ cup olive oil and remaining ingredients in a large jar. Cover tightly, and shake vigorously. Add oil mixture to vegetable mixture, tossing gently to coat. Cover and chill. Drain well before serving; serve with toast rounds. Yield: 16 appetizer servings.

HOLIDAY CHEESE SPREAD

3 cups (12 ounces) shredded sharp Cheddar cheese
1 (8-ounce) package cream cheese, softened
½ cup finely chopped onion
2 tablespoons mayonnaise or salad dressing

1 tablespoon prepared mustard
1 teaspoon celery seeds
1 teaspoon garlic powder
1 teaspoon Worcestershire sauce
1 teaspoon hot sauce

Position knife blade in food processor bowl; add all ingredients. Process 2 minutes or until mixture is smooth, stopping once to scrape down sides. Spoon cheese mixture into a serving container; cover and chill at least 8 hours and up to 5 days. Let stand at room temperature 1 hour before serving. Serve with unsalted crackers. Yield: 2½ cups.

CAVIAR-CREAM CHEESE SPREAD

2 (8-ounce) packages cream cheese, softened

1 (3-ounce) package cream cheese, softened

½ cup mayonnaise or salad dressing

½ cup grated onion

1 tablespoon lemon juice

1 teaspoon Worcestershire sauce

⅛ teaspoon hot sauce

1 (2-ounce) jar black caviar, drained

1 (2-ounce) jar red caviar, drained

4 hard-cooked egg yolks, sieved

⅓ cup minced fresh parsley

It's easy to create the dramatic design featured in the photograph below. Simply sketch the spoke design in the cream cheese mixture using a ruler and sharp knife; then fill in the triangles.

Beat cream cheese at medium speed of an electric mixer until smooth; add mayonnaise and next 4 ingredients, beating well. Spread mixture in a 10-inch quiche dish. Cover and chill at least 8 hours.

To serve, arrange caviar, egg yolks, and parsley over cream cheese mixture in spoke-fashion, creating a wheel design, if desired. Serve with assorted crackers. Yield: 20 to 25 appetizer servings.

Caviar-Cream Cheese Spread may take a little extra time to prepare if you choose a striking design such as this, but the compliments will make it worthwhile.

SUN-DRIED TOMATO AND CHEESE SPREAD

1 (7-ounce) jar sun-dried tomatoes in olive oil, undrained
1 (8-ounce) package cream cheese, softened
½ cup grated Parmesan cheese
½ cup unsalted butter, softened
1 tablespoon chopped fresh basil
Garnish: fresh basil sprigs

Drain tomatoes, reserving 2 tablespoons marinade. Set aside ¼ cup tomatoes; reserve remaining tomatoes and marinade for another use.

Position knife blade in food processor bowl; add ¼ cup tomatoes, 2 tablespoons marinade, cream cheese, and next 3 ingredients. Pulse 6 times or until well blended. Spoon mixture into a cheese crock or small bowl; cover and chill thoroughly. Let spread come to room temperature before serving. Garnish, if desired. Serve with pita chips. Yield: 2 cups.

BRANDIED PÂTÉ

Pâté, the French word for pie, generally refers to well-seasoned ground meat or vegetable spreads. Pâtés may be hot or cold and are usually served as an appetizer or first course.

8 slices bacon
1 pound chicken livers
½ cup brandy
¾ cup whipping cream
½ cup chopped onion
¼ cup mayonnaise or salad dressing
1 teaspoon dried thyme
¼ teaspoon salt
¼ teaspoon pepper
Pinch of ground nutmeg
½ cup coarsely chopped walnuts
3 tablespoons chopped fresh parsley
Garnishes: chopped fresh parsley, chopped walnuts

Cook bacon in a large skillet until crisp; remove bacon, reserving 2 tablespoons drippings in skillet. Crumble bacon, and set aside. Cook livers in drippings over medium-high heat until done. Drain livers, and set aside, reserving drippings in skillet. Remove skillet from heat. Pour brandy into skillet, stirring to loosen particles in pan; stir in whipping cream. Return skillet to heat, and bring mixture to a boil. Reduce heat to medium, and cook, stirring constantly, 4 minutes or until mixture is reduced to about 1 cup.

Position knife blade in food processor bowl; add livers, cream mixture, and onion. Process 1 minute or until smooth. Add mayonnaise and next 4 ingredients; process until blended. Add bacon, ½ cup walnuts, and 3 tablespoons parsley; process 10 seconds. Pour mixture into a lightly oiled 3-cup mold. Cover and chill at least 8 hours. Unmold pâté onto a serving platter; garnish, if desired. Serve with assorted crackers. Yield: 2⅔ cups.

MUSHROOM PÂTÉ

1 pound fresh mushrooms,
  chopped
2 tablespoons butter or margarine,
  melted
1 (8-ounce) package cream cheese,
  softened

1 teaspoon seasoned pepper
½ teaspoon garlic salt
Garnishes: fresh rosemary sprigs,
  sliced fresh mushrooms

Cook chopped mushrooms in butter in a large skillet over medium-high heat, stirring constantly, 5 minutes or until most of liquid evaporates and mushrooms are tender. Cool to room temperature.

Position knife blade in food processor bowl; add mushrooms, cream cheese, pepper, and garlic salt. Process 2 minutes or until smooth, scraping sides of processor bowl once. Spoon mixture into a greased 7½- x 3- x 2-inch loafpan. Cover and chill at least 8 hours. Unmold pâté onto a serving platter; garnish, if desired. Serve with toasted French baguette slices or assorted crackers. Yield: 2½ cups.

BUTTER-TOASTED PECANS

4 cups pecan halves
½ cup butter, melted

½ teaspoon salt

Spread pecans evenly in a 15- x 10- x 1-inch jellyroll pan. Pour butter over pecans, and sprinkle evenly with salt. Bake at 325° for 20 to 25 minutes or until pecans are toasted, stirring every 10 minutes. Spread pecans in a single layer on paper towels to drain; let cool completely. Store in an airtight container at room temperature up to 2 weeks. Yield: 4 cups.

BUTTERY CHEESE WAFERS

The logs of dough for Buttery Cheese Wafers may be tightly wrapped and refrigerated up to one week or frozen up to one month. Allow the frozen logs to thaw slightly before slicing.

½ cup butter, softened
2 cups (8 ounces) shredded sharp
   Cheddar cheese
1½ cups all-purpose flour

½ teaspoon salt
¼ to ½ teaspoon ground red
   pepper
Pecan halves

Beat butter at medium speed of an electric mixer until creamy. Add cheese and next 3 ingredients; beat until mixture forms a soft dough. Divide dough in half; shape each portion into a 6-inch log. Cover and chill at least 2 hours.

Cut logs into ¼-inch slices; place slices on ungreased baking sheets. Lightly press a pecan half into each slice. Bake at 350° for 10 to 12 minutes or until lightly browned. Cool 1 minute on baking sheets; transfer to wire racks, and let cool completely. Yield: 4 dozen.

HOLIDAY PASTRY SWIRLS

If the recipe for Holiday Pastry Swirls makes more than you need, freeze the extra rolls of dough for up to one month to have on hand for drop-in visitors.

1 large green pepper
1 large sweet red pepper
2 tablespoons sesame seeds,
   toasted
2 cups all-purpose flour

1 cup grated Parmesan cheese
½ teaspoon ground red pepper
¾ cup butter or margarine
⅓ cup plus 1 tablespoon water

Cut peppers in half; discard seeds and membranes. Place pepper halves, skin side up, on a foil-lined baking sheet; flatten with palm of hand. Broil 3 inches from heat (with electric oven door partially opened) 5 minutes or until blackened and charred. Place pepper halves in a heavy-duty, zip-top plastic bag; seal bag, and let stand 15 minutes to loosen skins. Peel and discard skins. Chop pepper halves finely. Combine chopped pepper and sesame seeds; set aside.

Combine flour, cheese, and ground red pepper; cut in butter with a pastry blender until mixture is crumbly. Add water, stirring just until dry ingredients are moistened. Divide dough into fourths; shape each portion into a ball. Cover and chill thoroughly.

Roll each ball of dough into a 10- x 7-inch rectangle on a lightly floured surface; spread each rectangle evenly with one-fourth of pepper mixture. Roll up tightly, beginning with long side. Pinch seams to seal, and fold ends under. Wrap rolls in wax paper, and chill at least 1 hour. (Rolls will be easier to slice if slightly frozen.)

Cut rolls into ¼-inch slices; place slices on lightly greased baking sheets. Bake at 400° for 11 to 12 minutes or until edges are lightly browned. Cool 1 minute on baking sheets; transfer to wire racks, and let cool completely. Yield: 13 dozen.

ROASTED PEPPER STRIPS AND ENDIVE

1 large sweet red pepper	Dash of ground white pepper
¼ cup olive oil	1 clove garlic, minced
1½ tablespoons minced fresh parsley	6 heads Belgian endive (about 1 pound)
1½ tablespoons balsamic vinegar	Garnish: small fresh parsley sprigs
¼ teaspoon salt	

Cut pepper in half; discard seeds and membrane. Place pepper halves, skin side up, on a foil-lined baking sheet; flatten with palm of hand. Broil 3 inches from heat (with electric oven door partially opened) 5 minutes or until blackened and charred. Place pepper halves in a heavy-duty, zip-top plastic bag; seal bag, and let stand 15 minutes to loosen skins. Peel and discard skins. Cut pepper halves into 2- x ¼-inch strips.

Combine olive oil and next 5 ingredients; stir in pepper strips. Cover and chill at least 8 hours. Slice stem ends from endive, and separate leaves; trim larger endive leaves to 3 inches. Drain pepper strips; place 1 pepper strip on each endive leaf. Garnish, if desired. Yield: 4 dozen.

CHEESY CHERRY TOMATOES

2 dozen cherry tomatoes	¼ teaspoon celery salt
1 (8-ounce) package cream cheese, softened	Dash of onion powder
4 slices bacon, cooked and crumbled	Garnish: small fresh parsley sprigs

Cut top off each tomato; scoop out pulp, leaving shells intact. Reserve pulp for another use. Invert tomato shells onto paper towels to drain.

Combine cream cheese and next 3 ingredients in a small mixing bowl; beat at medium speed of an electric mixer until creamy. Spoon or pipe cream cheese mixture into tomato shells. Garnish, if desired. Yield: 24 appetizers.

When piping the creamy filling into the tomato shells, use a large round tip to prevent the bacon pieces from clogging the opening of the tip.

Guests will line up for seconds once they sample cheesy Tarragon Cocktail Quiches and crispy Artichoke-Parmesan Phyllo Bites, so make plenty.

ARTICHOKE-PARMESAN PHYLLO BITES

3 (6-ounce) jars marinated artichoke hearts, undrained
¾ cup freshly grated Parmesan cheese, divided

1 clove garlic, minced
10 sheets commercial frozen phyllo pastry, thawed

Drain artichoke hearts, reserving marinade; set marinade aside. Position knife blade in food processor bowl; add artichoke hearts, ½ cup cheese, and garlic. Pulse 4 times or until artichoke hearts are finely chopped. Set aside.

Place 1 phyllo sheet on wax paper. (Keep remaining phyllo covered.) Lightly brush phyllo sheet with oil portion of reserved marinade; sprinkle with 2 teaspoons of remaining cheese. Top with another phyllo sheet; brush lightly with oil portion of reserved marinade. Cut phyllo sheet in half lengthwise. Cut each half crosswise into thirds, making 6 sections, each measuring approximately 6 x 5 inches.

Place a heaping teaspoon of artichoke mixture in center of each phyllo section. Gather corners of phyllo over filling, and gently twist to close. Place on a lightly greased baking sheet. Repeat procedure with remaining phyllo sheets, marinade, cheese, and artichoke mixture. Bake at 350° for 14 minutes or until golden. Serve immediately. Yield: 2½ dozen.

TARRAGON COCKTAIL QUICHES

1 cup (4 ounces) shredded
  Cheddar cheese
2 tablespoons chopped fresh
  chives
2 tablespoons chopped fresh
  tarragon or 2 teaspoons dried
  tarragon

Pastry Shells
3 large eggs, lightly beaten
¾ cup half-and-half
½ teaspoon salt
¼ teaspoon pepper
⅛ teaspoon ground nutmeg
Dash of hot sauce

Combine first 3 ingredients in a small bowl; spoon mixture evenly into Pastry Shells. Combine eggs and remaining ingredients; stir well. Spoon into Pastry Shells, filling three-fourths full. Bake at 350° for 30 to 35 minutes or until set. Yield: 3 dozen.

Pastry Shells

½ cup butter or margarine,
  softened
½ (8-ounce) package cream
  cheese, softened

1 cup plus 2 tablespoons
  all-purpose flour
1½ tablespoons sesame seeds
¼ teaspoon salt

Combine butter and cream cheese in a mixing bowl; beat at medium speed of an electric mixer until smooth and creamy. Stir in flour, sesame seeds, and salt. Cover and chill 1 hour.

Shape mixture into 36 (1-inch) balls. Place in lightly greased miniature (1¾-inch) muffin pans, shaping each ball into a shell. Yield: 3 dozen.

CHEESE WONTONS WITH HOT SAUCE

Get a head start on Cheese Wontons with Hot Sauce by preparing the wonton portion of the recipe up to four hours in advance. You may also prepare the sauce in advance—up to 24 hours. Place the wontons and the sauce in airtight containers, and chill. All that's left to do at serving time is to fry the wontons and reheat the sauce.

4 ounces Monterey Jack cheese with jalapeño peppers, cut into 24 cubes

24 (2-inch-square) wonton wrappers

Peanut or vegetable oil
Hot Sauce

Place 1 cheese cube in center of each wonton wrapper; moisten edges of wonton wrapper lightly with water. Fold each wonton wrapper in half diagonally to form a triangle, pressing edges together to seal.

Pour oil to depth of 1½ inches into a wok or large skillet; heat to 375°. Fry wontons, six at a time, 30 seconds on each side or until golden. Drain on paper towels. Serve immediately with Hot Sauce. Yield: 2 dozen.

Hot Sauce

⅓ cup chopped onion
1 clove garlic, minced
1 tablespoon vegetable oil
½ cup seeded and chopped tomato
1 tablespoon chopped canned jalapeño pepper

1½ tablespoons white vinegar
¼ teaspoon salt
¼ teaspoon dried oregano
¼ teaspoon ground cumin
1 (8-ounce) can tomato sauce

Cook onion and garlic in oil in a saucepan over medium heat, stirring constantly, until tender. Add tomato and remaining ingredients; cook until thoroughly heated, stirring occasionally. Serve warm. Yield: 1⅓ cups.

SESAME CHICKEN NUGGETS WITH PLUM SAUCE

6 skinned and boned chicken breast halves
2 (5½-ounce) packages pancake mix
1¾ cups water

2 tablespoons sesame seeds
1¼ teaspoons salt
½ teaspoon pepper
Vegetable oil
Plum Sauce

Cut chicken into 1-inch pieces. Combine pancake mix and next 4 ingredients in a large bowl; stir well. Add chicken nuggets, stirring gently to coat.

Pour oil to depth of 2 inches into a Dutch oven; heat to 375°. Fry chicken nuggets, a few at a time, until golden; drain on paper towels. Serve warm with Plum Sauce. Yield: 12 to 15 appetizer servings.

Plum Sauce

1 cup red plum jam
1 tablespoon prepared
   horseradish

1 tablespoon prepared mustard
1 teaspoon lemon juice

Combine all ingredients in a small saucepan. Cook over low heat, stirring constantly, until thoroughly heated. Serve warm or at room temperature. Yield: 1 cup.

ITALIAN SAUSAGE-STUFFED MUSHROOMS

24 large fresh mushrooms
1 tablespoon butter or margarine,
   melted
½ pound hot Italian sausage,
   casings removed

1 clove garlic, crushed
¼ teaspoon pepper
Grated Parmesan cheese

Clean mushrooms with damp paper towels; remove stems. Set stems aside. Cook mushroom caps in butter in a large skillet over medium-high heat, stirring constantly, 5 minutes. Drain. Place mushroom caps on rack of a broiler pan, stem side up. Set aside.

Combine sausage and garlic in a large skillet. Cook over medium-high heat until sausage browns, stirring until it crumbles; drain well. Position knife blade in food processor bowl; add mushroom stems, sausage mixture, and pepper. Process 20 seconds or until mixture is minced.

Spoon mixture evenly into mushroom caps; sprinkle with Parmesan cheese. Broil 5½ inches from heat (with electric oven door partially opened) 3 minutes or until thoroughly heated. Yield: 2 dozen.

ORANGE JUICY

1 (6-ounce) can frozen orange
   juice concentrate
1 cup water
1 cup milk

¼ cup sugar
1 teaspoon vanilla extract
2 cups ice cubes

Combine all ingredients in container of an electric blender; process until smooth. Serve immediately. Yield: 5 cups.

BRANDY VELVET

1 teaspoon instant coffee granules
½ cup hot water
1 quart coffee ice cream
½ cup brandy

½ cup chocolate syrup
Grated semisweet chocolate
   (optional)

Combine coffee granules and hot water in a small bowl or cup, stirring until granules dissolve. Combine coffee mixture, ice cream, brandy, and chocolate syrup in container of an electric blender; process until smooth. Pour beverage into glasses; sprinkle each serving with grated chocolate, if desired. Serve immediately. Yield: 5 cups.

HOLIDAY EGGNOG

2 cups sugar
4 cups half-and-half
1¼ cups milk
6 egg yolks, lightly beaten

1¼ cups bourbon, divided
2 cups whipping cream, whipped
Freshly grated nutmeg or ground
   nutmeg (optional)

Combine first 4 ingredients in a saucepan; cook over medium-low heat, stirring constantly, until mixture reaches 160°. Stir in ¾ cup bourbon. Cool; cover and chill.

Combine chilled mixture and remaining ½ cup bourbon in a punch bowl. Gently stir in whipped cream; sprinkle with nutmeg, if desired. Serve immediately. Yield: 14 cups.

Quick Party Eggnog offers a head start on preparation because it uses commercial eggnog as a base. It's sure to become a holiday favorite.

QUICK PARTY EGGNOG

½ gallon vanilla ice cream, softened

2 quarts commercial refrigerated eggnog

1½ cups bourbon (optional)

Freshly grated nutmeg or ground nutmeg (optional)

Spoon softened ice cream into a large punch bowl. Add eggnog and, if desired, bourbon, stirring gently to blend. Sprinkle with nutmeg, if desired. Serve immediately. Yield: about 18 cups.

MOCK CHAMPAGNE PUNCH

1 cup sugar
3 cups water
1 (12-ounce) can frozen lemonade
   concentrate, thawed and
   undiluted

2 cups sparkling Catawba, chilled
1 (2-liter) bottle ginger ale, chilled

Combine sugar and water in a saucepan; bring to a boil. Remove from heat; let cool. Stir in lemonade concentrate; chill. Combine chilled mixture, Catawba, and ginger ale in a punch bowl just before serving. Yield: 1 gallon.

SPARKLING CHAMPAGNE PUNCH

When stirring champagne or a carbonated beverage into punch, do so gently to prevent losing the bubbly effect.

Vegetable cooking spray
3¾ cups lemonade, divided
4 to 6 lemon slices
4 to 6 lime slices
4 to 6 maraschino cherries with
   stems
6 cups water
4 (6-ounce) cans frozen lemonade
   concentrate, thawed and
   undiluted

4 (6-ounce) cans frozen pineapple
   juice concentrate, thawed and
   undiluted
1 (2-liter) bottle ginger ale,
   chilled
1 (1-liter) bottle tonic water,
   chilled
1 (750-milliliter) bottle
   champagne, chilled

Lightly coat a 4½-cup ring mold with cooking spray. Pour 3 cups lemonade into mold; freeze until slushy. Arrange lemon slices, lime slices, and cherries in mold, securing fruit in slush mixture. Fill mold with remaining ¾ cup lemonade; freeze until firm.

Combine water, lemonade concentrate, and pineapple juice concentrate; chill thoroughly.

Remove ice ring from freezer; let stand at room temperature 5 minutes or until loosened. Unmold ice ring into bottom of a punch bowl. Pour chilled juice mixture into a large container; gently stir in ginger ale, tonic water, and champagne. Transfer mixture to punch bowl. Yield: 7 quarts.

WHITE CHRISTMAS PUNCH

1⅓ cups sugar
⅔ cup water
1 cup evaporated milk
2 teaspoons almond extract

2 (½-gallon) cartons vanilla ice cream, softened
4 (2-liter) bottles lemon-lime carbonated beverage, chilled

Combine sugar and water in a saucepan; cook over medium heat, stirring constantly, until sugar dissolves. Remove from heat. Stir in evaporated milk and almond extract; let cool. Chill until ready to serve.

Combine milk mixture, ice cream, and carbonated beverage in a large container just before serving; stir gently to break ice cream into small pieces. Transfer mixture to a punch bowl. Yield: about 3 gallons.

For smaller gatherings, you can easily halve the ingredients in White Christmas Punch.

PLANTATION COFFEE PUNCH

2 quarts hot brewed coffee
½ cup sugar
2 quarts coffee ice cream, softened
1 quart chocolate milk

1 tablespoon vanilla extract
Whipped cream
Shaved semisweet chocolate (optional)

Combine hot coffee and sugar, stirring until sugar dissolves. Cover and chill thoroughly. Combine chilled coffee mixture, ice cream, milk, and vanilla in a punch bowl; stir gently until ice cream melts. Top with dollops of whipped cream; sprinkle with shaved chocolate, if desired. Yield: 5 quarts.

WHITE SANGRÍA SLUSH

1 (12-ounce) can frozen lemonade concentrate, thawed and undiluted
1 (6-ounce) can frozen orange juice concentrate, thawed and undiluted

1½ cups water
1 (750-milliliter) bottle Chablis or other dry white wine, chilled
1 (10-ounce) bottle club soda, chilled
Lemon, lime, or orange slices

Combine first 3 ingredients in a 13- x 9- x 2-inch pan; freeze until firm. To serve, spoon frozen mixture into a large pitcher. Add wine and club soda, stirring gently until mixture is slushy. Stir in sliced fruit. Yield: 2 quarts.

CINNAMON HOT CHOCOLATE

1 (6-ounce) package semisweet
  chocolate morsels
½ cup sugar
⅓ cup water

¼ teaspoon ground cinnamon
1 cup whipping cream
Hot milk

Combine first 4 ingredients in a heavy saucepan; cook over low heat, stirring frequently, until chocolate melts. Cool slightly.

Beat whipping cream at high speed of an electric mixer until soft peaks form; fold whipped cream into chocolate mixture. Store in an airtight container in refrigerator up to 1 week.

For each serving, place 3 tablespoons chocolate mixture in a mug; add ¾ cup hot milk, stirring until blended. Yield: 17 servings.

SPICED APPLE CIDER

10 whole cloves
10 whole allspice
4 (3-inch) sticks cinnamon

1 (64-ounce) bottle apple cider
¼ cup firmly packed brown sugar
Cinnamon sticks (optional)

Cut a 6-inch square of cheesecloth; place first 3 ingredients in center, and tie with string. Combine spice bag, cider, and brown sugar in a Dutch oven. Bring to a boil; reduce heat, and simmer 5 minutes. Remove and discard spice bag. Serve warm with cinnamon-stick stirrers, if desired. Yield: 2 quarts.

MEXICAN COFFEE

12 cups hot brewed coffee
1 cup chocolate syrup
½ cup Kahlúa or other coffee-
  flavored liqueur

¼ to ½ teaspoon ground
  cinnamon
Whipped cream
Ground cinnamon

Combine first 4 ingredients in a large container; stir well. Ladle beverage into individual cups; top each serving with whipped cream, and sprinkle with cinnamon. Serve immediately. Yield: 13 cups.

HOT WINE PUNCH

1 quart Burgundy or other
   dry red wine
2 cups orange juice
½ cup sugar

½ cup lemon juice
4 whole cloves
1 (3-inch) stick cinnamon

Combine all ingredients in a large saucepan; cook over medium heat 20 minutes or just until mixture begins to simmer, stirring occasionally. Remove and discard spices. Serve warm. Yield: 6 cups.

PERKY CRANBERRY PUNCH

2 (32-ounce) bottles cranberry
   juice
1 (46-ounce) can unsweetened
   pineapple juice
2 cups water

1 cup firmly packed brown sugar
2 tablespoons whole allspice
2 tablespoons whole cloves
6 (3-inch) sticks cinnamon

Pour first 3 ingredients into a large percolator. Place brown sugar and remaining ingredients in percolator basket. Perk through complete cycle of electric percolator. Yield: 1 gallon.

Perky Cranberry Punch is the percolator punch that folks enjoy so much during the holidays. It's the perfect substitute for coffee at a Christmas get-together.

HOLIDAY WASSAIL

1 orange
1 lemon
1½ teaspoons whole cloves
3 (3-inch) sticks cinnamon
½ cup sugar

1 gallon apple cider
2 cups orange juice
½ cup lemon juice
Garnish: orange and lemon slices
   studded with whole cloves

Peel orange and lemon, keeping rinds intact. Insert cloves into strips of rind. Combine rinds, cinnamon sticks, sugar, and cider in a large Dutch oven. Bring to a boil; cover, reduce heat, and simmer 10 minutes. Cool completely.

Add orange and lemon juices to mixture; cook over medium heat, stirring frequently, just until thoroughly heated. Remove and discard rinds and cinnamon sticks. Transfer mixture to a heat-proof punch bowl, if desired. Garnish, if desired. Yield: 17 cups.

Entrées For the Feast

Whether you're serving traditional turkey and dressing, a glazed baked ham, or a regal crown roast of pork, holiday feasting calls for something extra special. Along with a beautifully appointed table, you'll want an exceptional entrée to make the meal distinctive. You may choose to prepare your family's favorite holiday stand-bys the same way your mother did—and her mother before her. But for those of you who want to start a new tradition, or want to add variety to your holiday feast, do we have some surprises for you! How about a rich, creamy seafood casserole? Or smoked quail? Or peppered beef tenderloin medaillons wrapped in phyllo pastry? Whatever your choice, these elegant entrées suit the season and promise to be selections you'll serve with pride.

Apricot-Glazed Cornish Hens (page 133)

CHESAPEAKE BAY CRAB CAKES

¼ cup minced onion
2 tablespoons minced green
  pepper
¼ cup butter or margarine,
  melted
1 pound fresh crabmeat,
  drained and flaked
1 to 1¼ cups fine, dry
  breadcrumbs, divided
1 tablespoon dried parsley flakes

1 tablespoon mayonnaise or
  salad dressing
1 tablespoon lemon juice
1 teaspoon Old Bay seasoning
1 teaspoon dry mustard
1 teaspoon Worcestershire sauce
Dash of ground red pepper
1 large egg, lightly beaten
Vegetable oil

Cook onion and green pepper in butter in a large skillet over medium-high heat, stirring constantly, until tender. Remove from heat; stir in crabmeat, ¾ cup breadcrumbs, and next 8 ingredients. Shape mixture into 8 patties; dredge patties in remaining breadcrumbs.

Pour oil to depth of ¼ inch into a large heavy skillet. Fry patties in hot oil over medium-high heat 3 minutes on each side or until golden. Yield: 4 servings.

SEAFOOD CASSEROLE

1 pound unpeeled medium-size
  fresh shrimp
1 cup Chablis or other dry white
  wine
1 tablespoon chopped fresh parsley
1 tablespoon butter or margarine
1 teaspoon salt
1 medium onion, thinly sliced
1 pound fresh bay scallops
3 tablespoons butter or margarine
3 tablespoons all-purpose flour
1 cup half-and-half
½ cup (2 ounces) shredded Swiss
  cheese

2 teaspoons lemon juice
⅛ teaspoon pepper
½ pound crab-flavored seafood
  product, flaked
1 (4½-ounce) can sliced
  mushrooms, drained
1 cup soft breadcrumbs
¼ cup grated Parmesan cheese
Paprika
Garnishes: 3 peeled and deveined
  cooked shrimp, fresh parsley
  sprigs

Peel and devein shrimp. Combine wine and next 4 ingredients in a large Dutch oven; bring to a boil. Add shrimp and scallops. Cook 3 to 5 minutes or until shrimp turn pink, stirring frequently. Drain, reserving ⅔ cup cooking liquid. Set aside 3 shrimp for garnish, if desired.

Melt 3 tablespoons butter in Dutch oven over low heat; add flour, stirring until smooth. Cook, stirring constantly, 1 minute. Gradually add half-and-half; cook over medium heat, stirring constantly, until thickened and bubbly. Stir in Swiss cheese. Gradually stir in reserved cooking liquid, lemon juice, and pepper. Stir in shrimp mixture, seafood product, and mushrooms.

Spoon mixture into a lightly greased 11- x 7- x 1½-inch baking dish. Cover and bake at 350° for 40 minutes or until bubbly. Combine breadcrumbs and Parmesan cheese; sprinkle over casserole. Bake, uncovered, an additional 5 minutes. Sprinkle with paprika. Let stand 10 minutes before serving. Garnish, if desired. Yield: 6 servings.

PEPPERED BEEF TENDERLOIN BUNDLES

1 cup chopped zucchini	¼ teaspoon salt
1 cup chopped fresh mushrooms	8 (4-ounce) beef tenderloin steaks
½ cup chopped onion	2 tablespoons cracked pepper
1 clove garlic, minced	Vegetable cooking spray
3 tablespoons butter or margarine, melted	16 sheets commercial frozen phyllo pastry, thawed

Cook first 4 ingredients in butter in a large skillet over medium-high heat, stirring constantly, until tender. Stir in salt. Remove mixture from skillet; set aside. Sprinkle both sides of steaks with pepper. Coat skillet with cooking spray; place over high heat until hot. Add steaks, and cook 1½ to 2 minutes on each side or until lightly browned. Set aside.

Place 1 phyllo sheet on a towel. (Keep remaining phyllo covered.) Coat phyllo sheet with cooking spray; fold in half lengthwise. Place 1 steak 3 inches from end of sheet. Spoon 2 tablespoons zucchini mixture onto steak; fold short end of sheet over stuffing. Fold sides of sheet over steak, and roll up.

Place a second phyllo sheet on a towel; cut into a 12-inch square, and coat with cooking spray. Place wrapped steak, vegetable side up, in center of phyllo square. Bring corners of square to the middle, gently pressing together in center. Pull ends up and out to resemble a package. Coat bundle with cooking spray, and place on a baking sheet coated with cooking spray. Repeat procedure with remaining phyllo sheets, steaks, and zucchini mixture.

Bake at 400° for 15 minutes for rare, 17 minutes for medium-rare, or 20 minutes for medium. Serve immediately. Yield: 8 servings.

Phyllo pastry is tissue-thin layers of dough used to encase foods such as these beef tenderloin bundles or to create flaky desserts such as baklava. Phyllo (sometimes spelled "filo") will dry out and become too fragile to work with if not kept covered and moist during recipe preparation.

BEEF MEDAILLONS WITH HORSERADISH CREAM

¼ cup red wine vinegar
2 tablespoons vegetable oil
¾ teaspoon chopped fresh thyme
  or ¼ teaspoon dried thyme
¼ teaspoon salt
¼ teaspoon pepper
4 (4-ounce) beef tenderloin steaks
½ pound carrots, scraped and cut
  into very thin strips

2 tablespoons butter or margarine
¼ teaspoon salt
¼ teaspoon ground nutmeg
⅛ teaspoon ground white pepper
Horseradish Cream
Garnish: fresh thyme sprigs

Combine first 5 ingredients in a shallow dish. Add steaks, turning to coat both sides. Cover and marinate in refrigerator 4 hours, turning once.

Cook carrot in boiling water to cover 4 minutes or until crisp-tender; drain. Combine carrot, butter, and next 3 ingredients, tossing to coat. Set aside, and keep warm.

Remove steaks from marinade, reserving marinade. Broil steaks 3 inches from heat (with electric oven door partially opened) 3 to 4 minutes on each side or to desired degree of doneness, basting with marinade just before turning.

Place 1 steak in center of each of 4 dinner plates. Spoon 3 tablespoons Horseradish Cream along 1 side of each steak; spoon carrot mixture evenly along other side of each steak. Garnish, if desired. Yield: 4 servings.

Horseradish Cream

1¼ cups whipping cream
2½ tablespoons prepared
  horseradish

⅛ teaspoon salt
⅛ teaspoon pepper
Pinch of ground nutmeg

Cook whipping cream in a medium saucepan over medium heat, stirring frequently, until reduced to ¾ cup (about 15 minutes). Stir in horseradish and remaining ingredients; cook, stirring constantly, just until mixture is thoroughly heated. Yield: ¾ cup.

SPINACH-STUFFED BEEF TENDERLOIN

½ pound fresh spinach
¼ pound fresh mushrooms, diced
2 tablespoons butter or margarine, melted
¼ cup grated Parmesan cheese
½ teaspoon fennel seeds
½ teaspoon ground sage
½ teaspoon salt
½ teaspoon freshly ground pepper
1 large egg, lightly beaten
1 (5- to 6-pound) beef tenderloin, trimmed
1 teaspoon freshly ground pepper
¾ teaspoon fennel seeds
3 cloves garlic, crushed

Remove stems from spinach; wash leaves thoroughly, and drain. Place spinach in a medium skillet; cover and cook over medium heat just until spinach wilts (about 3 minutes), stirring once. Remove from heat; uncover and let cool. Chop spinach; drain well, pressing spinach between layers of paper towels. Set aside.

Cook mushrooms in butter in a medium skillet over medium-high heat, stirring constantly, until tender. Remove from heat; stir in chopped spinach, Parmesan cheese, and next 5 ingredients.

Slice tenderloin lengthwise down center, cutting to, but not through, bottom. Spoon spinach mixture into opening of tenderloin. Press sides of tenderloin together over filling, and tie securely with heavy string at 2-inch intervals. Combine 1 teaspoon pepper, ¾ teaspoon fennel seeds, and garlic; rub over entire surface of tenderloin.

Place tenderloin on a lightly greased rack in a shallow roasting pan; insert meat thermometer into thickest portion of tenderloin. Place tenderloin in a 500° oven; immediately reduce oven temperature to 350°. Bake, uncovered, for 55 to 60 minutes or until meat thermometer registers desired degree of doneness (rare 140°, medium-rare 150°, or medium 160°). Let stand 10 minutes before slicing. Yield: 12 to 14 servings.

Our home economists recommend using a meat thermometer to ensure the exact doneness of large cuts of meat. If you rely on the cooking time alone, you risk overcooking a large cut of meat such as this beef tenderloin or the standing rib roast on the following page.

STANDING RIB ROAST WITH YORKSHIRE PUDDING

Yorkshire pudding isn't really a pudding. It actually resembles a popover in appearance and has the texture of a soufflé. It's the traditional British accompaniment to a stately rib roast.

1 (6½- to 7-pound) standing
   rib roast
Salt

Pepper
Yorkshire Pudding

Sprinkle roast with salt and pepper. Place roast, fat side up, on a lightly greased rack in a shallow roasting pan. Insert meat thermometer, making sure it does not touch fat or bone. Bake at 325° for 1½ hours or until meat thermometer registers desired degree of doneness (rare 140°, medium-rare 150°, or medium 160°).

Transfer roast to a serving platter, reserving ¼ cup clear pan drippings for Yorkshire Pudding recipe. Let stand 10 minutes before carving. Serve roast with Yorkshire Pudding. Yield: 12 servings.

Yorkshire Pudding

1 cup all-purpose flour
1 cup milk
¼ teaspoon salt

2 large eggs
¼ cup clear pan drippings from
   roasted standing rib roast

Combine first 4 ingredients in a medium mixing bowl; beat at low speed of an electric mixer until smooth. Spoon 1 teaspoon pan drippings into each muffin pan; tilt to coat evenly. Spoon batter into pans, filling half full. Bake at 425° for 15 minutes. Reduce heat to 350°, and bake an additional 18 to 20 minutes or until golden. Serve immediately. Yield: 1 dozen.

ITALIAN VEAL ROLLS

6 (4-ounce) veal cutlets
6 slices prosciutto (about
   2 ounces)
4 ounces fontina cheese, cut
   into 6 strips
¼ teaspoon salt
¼ teaspoon pepper

½ cup all-purpose flour
1 tablespoon butter or margarine,
   melted
1 tablespoon vegetable oil
1 cup Chablis or other dry
   white wine
Hot cooked angel hair pasta

Place cutlets between 2 sheets of heavy-duty plastic wrap; flatten to ⅛-inch thickness, using a meat mallet or rolling pin. Wrap 1 slice of prosciutto around a cheese strip, and place in center of a cutlet. Roll up cutlet lengthwise, and secure with a wooden pick. Repeat procedure with remaining prosciutto, cheese strips, and cutlets.

Sprinkle veal rolls with salt and pepper; dredge in flour. Cook in butter and oil in a large heavy skillet over medium-high heat, turning occasionally, until browned on all sides. Remove from skillet, and keep warm.

Add wine to skillet. Bring to a boil, and cook until wine is reduced to ½ cup. Return veal rolls to skillet. Cover, reduce heat, and simmer 7 minutes. Serve sliced or whole veal rolls over pasta. Yield: 6 servings.

Italian Veal Rolls are filled with smooth fontina cheese and slices of prosciutto. Slice the rolls and serve over a bed of angel hair pasta for an elegant main course.

CRANBERRY LEG OF LAMB

1 (3- to 4-pound) shank-half
  leg of lamb
1 clove garlic, sliced
1 teaspoon ground ginger
1 teaspoon dry mustard
½ cup whole-berry cranberry
  sauce

¼ cup cherry preserves
1 tablespoon port wine
2 tablespoons all-purpose flour
¼ cup water
¼ teaspoon salt
⅛ teaspoon pepper

Cut several ½-inch slits in top of leg of lamb; insert garlic slices into slits. Combine ginger and mustard; rub over lamb. Place lamb, fat side up, on a lightly greased rack in a shallow roasting pan; insert meat thermometer, making sure it does not touch fat or bone. Bake at 325° for 45 minutes.

Combine cranberry sauce and preserves in a saucepan; cook over low heat until mixture melts, stirring occasionally. Stir in wine. Spoon mixture over lamb; bake 1 hour and 15 minutes or until thermometer registers desired degree of doneness (medium-rare 150° or medium 160°). Transfer lamb to a platter, reserving drippings. Let stand 10 minutes before carving.

Skim fat from drippings; add enough water to drippings to measure 1¼ cups. Pour into a saucepan. Combine flour and ¼ cup water; add to drippings. Cook over medium heat, stirring constantly, until thickened and bubbly; stir in salt and pepper. Serve mixture with lamb. Yield: 6 to 8 servings.

PORK MEDAILLONS IN MUSTARD SAUCE

3 tablespoons vegetable oil
1 tablespoon coarse-grained
  mustard
½ teaspoon salt
½ teaspoon pepper

2 (¾-pound) pork tenderloins
¼ cup Chablis or other dry white
  wine
Mustard Sauce
Garnish: fresh basil sprigs

Combine first 4 ingredients; rub over tenderloins. Place tenderloins in a large heavy-duty, zip-top plastic bag. Seal bag; marinate in refrigerator 8 hours, turning bag occasionally.

Place tenderloins on a lightly greased rack in a shallow roasting pan; brush with half of wine. Insert meat thermometer into thickest portion of 1 tenderloin. Bake at 400° for 25 minutes or until meat thermometer registers 160°, brushing with remaining half of wine after 10 minutes. Let stand

10 minutes before slicing. Cut tenderloins into ¼-inch slices; arrange slices evenly on 4 dinner plates. Spoon Mustard Sauce evenly around slices. Garnish, if desired. Yield: 4 servings.

Mustard Sauce

1¾ cups whipping cream
¼ cup coarse-grained mustard

¼ teaspoon salt
⅛ teaspoon ground white pepper

Cook whipping cream in a medium saucepan over medium heat, stirring frequently, until reduced to 1¼ cups (about 15 minutes). Add mustard, salt, and pepper; cook, stirring constantly, just until mixture is thoroughly heated. Yield: 1⅓ cups.

STUFFED CROWN ROAST OF PORK

1 (12-rib) crown roast of pork
   (about 6 pounds)
½ teaspoon salt
½ teaspoon pepper
1 (6-ounce) package long-grain
   and wild rice mix
2 cups chicken broth
1 cup raisins

½ cup sliced green onions
2 tablespoons butter or margarine
½ cup canned garbanzo beans or
   chick peas, rinsed and drained
½ cup chopped pecans, toasted
Garnishes: spiced crabapples,
   fresh parsley sprigs

The butcher makes a crown roast of pork or lamb by tying a strip of the rib section into a circle with the rib tips turned up. The center of a crown roast is usually filled with stuffing or a vegetable mixture.

Sprinkle roast on all sides with salt and pepper. Place roast, bone ends up, on a lightly greased rack in a shallow roasting pan. Bake at 325° for 1 hour.

Combine rice mix, contents of seasoning packet, chicken broth, and next 3 ingredients in a medium saucepan. Bring to a boil; cover, reduce heat, and simmer 25 minutes or until rice is tender and liquid is absorbed. Add garbanzo beans and pecans, tossing gently to combine.

Spoon rice mixture into center of roast. Cover stuffing and exposed ends of ribs with aluminum foil. Insert meat thermometer, making sure it does not touch fat or bone. Bake at 325° for 1½ hours or until meat thermometer registers 160°.

Transfer roast to a large serving platter; remove aluminum foil and string. Spoon half of rice mixture around roast, leaving center of roast filled with remaining rice mixture. Let stand 10 minutes before carving. Garnish, if desired. Yield: 8 to 10 servings.

Special entrées don't have to contain lots of fancy ingredients. You probably have most of the ingredients for Roast Pork Loin with Glazed Apples on hand.

ROAST PORK LOIN WITH GLAZED APPLES

1 (3- to 4-pound) boneless pork
  loin roast, tied
1 teaspoon dried thyme
¼ teaspoon salt
¼ teaspoon pepper
2 large Granny Smith apples

¼ cup lemon juice
1 cup water
½ cup sugar
¼ cup light corn syrup
Garnish: fresh thyme sprigs

Sprinkle roast with thyme, salt, and pepper. Place roast, fat side up, in a lightly greased 13- x 9- x 2-inch pan. Insert meat thermometer into thickest portion, making sure it does not touch fat. Bake at 450° for 20 minutes; reduce heat to 325°, and bake 1 hour and 15 minutes or until thermometer registers 160°. Transfer to a platter; let stand 10 minutes before slicing.

Core apples, and cut into ½-inch-thick rings. Cut rings in half crosswise, and toss with lemon juice. Combine water, sugar, corn syrup, and any remaining lemon juice in a large skillet. Bring to a boil; boil 5 minutes. Layer apple slices in skillet; bring to a boil. Reduce heat, and simmer, uncovered, 8 minutes or until apple slices are tender, turning once. Arrange apple slices on platter around roast. Garnish, if desired. Yield: 8 to 10 servings.

MARINATED BAKED HAM

1 (7- to 8-pound) fully cooked
  ham half
2 cups orange juice
2 cups ginger ale

⅓ cup firmly packed brown sugar
¼ cup orange marmalade
1 teaspoon dry mustard

Place first 3 ingredients in a large heavy-duty, zip-top plastic bag. Seal bag; marinate in refrigerator 8 hours, turning bag occasionally.

Remove ham from marinade, reserving marinade. Place ham, fat side up, in a shallow roasting pan lined with heavy-duty aluminum foil. Bake, uncovered, at 325° for 1½ hours, basting frequently with marinade.

Remove ham from oven; reduce oven temperature to 300°. Slice skin from ham; score fat in a diamond design. Combine brown sugar, marmalade, and mustard; spread over scored fat. Bake, uncovered, an additional 30 minutes. Let stand 10 minutes before carving. Yield: 14 to 16 servings.

SHERRIED CHICKEN WITH ARTICHOKES

6 skinned and boned chicken
  breast halves
1 teaspoon paprika
½ teaspoon pepper
2 tablespoons butter or
  margarine, melted
1 (14-ounce) can artichoke hearts,
  drained and halved
1⅓ cups sliced fresh mushrooms
3 tablespoons sliced green onions

2 tablespoons butter or
  margarine, melted
1 tablespoon cornstarch
1 teaspoon chicken-flavored
  bouillon granules
½ teaspoon dried rosemary,
  crushed
⅔ cup water
¼ cup dry sherry

Sprinkle chicken on both sides with paprika and pepper. Cook chicken in 2 tablespoons butter in a large skillet over medium-high heat 2 minutes on each side or until lightly browned. Place chicken in a lightly greased 11- x 7- x 1½-inch baking dish. Arrange artichoke hearts around chicken; set aside.

Cook mushrooms and green onions in 2 tablespoons butter in a skillet over medium heat, stirring constantly, until tender. Combine cornstarch and remaining ingredients; add to skillet. Bring to a boil; cook, stirring constantly, 1 minute. Pour mixture over chicken and artichokes. Cover and bake at 375° for 30 minutes or until chicken is done. Yield: 6 servings.

HEARTS OF PALM CHICKEN ROLLS

Béarnaise sauce, a classic French sauce, is made from a reduction of wine vinegar and shallots. Tarragon gives the sauce its characteristic flavor. The rich sauce gets its yellow color from egg yolks and butter, and it is served with meat, fish, eggs, or vegetables.

6 skinned and boned chicken
   breast halves
½ teaspoon salt
¼ teaspoon ground white pepper
¼ cup butter or margarine,
   melted and divided

1 (14.4-ounce) can hearts of palm,
   drained
Garnish: fresh tarragon sprigs
Béarnaise Sauce

Place chicken breast halves between 2 sheets of heavy-duty plastic wrap; flatten to ¼-inch thickness using a meat mallet or rolling pin. Sprinkle with salt and pepper; brush with 2 tablespoons melted butter.

Place a heart of palm on each chicken breast half; roll up from short side, and secure each with a wooden pick. Place chicken rolls on a lightly greased rack in a roasting pan; brush with remaining 2 tablespoons melted butter. Cover and bake at 325° for 1 hour. Transfer chicken rolls to a serving platter; garnish, if desired. Serve with Béarnaise Sauce. Yield: 6 servings.

Béarnaise Sauce

3 tablespoons white wine vinegar
2 teaspoons minced shallots
1½ teaspoons chopped fresh
   tarragon or ½ teaspoon dried
   tarragon

3 egg yolks, lightly beaten
⅛ teaspoon salt
⅛ teaspoon ground red pepper
2 tablespoons lemon juice
½ cup butter or margarine

Combine vinegar and shallots in a small saucepan; bring to a boil over medium heat. Reduce heat, and simmer until vinegar is reduced by half. Pour mixture through a wire-mesh strainer into a bowl, discarding shallots. Let vinegar cool slightly; stir in tarragon. Set aside.

Combine egg yolks, salt, and pepper in top of a double boiler; gradually add lemon juice, stirring constantly. Add one-third of butter to egg mixture; cook over hot (not boiling) water, stirring constantly with a wire whisk until butter melts. Add another third of butter, stirring constantly. As sauce thickens, stir in remaining third of butter. Cook, stirring constantly, until mixture is thickened. Remove from heat immediately. Add vinegar mixture to sauce, stirring well. Serve immediately. Yield: ¾ cup.

APRICOT-GLAZED CORNISH HENS

¾ cup apricot preserves
2 teaspoons grated orange rind
2 tablespoons orange juice
4 (1- to 1¼-pound) Cornish hens
¼ teaspoon paprika
½ cup cashews
2 tablespoons butter or margarine,
   melted

½ cup sliced green onions
1 (6-ounce) package long-grain
   and wild rice mix
2⅓ cups chicken broth
Garnish: dried apricot roses

Combine first 3 ingredients in a small bowl; set aside.

Remove giblets from hens; reserve for another use. Rinse hens with cold water, and pat dry. Lift wingtips up and over back, and tuck under hens. Close cavities, and secure with wooden picks. Tie ends of legs together with string. Sprinkle hens with paprika.

Place hens, breast side up, on a lightly greased rack in a shallow roasting pan. Bake, uncovered, at 350° for 45 minutes. Brush hens with ⅓ cup apricot mixture. Bake an additional 30 to 45 minutes or until juices run clear when thigh is pierced with a fork, basting occasionally with ⅓ cup apricot mixture.

Cook cashews in butter in a large skillet over medium heat, stirring frequently, until lightly browned. Remove cashews from skillet using a slotted spoon, reserving butter in skillet. Set cashews aside.

Add green onions to butter in skillet, and cook over medium-high heat, stirring constantly, until tender. Add rice mix, contents of seasoning packet, and chicken broth; bring to a boil. Cover, reduce heat, and simmer 25 minutes or until rice is tender and liquid is absorbed. Stir in cashews.

Place rice mixture on a serving platter. Arrange hens on top of rice mixture. Brush hens with remaining apricot mixture, and garnish, if desired. Yield: 4 servings.

TURKEY BREAST WITH VEGETABLE STUFFING

1 (5-pound) skinned and boned
turkey breast
1½ cups chopped sweet red
pepper
1 cup chopped purple onion
1 (8-ounce) can water chestnuts,
drained and chopped
1 tablespoon olive oil
1 (10-ounce) package frozen
chopped spinach, thawed and
drained

¾ cup Chablis or other dry white
wine, divided
½ teaspoon salt
½ teaspoon pepper
½ teaspoon poultry seasoning
½ teaspoon dried savory
¼ cup olive oil
Garnishes: kale, sweet red pepper
strips, green onions
White Wine Gravy (facing page)

Trim fat from turkey breast; remove tendons. Place outer side of turkey breast on heavy-duty plastic wrap. Starting from center, slice horizontally through thickest portion of each side of breast almost to, but not through, outer edges. Flip cut pieces over to enlarge breast. Place heavy-duty plastic wrap over turkey, and pound to a more even thickness using a meat mallet or rolling pin.

Cook chopped sweet red pepper, chopped onion, and water chestnuts in 1 tablespoon oil in a large skillet over medium heat, stirring constantly, until tender. Add spinach, ½ cup wine, and next 4 ingredients. Cook, stirring constantly, until liquid evaporates.

Spread spinach mixture over turkey breast to within 2 inches of edges; roll up turkey breast, jellyroll fashion, starting with short side. Tie securely at 1½-inch intervals with heavy string. Place turkey roll, seam side down, on a lightly greased rack in a shallow roasting pan. Combine ¼ cup oil and remaining ¼ cup wine; brush over turkey roll. Reserve any remaining wine mixture. Insert meat thermometer into thickest portion of turkey roll.

Bake, uncovered, at 325° for 1 hour and 45 minutes or until meat thermometer registers 170°, basting frequently with reserved wine mixture. Transfer turkey roll to a large serving platter, reserving pan drippings for White Wine Gravy. Let turkey roll stand 10 minutes. Remove strings; cut turkey roll into 12 slices. Garnish, if desired. Serve with White Wine Gravy. Yield: 12 servings.

White Wine Gravy

Pan drippings from 1 roasted
turkey breast
½ cup Chablis or other dry white
wine
1 to 1½ cups chicken broth

½ teaspoon salt
½ teaspoon pepper
2 tablespoons cornstarch
¼ cup water

Spoon pan drippings from turkey breast into a 2-cup liquid measuring cup; add wine and enough chicken broth to make 2 cups. Combine wine mixture, salt, and pepper in a medium saucepan. Combine cornstarch and water; add to wine mixture. Bring to a boil over medium heat; boil, stirring constantly, 1 minute. Yield: 2 cups.

SMOKED TURKEY BREAST

1 (5- to 6-pound) bone-in turkey
breast
1 teaspoon seasoned salt
1 teaspoon dried crushed red
pepper

1 tablespoon seasoned salt
1½ teaspoons dried basil
1 teaspoon paprika
Vegetable cooking spray
Hickory chips

You won't need a smoker or gas grill for this smoked turkey recipe. Three hours on your charcoal grill gives this bird its unbeatable smoky flavor.

Split turkey breast through center so it will lie flat on grill. Combine 1 teaspoon seasoned salt and crushed red pepper; sprinkle mixture over underside of turkey breast. Combine 1 tablespoon seasoned salt, basil, and paprika; sprinkle mixture over top of turkey breast. Coat both sides of turkey breast with cooking spray.

Prepare charcoal fire in end of grill; let burn 15 to 20 minutes. Soak hickory chips in water at least 15 minutes; place chips on coals. Place turkey breast on end of grill opposite hot coals; close grill hood. Cook 2½ to 3 hours or until a meat thermometer registers 170° when inserted into thickest portion of breast. Let stand 10 minutes before carving. Yield: 10 to 12 servings.

ROAST TURKEY WITH CORNBREAD DRESSING

Every holiday season, our test kitchens receive countless requests for a good, basic giblet gravy recipe. Featured on the facing page is an outstanding version of this traditional gravy.

1 (12- to 14-pound) turkey
Salt
Vegetable oil or melted butter or margarine

Garnishes: orange slices, fresh sage sprigs, celery leaves
Cornbread Dressing
Giblet Gravy (facing page)

Remove giblets and neck from turkey; reserve for Giblet Gravy. Rinse turkey thoroughly with cold water; pat dry. Sprinkle cavity with salt. Tie ends of legs to tail with cord or tuck them under flap of skin around tail. Lift wingtips up and over back, and tuck under bird.

Place turkey on a lightly greased rack in a roasting pan, breast side up; brush entire bird with oil. Insert meat thermometer into meaty portion of thigh, making sure it does not touch bone. Bake at 325° until meat thermometer registers 180° (about 3 hours). If turkey starts to brown too much, cover loosely with aluminum foil.

When turkey is two-thirds done, cut the cord or band of skin holding the drumstick ends to the tail; this will ensure that the inside of the thighs is cooked. Turkey is done when drumsticks are easy to move up and down. Let stand 15 minutes before carving. Garnish, if desired. Serve turkey with Cornbread Dressing and Giblet Gravy. Yield: 14 to 16 servings.

Cornbread Dressing

2 cups finely chopped celery
1 small onion, finely chopped
½ cup butter or margarine, melted
5 cups crumbled cornbread

2 cups herb-seasoned stuffing mix
2 teaspoons rubbed sage
2 (14½-ounce) cans ready-to-serve chicken broth
3 large eggs, lightly beaten

Cook celery and onion in butter in a large skillet over medium heat, stirring constantly, until tender. Combine vegetable mixture, cornbread, and remaining ingredients in a large bowl; stir well. Spoon mixture into a lightly greased 13- x 9- x 2-inch baking dish. Bake, uncovered, at 325° for 40 minutes or until lightly browned. Yield: 10 servings.

Giblet Gravy

Giblets and neck from 1 turkey
2 stalks celery, chopped
1 small onion, chopped
½ teaspoon salt
2½ cups water
Pan drippings from roasted
    turkey
3 tablespoons all-purpose flour
¼ cup water
1 hard-cooked egg, chopped
¼ teaspoon pepper

Combine giblets (except liver), neck, celery, onion, and salt in a medium saucepan; add 2½ cups water. Bring to a boil; cover, reduce heat, and simmer 45 minutes or until giblets are tender. Add liver; simmer an additional 10 minutes. Pour mixture through a wire-mesh strainer into a bowl, discarding celery and onion. Set strained broth aside. Remove meat from neck; coarsely chop neck meat and giblets (including liver). Set aside.

Skim fat from pan drippings of roasted turkey; discard fat. Add enough strained broth to pan drippings to equal 1½ cups.

Combine flour and ¼ cup water in a medium saucepan; stir until smooth. Add broth mixture to flour mixture. Cook over medium heat, stirring constantly, until thickened and bubbly. Stir in chopped neck meat, chopped giblets, egg, and pepper. Yield: 2½ cups.

SMOKED HATCREEK QUAIL

12 quail, dressed
2 cups orange juice
Hickory chips
5 cups cola-flavored beverage
Olive oil
2 oranges

Place quail in a large heavy-duty, zip-top plastic bag; add orange juice. Seal bag; marinate in refrigerator 8 hours, turning bag occasionally.

Prepare charcoal fire in smoker; let burn 20 minutes. Soak hickory chips in water at least 15 minutes; place chips on coals. Place water pan in smoker; add cola-flavored beverage to pan.

Drain quail, and brush with olive oil. Tie ends of legs together with string or cord. Cut each orange into 6 slices; arrange orange slices over rack. Arrange quail on top of orange slices. Cover with smoker lid, and cook 1 to 1½ hours or until quail is done. Clip string holding legs together. Arrange quail on serving platter over orange slices. Yield: 6 servings.

Cozy Casual Entrées

If the holidays find you in a state of panic rather than good cheer, take a look at these casual entrées. They're streamlined to make family mealtime or entertaining a little easier. With many of these recipes, preparation time is minimal, and some take shortcuts by using convenience products. We've even included a few that can be made a day ahead, requiring only finishing touches before serving. Consider a soup-and-sandwich combo or perhaps an entrée that needs only a salad and bread to round out the menu. To enhance the ease of casual entertaining, set up a buffet and invite guests to serve themselves.

Mexican Chili (page 151), Turkey Hero with Garlic Sauce (page 149).

SAUSAGE BREAKFAST CASSEROLE

6 slices white bread
Butter or margarine
1 pound ground pork sausage
1½ cups (6 ounces) shredded
  Longhorn cheese

6 large eggs, lightly beaten
2 cups half-and-half
½ teaspoon salt

Trim crust from bread slices; reserve crusts for another use. Spread butter over 1 side of each bread slice. Place bread slices, buttered side up, in bottom of a lightly greased 13- x 9- x 2-inch baking dish. Set aside.

Brown sausage in a large skillet, stirring until it crumbles; drain. Spoon sausage over bread; sprinkle with cheese. Combine eggs, half-and-half, and salt; pour over cheese. Cover and chill 8 hours or overnight.

Remove from refrigerator; let stand, covered, 15 minutes. Uncover and bake at 350° for 45 minutes or until golden. Yield: 8 servings.

BREAKFAST PIZZA

1 pound ground pork sausage
1 (8-ounce) can refrigerator
  crescent rolls
1 cup (4 ounces) shredded sharp
  Cheddar cheese
1 cup (4 ounces) shredded
  mozzarella cheese

5 large eggs, lightly beaten
½ cup milk
¾ teaspoon dried oregano
⅛ teaspoon pepper

Brown sausage in a large skillet, stirring until it crumbles; drain. Set aside.

Unroll crescent rolls, separating into 8 triangles. Place triangles with elongated points toward center on a greased 12-inch pizza pan. Press perforations together to form a crust. Bake at 375° for 8 minutes on lower rack of oven. (Crust will be puffy when removed from oven.) Reduce oven temperature to 350°. Spoon sausage over dough; sprinkle with cheeses.

Combine eggs and remaining ingredients; pour over sausage mixture. Bake at 350° on lower rack of oven 30 to 35 minutes or until crust is golden. Cut into wedges to serve. Yield: 6 to 8 servings.

ROLLED OMELET WITH CHEESE SAUCE

⅓ cup sour cream
1 (3-ounce) package cream cheese, softened
6 large eggs, separated
1½ teaspoons cream of tartar
2 green onions, thinly sliced

2 ounces cooked ham, cut into thin strips
Cheese Sauce
4 slices bacon, cooked and crumbled

Grease a 9-inch square pan; line bottom of pan with wax paper. Grease wax paper; set pan aside. Beat sour cream and cream cheese at medium speed of an electric mixer until smooth and creamy; set aside.

Beat egg whites and cream of tartar at high speed of electric mixer until foamy; set aside. Beat egg yolks at high speed until thick and pale. Fold beaten egg whites into yolks; pour mixture into prepared pan. Bake at 350° for 10 minutes or until set. Broil 5½ inches from heat (with electric oven door partially opened) 1 minute or until top of omelet is lightly browned.

Immediately transfer omelet to a serving platter. Spread cream cheese mixture evenly over omelet; sprinkle with green onions and ham. Roll up omelet, jellyroll fashion. Spoon Cheese Sauce over rolled omelet; sprinkle with bacon. Serve immediately. Yield: 2 to 4 servings.

Cheese Sauce

2 tablespoons butter or margarine
2 tablespoons all-purpose flour
1 cup milk

½ cup (2 ounces) shredded sharp Cheddar cheese
¼ teaspoon salt

Melt butter in a small heavy saucepan over low heat; add flour, stirring until mixture is smooth. Cook, stirring constantly, 1 minute. Gradually add milk; cook over medium heat, stirring constantly, until mixture is thickened and bubbly. Add cheese and salt; stir until cheese melts. Yield: 1¼ cups.

CHILE-CHEESE QUICHE

If you don't have time to prepare pastry for the crust of Chile-Cheese Quiche or Pizza Quiche (below), use a refrigerated piecrust.

Pastry for 9-inch pie
1 cup (4 ounces) shredded
   Cheddar cheese
1½ cups (6 ounces) shredded
   Monterey Jack cheese, divided

1 (4-ounce) can chopped green
   chiles, drained
3 large eggs, lightly beaten
1 cup half-and-half

Line a 9-inch quiche dish or pieplate with pastry; trim excess pastry around edges. Prick bottom and sides of pastry with a fork. Bake at 400° for 3 minutes; remove pastry shell from oven, and gently prick again. Bake an additional 5 minutes. Cool completely on a wire rack.

Layer Cheddar cheese, ¾ cup Monterey Jack cheese, green chiles, and remaining ¾ cup Monterey Jack cheese in pastry shell. Combine eggs and half-and-half; pour into pastry shell. Bake at 350° for 50 minutes or until set. Let stand 10 minutes before serving. Yield: 6 servings.

PIZZA QUICHE

½ pound hot Italian sausage
Pastry for double-crust 9-inch pie
1 cup ricotta cheese
3 large eggs
1 cup (4 ounces) shredded
   mozzarella cheese

¼ cup grated Parmesan cheese
1 (3½-ounce) package sliced
   pepperoni, chopped
1 tablespoon milk
Commercial pizza sauce

Remove and discard casings from sausage. Brown sausage in a large skillet, stirring until it crumbles; drain well, and set aside.

Line a 9-inch quiche dish or pieplate with half of pastry; trim excess pastry around edges. Prick bottom and sides of pastry with a fork. Bake at 400° for 8 minutes. Remove from oven; reduce oven temperature to 350°.

Combine ricotta cheese and eggs in a large mixing bowl; beat at medium speed of an electric mixer until smooth. Stir in sausage, mozzarella cheese, Parmesan cheese, and pepperoni. Spoon mixture into pastry shell.

Cut an 8-inch circle out of remaining pastry; cut circle into 6 wedges. Arrange pastry wedges on top of filling. Bake at 350° for 20 minutes. Brush top of pastry with milk; bake an additional 20 to 25 minutes or until golden. Cool 10 minutes before serving. Cook pizza sauce over medium heat just until thoroughly heated; serve with quiche. Yield: 6 servings.

Spicy Barbecued Shrimp is a quick fix that makes the most of a favorite shellfish. The succulent shrimp are baked in a spicy butter mixture with lemon slices.

SPICY BARBECUED SHRIMP

1 cup butter or margarine, melted
1 cup lemon juice
1 cup Worcestershire sauce
2 tablespoons chopped fresh
 rosemary or 2 teaspoons dried
 rosemary
1 tablespoon salt
1 tablespoon coarsely ground
 black pepper
1 tablespoon hot sauce

¼ teaspoon ground red pepper
4 cloves garlic, minced
3 pounds unpeeled large or jumbo
 fresh shrimp
2 large lemons, thinly sliced
Garnishes: fresh rosemary sprigs,
 lemon wedges
French bread (optional)

Combine first 9 ingredients; stir well, and set aside. Rinse shrimp; drain well. Layer shrimp and lemon slices in a shallow 3-quart baking dish; pour butter mixture over shrimp. Bake, uncovered, at 400° for 25 to 30 minutes or until shrimp are done and shells start to pull away, stirring once. Garnish, if desired. Serve with French bread, if desired. Yield: 6 servings.

PEPPERONI SPAGHETTI

Pepperoni Spaghetti is a flavorful combination of ingredients from two all-time favorites—pizza and spaghetti. A green salad and bread are all you need to round out this easy entrée.

1 pound ground beef
1 (3-ounce) package sliced pepperoni, chopped
1 large onion, chopped
1 medium-size green pepper, chopped
1 (32-ounce) jar spaghetti sauce with mushrooms

1 (12-ounce) package spaghetti, uncooked
1 cup (4 ounces) shredded mozzarella cheese
1 tablespoon grated Parmesan cheese

Cook first 4 ingredients in a large skillet over medium-high heat until beef is browned, stirring until beef crumbles; drain well. Return mixture to skillet; stir in spaghetti sauce. Bring to a boil; cover, reduce heat, and simmer 20 minutes, stirring occasionally.

Cook spaghetti according to package directions, omitting salt; drain. Arrange cooked spaghetti on an ovenproof platter. Spoon meat sauce over spaghetti; sprinkle with mozzarella cheese. Broil 5½ inches from heat (with electric oven door partially opened) 1 to 2 minutes or until cheese melts. Remove from oven; sprinkle with Parmesan cheese. Yield: 6 to 8 servings.

DOUBLE-CRUST TACO SQUARES

1 pound ground beef
1 (1¼-ounce) package taco seasoning mix
2 (8-ounce) cans refrigerator crescent rolls

4 cups (16 ounces) shredded Monterey Jack cheese, divided
Sour cream
Commercial salsa
Jalapeño pepper slices (optional)

Brown ground beef in a large skillet, stirring until it crumbles; drain. Add taco seasoning mix, preparing according to package directions. Set aside.

Unroll 1 can of rolls onto a lightly greased baking sheet; press perforations together to make a 13- x 8-inch rectangle. Sprinkle with 2 cups cheese. Spread beef mixture over cheese; sprinkle with remaining 2 cups cheese. Unroll second can of rolls onto a flat surface; press perforations together to make a 13- x 8-inch rectangle. Place rectangle over cheese; press edges together to seal.

Bake at 400° for 12 to 15 minutes or until browned. Cool 5 minutes; cut into squares. Serve with sour cream, salsa, and, if desired, jalapeño pepper slices. Yield: 6 servings.

CHICKEN ENCHILADAS

1½ tablespoons chopped onion
1½ tablespoons chopped fresh
   cilantro
1 jalapeño pepper, seeded and
   chopped
1½ teaspoons butter or
   margarine, melted
5 cups shredded, cooked chicken

3 (10-ounce) cans enchilada sauce,
   divided
8 (6-inch) corn tortillas
1½ cups (6 ounces) shredded
   Cheddar cheese
½ cup diced tomato
⅓ cup sliced ripe olives
4 cups shredded iceberg lettuce

Cook first 3 ingredients in butter in a large skillet over medium-high heat, stirring constantly, until tender. Stir in chicken and 1 can enchilada sauce; reduce heat, and cook 5 minutes, stirring occasionally.

Wrap tortillas in aluminum foil; bake at 350° for 12 minutes or until thoroughly heated. Work with 1 tortilla at a time, keeping remaining tortillas covered and warm. Spoon ¼ cup chicken mixture down center of tortilla. Roll up tightly, and place in a 13- x 9- x 2-inch baking dish, seam side down. Repeat procedure with remaining tortillas and chicken mixture.

Heat remaining 2 cans enchilada sauce; pour over enchiladas. Top with cheese, tomato, and olives. Bake at 350° for 10 to 12 minutes or until cheese melts and enchiladas are thoroughly heated. Serve enchiladas on bed of shredded lettuce. Yield: 4 servings.

QUICK CURRIED CHICKEN

1 pound skinned and boned
   chicken breast halves, cubed
¾ cup chopped onion
3 tablespoons butter or margarine,
   melted
1 (10¾-ounce) can cream of
   mushroom soup, undiluted

1½ teaspoons curry powder
1 (8-ounce) carton sour cream
Hot cooked rice
Assorted condiments: flaked
   coconut, dry-roasted peanuts,
   chopped green onions, raisins,
   crumbled cooked bacon

Cook chicken and ¾ cup chopped onion in butter in a large skillet over medium heat, stirring constantly, until chicken is done. Stir in soup and curry powder. Bring to a boil, stirring frequently. Reduce heat to low; stir in sour cream. Cook, stirring frequently, until thoroughly heated. Serve over rice. Top with your choice of assorted condiments. Yield: 4 to 6 servings.

The assorted condiments listed with the ingredients are what give Quick Curried Chicken its flair. Let family members or guests personalize their plates by adding their choice of the suggested condiments.

EASY RED BEANS AND RICE

Easy Red Beans and Rice is quick to fix—it uses canned beans and is ready in about 30 minutes.

1 pound smoked link sausage, cut into ¼-inch slices
1 medium onion, chopped
1 green pepper, chopped
1 clove garlic, minced
2 (15-ounce) cans kidney beans, drained

1 (16-ounce) can whole tomatoes, undrained and chopped
½ teaspoon dried oregano
½ teaspoon ground black pepper
Hot cooked rice

Cook sausage in a Dutch oven over medium-high heat until browned, stirring frequently. Add onion, green pepper, and garlic; cook until tender, stirring occasionally. Stir in beans and next 3 ingredients. Bring to a boil; cover, reduce heat, and simmer 20 minutes, stirring occasionally. Serve over rice. Yield: 4 to 6 servings.

HAM-AND-BLUE CHEESE PASTA SALAD

3 cups bow tie pasta, uncooked
1 cup coarsely chopped pecans
⅓ cup grated Parmesan cheese
2 tablespoons chopped fresh parsley
1 tablespoon minced fresh rosemary
½ to ¾ teaspoon freshly ground pepper

4 ounces cooked ham, cut into strips
1 (4-ounce) package blue cheese, crumbled
1 clove garlic, minced
¼ cup olive oil

Cook pasta according to package directions. Drain well, and place in a large serving bowl. Add pecans and next 7 ingredients, tossing gently to combine. Add oil, stirring gently to coat mixture. Serve immediately or cover and chill thoroughly, if desired. Yield: 4 to 6 servings.

Taco Salad is perfect for those nights when you have only a few minutes to fix dinner. This main-dish salad also makes a great Saturday lunch.

TACO SALAD

1 (5.6-ounce) package flour
   tortilla salad shells
1 pound ground beef
$\frac{2}{3}$ cup water
$\frac{1}{4}$ cup taco seasoning mix
$\frac{1}{4}$ cup chopped green onions
$\frac{1}{2}$ medium head iceberg lettuce,
   shredded

1 large tomato, chopped
1 ($2\frac{1}{4}$-ounce) can sliced ripe
   olives, drained
1 medium avocado, peeled and
   sliced
Shredded Cheddar cheese
Sour cream
Commercial picante sauce

Bake salad shells according to package directions; set aside. Brown ground beef in a large skillet, stirring until it crumbles; drain. Return to skillet; add water, taco seasoning mix, and green onions. Bring to a boil; reduce heat, and simmer 10 minutes, stirring occasionally.

Layer lettuce and next 3 ingredients in salad shells; top with meat mixture. Serve with cheese, sour cream, and picante sauce. Yield: 4 servings.

CURRIED TURKEY SALAD

Raisins and chopped Red Delicious apple add a slightly sweet touch to Curried Turkey Salad. This salad is the perfect entrée for a ladies' luncheon.

2 cups unpeeled chopped Red
   Delicious apple
2 tablespoons lemon juice
2 cups cubed cooked turkey breast
1 cup thinly sliced celery
1 cup chopped pecans
½ cup raisins
2 tablespoons minced onion
⅓ cup whipping cream
2 teaspoons curry powder

¾ teaspoon salt
¼ teaspoon pepper
½ cup mayonnaise or salad
   dressing
Lettuce leaves
1 medium-size Red Delicious
   apple, thinly sliced
Lemon juice
¼ cup flaked coconut, toasted

Combine chopped apple and 2 tablespoons lemon juice in a large bowl, tossing to coat. Add turkey and next 4 ingredients, tossing to combine. Set aside.

Combine whipping cream, curry powder, salt, and pepper in a small mixing bowl; beat at medium speed of an electric mixer until soft peaks form. Fold whipped cream mixture into mayonnaise; fold mayonnaise mixture into turkey mixture. Cover and chill thoroughly.

Spoon turkey mixture onto individual lettuce-lined plates. Brush apple slices with lemon juice, and arrange slices on plates. Sprinkle salads with toasted coconut, and serve immediately. Yield: 6 servings.

HOT CRAB-AND-CHEESE SANDWICHES

½ cup chopped green onions
½ cup chopped sweet red pepper
1 tablespoon butter or margarine,
   melted
½ pound fresh crabmeat, drained
   and flaked
1 cup (4 ounces) shredded
   Cheddar cheese

1 cup (4 ounces) shredded
   Monterey Jack cheese
⅓ cup cream of celery soup,
   undiluted
3 English muffins, split and
   toasted

Cook green onions and pepper in butter in a skillet over medium-high heat, stirring constantly, until tender. Remove from heat; stir in crabmeat and next 3 ingredients. Mound mixture in centers of muffin halves. (Do not spread to edges.) Place muffin halves on a lightly greased baking sheet. Bake at 350° for 15 minutes or until thoroughly heated. Yield: 3 to 6 servings.

MUFFALETTA-STYLE PO-BOYS

6 French rolls, split
¼ cup mayonnaise or salad
   dressing
1 tablespoon plus 1 teaspoon salad
   olive juice
½ pound thinly sliced deli ham

¼ cup plus 2 tablespoons chopped
   salad olives
¼ pound thinly sliced salami
2 tablespoons chopped ripe olives
1 (6-ounce) package sliced
   mozzarella cheese

Place roll halves, cut side up, on an ungreased baking sheet. Combine mayonnaise and olive juice; spread mixture on cut side of each roll half. Layer bottom halves of rolls evenly with ham, salad olives, salami, and ripe olives. Place 1 cheese slice on top half of each roll.

   Broil 3 inches from heat (with electric oven door partially opened) 2 to 3 minutes or until cheese melts. Invert cheese halves of rolls onto meat halves; serve immediately. Yield: 6 servings.

TURKEY HERO WITH GARLIC SAUCE

¼ cup mayonnaise or salad
   dressing
1 tablespoon minced fresh chives
1 tablespoon vegetable oil
1 tablespoon Dijon mustard
1 teaspoon sugar
1 teaspoon lemon juice

1 large clove garlic, minced
1 (16-ounce) loaf French bread
Lettuce leaves
12 ounces sliced cooked turkey
2 medium tomatoes, sliced
1 small purple onion, sliced and
   separated into rings

Combine first 7 ingredients in container of an electric blender; process until smooth, stopping once to scrape down sides. Slice bread in half horizontally; spread mayonnaise mixture on cut sides of bread. Layer lettuce leaves, turkey, tomato, and onion on bottom half of bread. Cover with top half of bread. Secure sandwich with long wooden picks, if necessary. To serve, cut sandwich into 6 equal portions. Yield: 6 servings.

Turkey Hero with Garlic Sauce will feed a hungry bunch and make mealtime easy on the cook. Garnish each section of the sandwich with a small sweet pickle or green olive attached with a long wooden pick.

While Chunky Potato Soup cooks, you'll have just enough time to toss a salad and heat commercial rolls for a sure-to-please family supper.

CHUNKY POTATO SOUP

3 tablespoons butter or margarine
¼ cup all-purpose flour
4 cups milk
2 cups peeled, chopped baking potato

½ cup minced onion
¾ teaspoon salt
½ teaspoon freshly ground pepper
Garnish: fresh chives

Melt butter in a heavy saucepan over low heat; add flour, stirring until smooth. Cook, stirring constantly, 1 minute. Gradually stir in milk. Stir in potato and next 3 ingredients. Cook over medium heat, stirring frequently, 30 minutes or until mixture is thickened and potato is done. Garnish, if desired. Yield: 5 cups.

CHEESY BROCCOLI SOUP

1 (10-ounce) package frozen
   chopped broccoli
½ cup chopped onion
¼ cup chopped green pepper
1½ tablespoons butter or
   margarine, melted

1½ cups milk
1 cup water
1 (10¾-ounce) can cream of
   chicken soup, undiluted
12 ounces loaf process cheese
   spread, cubed

Cook broccoli according to package directions, omitting salt; drain well.

Cook onion and pepper in butter in a large saucepan over medium heat, stirring constantly, until tender. Add broccoli, milk, and remaining ingredients; cook, stirring frequently, until cheese melts and mixture is thoroughly heated. Yield: 6 cups.

MEXICAN CHILI

2 pounds ground beef
1 cup chopped onion
¾ cup chopped green pepper
1 clove garlic, minced
1 (16-ounce) can kidney beans,
   drained
1 (16-ounce) can whole tomatoes,
   undrained and chopped
2 (8-ounce) cans tomato sauce
1 tablespoon plus 1 teaspoon chili
   powder

2 teaspoons ground cumin
½ teaspoon salt
½ teaspoon dried basil
¼ teaspoon pepper
¼ teaspoon hot sauce
1 fresh or canned green chile,
   seeded and chopped
Shredded Cheddar cheese
   (optional)
Corn chips (optional)

You can make rich and meaty Mexican Chili a day or two ahead; then simply reheat and serve. To freeze, prepare the chili, and let cool completely. Place in an airtight container, and freeze up to one month. Thaw before reheating.

Combine first 4 ingredients in a Dutch oven; cook over medium heat until beef is browned, stirring until it crumbles. Drain. Add beans and next 9 ingredients; cover, reduce heat, and simmer 20 minutes, stirring occasionally. If desired, top with shredded Cheddar cheese, and serve with corn chips. Yield: 9 cups.

All The Trimmings

'Tis the season for traditions, and many of them come in the form of delicious side dishes reserved just for the holidays. Salads and vegetables that are prepared simply the rest of the year now arrive at the dinner table embellished in exceptional ways and served in the finest china and silver. Although lavish attention is given to entrées and desserts, it's the classic trimmings—sweet potato casserole, cranberry salad, and oyster dressing, to name a few—that family members request and expect for the holiday feast. These are the treasured flavors and aromas that mean Christmas to the families who share them. May these side dishes become a part of your family's traditions.

Walnut-Goat Cheese Salad (page 158), Pepper Pasta (page 154).

153

CHEESE GRITS CASSEROLE

4 cups water
1 teaspoon salt
1 cup quick-cooking grits
2 cups (8 ounces) shredded sharp
  Cheddar cheese
⅔ cup milk

⅓ cup butter or margarine
1 teaspoon Worcestershire sauce
¼ teaspoon ground red pepper
4 large eggs, lightly beaten
Paprika

Bring water and salt to a boil in a large saucepan; stir in grits. Return to a boil. Cover, reduce heat, and simmer 5 minutes, stirring occasionally. Remove from heat. Add cheese and next 4 ingredients, stirring until cheese and butter melt. Add eggs; stir well.

Spoon mixture into a lightly greased 2-quart casserole; sprinkle with paprika. Bake at 350° for 1 hour or until thoroughly heated and lightly browned. Let stand 5 minutes before serving. Yield: 8 servings.

PEPPER PASTA

Pepper Pasta gets its festive holiday color from sweet red pepper and green pepper strips. You can use two peppers of the same color, if you'd like.

4 cloves garlic, minced
1 teaspoon grated lemon rind
½ teaspoon dried crushed red
  pepper
¼ cup butter or margarine,
  melted
3 tablespoons olive oil
1 (14½-ounce) can ready-to-serve
  chicken broth
3 tablespoons lemon juice

½ teaspoon salt
½ teaspoon freshly ground
  pepper
1 (16-ounce) package fettuccine,
  uncooked
1 medium-size sweet red pepper,
  cut into thin strips
1 medium-size green pepper, cut
  into thin strips

Cook first 3 ingredients in butter and oil in a medium saucepan over medium heat 2 minutes, stirring occasionally. Stir in chicken broth and lemon juice; cook until mixture is reduced to 1¼ cups (about 25 minutes), stirring occasionally. Stir in salt and ground pepper. Set aside.

Cook fettuccine in a Dutch oven according to package directions; drain well. Return fettuccine to Dutch oven; add broth mixture and pepper strips. Cook over low heat, tossing gently, until mixture is thoroughly heated. Serve immediately. Yield: 8 to 10 servings.

ORANGE-HERB RICE

2 tablespoons chopped onion
2 tablespoons butter or margarine, melted
2 cups water
½ teaspoon grated orange rind
½ cup orange juice
1 teaspoon salt
⅛ teaspoon dried marjoram
⅛ teaspoon dried thyme
1 cup long-grain rice, uncooked

Cook onion in butter in a large saucepan over medium-high heat, stirring constantly, until tender. Add water and next 5 ingredients; bring to a boil. Stir in rice. Cover, reduce heat, and simmer 25 minutes or until rice is tender and liquid is absorbed. Yield: 6 to 8 servings.

CORNBREAD-OYSTER DRESSING

7 slices whole wheat bread, toasted and cut into ½-inch cubes
6 cups cornbread crumbs
2 tablespoons dried parsley flakes
1 teaspoon rubbed sage
1 cup finely chopped celery
1 cup chopped onion
¼ cup butter or margarine, melted
2 large eggs, lightly beaten
3½ to 4 cups chicken broth
1 (12-ounce) container fresh Standard oysters, drained and chopped
1 teaspoon salt
1 teaspoon pepper

Combine first 4 ingredients in a large bowl; set aside. Cook celery and onion in butter in a large skillet over medium-high heat, stirring constantly, until tender; let cool. Add vegetable mixture and eggs to bread mixture; stir in enough chicken broth to moisten bread. Stir in oysters, salt, and pepper.

Spoon mixture into a greased 13- x 9- x 2-inch baking dish. Bake at 350° for 40 minutes or until thoroughly heated and edges of dressing are lightly browned. Yield: 10 to 12 servings.

Rice Dressing brings out the best in pork chops. This side dish can even stand alone as a hearty but not-too-filling entrée.

RICE DRESSING

1 (6-ounce) package long-grain
  and wild rice mix
¾ pound ground pork sausage
1 tablespoon vegetable oil
1 tablespoon all-purpose flour
1 cup chopped onion
¾ cup chopped celery
¾ cup sliced green onions

½ cup chopped green pepper
1 teaspoon Worcestershire sauce
⅛ teaspoon hot sauce
2 cloves garlic, minced
1 chicken-flavored bouillon cube
1 (4.5-ounce) jar sliced
  mushrooms

Cook rice mix according to package directions. Set aside. Brown sausage in a Dutch oven, stirring until it crumbles. Drain and set aside.

Combine oil and flour in Dutch oven; cook over medium heat, stirring constantly, until mixture is caramel-colored. Stir in chopped onion and next

7 ingredients. Drain mushrooms, reserving liquid; add water to mushroom liquid to equal 1 cup. Add mushrooms and 1 cup liquid to Dutch oven.

Bring mixture to a boil; cover, reduce heat, and simmer 15 minutes or until vegetables are tender. Stir in rice and sausage; cook until thoroughly heated. Yield: 8 servings.

CITRUS-BLUE CHEESE SALAD

2 medium-size pink grapefruit
1 (0.7-ounce) envelope Italian salad dressing mix
½ cup vegetable oil
2 tablespoons water

10 cups mixed salad greens
2 oranges, peeled, seeded, and sectioned
1 (4-ounce) package crumbled blue cheese

Citrus-Blue Cheese Salad is a smart choice as a first course for an elegant dinner party. It not only serves a lot of guests but also can be made ahead.

Peel and section grapefruit, catching juice in a bowl. Reserve ¼ cup juice; set grapefruit sections aside. Combine reserved juice, dressing mix, oil, and water in a jar. Cover tightly, and shake vigorously. Chill at least 3 hours.

Layer half each of salad greens, grapefruit sections, and orange sections in a large salad bowl. Repeat procedure with remaining greens and fruit sections. Sprinkle with blue cheese. Cover and chill at least 3 hours. Pour dressing over salad, tossing to coat. Serve immediately. Yield: 10 servings.

Note: Any combination of leaf, romaine, and Bibb lettuces and fresh spinach will work well in this salad.

GREEK SALAD

6 cups torn iceberg lettuce
4 cups torn romaine lettuce
1 cup pitted ripe olives
2 tomatoes, cut into wedges
1 large cucumber, sliced
½ cup olive oil

3 tablespoons red wine vinegar
1 teaspoon dried oregano
½ teaspoon freshly ground pepper
1 cup crumbled feta cheese

Serve our version of classic Greek Salad with your favorite veal piccata and creamy fettuccine Alfredo recipes.

Combine first 5 ingredients in a large bowl; toss well. Combine olive oil, vinegar, oregano, and pepper in a jar. Cover tightly, and shake vigorously. Pour dressing over salad, tossing to coat. Sprinkle with feta cheese. Serve immediately. Yield: 10 servings.

GREEN SALAD VINAIGRETTE

You'll want to have Roasted Pecans on hand not only for the salad but also for munching or gift giving. You can easily double or triple the recipe.

6 cups mixed salad greens
4 slices bacon, cooked and
  crumbled
1 small purple onion, thinly sliced
Roasted Pecans

¼ cup olive oil
2 tablespoons raspberry vinegar
1½ teaspoons sugar
⅛ teaspoon salt
Dash of ground white pepper

Combine first 4 ingredients in a large bowl; toss well. Combine olive oil and remaining ingredients in a jar. Cover tightly, and shake vigorously. Pour dressing over salad, tossing to coat. Serve immediately. Yield: 6 servings.

Roasted Pecans

1 tablespoon butter or margarine
2 tablespoons sugar
1 tablespoon orange juice

¼ teaspoon ground cinnamon
⅛ teaspoon ground red pepper
1 cup pecan halves

Melt butter in a large skillet over medium heat; stir in sugar and next 3 ingredients. Add pecans, stirring to coat. Spread pecans on a lightly greased baking sheet. Bake at 325° for 15 minutes, stirring every 5 minutes. Cool completely. Yield: 1 cup.

WALNUT-GOAT CHEESE SALAD

¼ cup orange juice
3 tablespoons white wine vinegar
⅛ teaspoon salt
⅛ teaspoon ground white pepper
½ cup vegetable oil
¼ cup olive oil

6 cups mixed baby lettuce or
  mixed salad greens
½ cup chopped walnuts, toasted
6 ounces goat cheese, cut into
  ¼-inch-thick slices
Garnish: edible flowers

Combine first 4 ingredients in container of an electric blender. With blender on high, gradually add oils in a slow, steady stream, processing until blended.
　Arrange lettuce, walnuts, and goat cheese slices on individual salad plates. Garnish, if desired. Serve dressing with salad. Yield: 6 servings.

Proudly present Frozen Cranberry Salad with this year's holiday dinner. You'll enjoy this refreshing alternative to the traditional congealed salad.

FROZEN CRANBERRY SALAD

2 (3-ounce) packages cream
   cheese, softened
2 tablespoons sugar
2 tablespoons mayonnaise or salad
   dressing
1 (16-ounce) can whole-berry
   cranberry sauce
1 (8-ounce) can crushed
   pineapple, drained

½ cup chopped pecans
1 cup whipping cream
½ cup sifted powdered sugar
1 teaspoon vanilla extract
Lettuce leaves
Garnishes: fresh cranberries,
   fresh mint sprigs

To make individual salads, freeze the mixture for Frozen Cranberry Salad in lightly oiled muffin pans.

Combine first 3 ingredients, stirring until smooth. Stir in cranberry sauce, pineapple, and pecans.

Beat whipping cream until foamy; gradually add powdered sugar, beating until soft peaks form. Stir in vanilla. Fold whipped cream mixture into cranberry mixture. Spoon mixture into an 8-inch square dish. Cover and freeze until firm. Cut into squares, and serve on lettuce leaves. Garnish, if desired. Yield: 9 servings.

RASPBERRY RIBBON SALAD

For variety, substitute strawberry-flavored gelatin and frozen strawberries in syrup for the raspberry-flavored gelatin and raspberries in syrup.

2 (3-ounce) packages raspberry-flavored gelatin
1¼ cups boiling water
2 (10-ounce) packages frozen raspberries in syrup, thawed and undrained
1 (15¼-ounce) can crushed pineapple, undrained
½ cup chopped pecans
2 cups sour cream, divided
Lettuce leaves

Combine gelatin and boiling water, stirring 2 minutes or until gelatin dissolves. Chill until the consistency of unbeaten egg white. Fold in raspberries, pineapple, and pecans. Spoon 1½ cups gelatin mixture into a lightly oiled 9-cup mold; chill until set. (Keep remaining gelatin mixture at room temperature.) Spread 1 cup sour cream over raspberry layer. Spoon half of remaining raspberry mixture over sour cream layer; chill until set.

Spread remaining 1 cup sour cream over raspberry layer; top with remaining raspberry mixture. Cover and chill until set. Unmold onto a lettuce-lined serving plate. Yield: 14 servings.

MARINATED ASPARAGUS AND HEARTS OF PALM

Hearts of palm are the edible inner portion of the stem of the cabbage palm tree. Hearts of palm resemble white asparagus (without the tip), and their taste is similar to that of an artichoke.

3 pounds fresh asparagus
2 (14.4-ounce) cans hearts of palm, drained and cut into ½-inch slices
1 pint teardrop or cherry tomatoes
¾ cup vegetable oil
½ cup cider vinegar
1½ teaspoons salt
1 teaspoon pepper
3 cloves garlic, crushed
Bibb lettuce leaves

Snap off tough ends of asparagus. Remove scales from stalks with a knife or vegetable peeler, if desired. Arrange asparagus, in batches, in a vegetable steamer over boiling water. Cover and steam 4 to 5 minutes or until crisp-tender. Plunge asparagus into ice water to stop cooking process; drain.

Combine asparagus, hearts of palm, and tomatoes in a large heavy-duty, zip-top plastic bag. Combine oil and next 4 ingredients in a small jar. Cover tightly, and shake vigorously. Pour dressing mixture over vegetable mixture in bag. Seal bag, and marinate in refrigerator 8 hours, turning bag occasionally.

To serve, drain vegetable mixture, discarding marinade. Arrange vegetable mixture on a lettuce-lined platter. Yield: 12 servings.

SALADE RIVIERA

1 (14.4-ounce) can hearts of palm, drained and sliced
1 (14-ounce) can artichoke hearts, drained and quartered
10 pimiento-stuffed olives, halved
10 pitted ripe olives, halved
½ cup chopped green pepper
½ cup chopped sweet red pepper
Vinaigrette Dressing
Boston lettuce leaves
12 cherry tomatoes, halved
2 hard-cooked eggs, quartered

Combine first 6 ingredients in a large bowl. Pour Vinaigrette Dressing over salad, tossing gently to coat. Cover and chill at least 1 hour. To serve, arrange salad mixture on a lettuce-lined platter, and top with tomato halves and egg quarters. Yield: 4 to 6 servings.

Vinaigrette Dressing

3 tablespoons white wine vinegar
3 tablespoons olive oil
3 tablespoons vegetable oil
½ teaspoon salt
½ teaspoon pepper
½ teaspoon Dijon mustard

Combine all ingredients in a small jar. Cover tightly, and shake vigorously. Yield: ½ cup.

ZESTY BLACK-EYED PEA SALAD

2 (15.8-ounce) cans black-eyed peas, rinsed and drained
1 cup chopped celery
1 cup chopped green pepper
1 cup peeled, chopped tomato
⅓ cup sliced green onions
1 clove garlic, minced
1 (4.5-ounce) jar sliced mushrooms, drained
1 (4-ounce) jar diced pimiento, drained
1 (8-ounce) bottle Italian salad dressing
Lettuce leaves
½ cup sliced green onions
3 slices bacon, cooked and crumbled

Combine first 9 ingredients in a large bowl, tossing gently. Cover and chill at least 8 hours, stirring occasionally. Drain vegetable mixture, and spoon into a lettuce-lined serving bowl; sprinkle with ½ cup sliced green onions and crumbled bacon. Yield: 8 to 10 servings.

CHAMPAGNE ORANGES

Serve Champagne Oranges as a side dish with dinner or as a breakfast or brunch accompaniment. Sparkling white grape juice may be substituted for the champagne.

½ cup sugar
½ cup orange marmalade
1½ cups champagne

8 large navel oranges, peeled and sectioned
⅓ cup slivered almonds, toasted

Combine sugar and marmalade in a small saucepan; cook over medium heat, stirring frequently, until sugar dissolves. Cool slightly. Combine marmalade mixture, champagne, and orange sections in a large bowl, stirring gently. Cover and chill 8 hours.

Transfer orange mixture to a serving dish, and sprinkle with slivered almonds. Yield: 10 to 12 servings.

Every delectable bite of Champagne Oranges combines the sweetness of oranges with the tartness of champagne. The oranges marinate for eight hours, so make it ahead.

CRANBERRY-ORANGE CHUTNEY

2 oranges, peeled, seeded, and
  sectioned
1 (16-ounce) can whole-berry
  cranberry sauce
1 (16-ounce) can pear halves,
  drained and chopped
1 cooking apple, chopped

1 cup sugar
½ cup raisins
¼ cup chopped pecans
1 tablespoon white vinegar
½ teaspoon ground ginger
½ teaspoon ground cinnamon

Chop orange sections. Combine chopped orange, cranberry sauce, and remaining ingredients in a large saucepan. Cook over medium heat, stirring frequently, 45 to 50 minutes or until mixture is very thick; cool. Store in an airtight container in refrigerator. Yield: 4 cups.

Chutney, from the East Indian word "chatni," is a thick condiment containing fruit, sugar, vinegar, and spices. Serve Cranberry-Orange Chutney with grilled or roasted pork or poultry or with cheese or bread.

HOT CURRIED FRUIT

1 (29-ounce) can pear halves,
  undrained
1 (29-ounce) can peach halves,
  undrained
1 (20-ounce) can pineapple
  chunks, undrained
1 (17-ounce) can apricot halves,
  undrained

1 (16½-ounce) can pitted Royal
  Anne cherries, undrained
¼ cup sugar
3 tablespoons all-purpose flour
3 tablespoons butter or margarine
¼ cup Chablis or other dry
  white wine*
1 teaspoon curry powder

Drain first 5 ingredients, reserving juices in a bowl. Combine fruit in a large bowl; set aside. Stir juice mixture, and reserve ¾ cup. Reserve remaining juice mixture for another use.

Combine sugar and flour in a heavy saucepan; gradually stir in reserved ¾ cup juice mixture. Add butter, and cook over medium heat, stirring constantly, until mixture is thickened and bubbly. Remove from heat; stir in wine and curry powder.

Add sauce mixture to fruit mixture, stirring gently. Spoon mixture into a lightly greased 13- x 9- x 2-inch baking dish. Bake at 350° for 30 minutes or until thoroughly heated. Yield: 10 to 12 servings.

*One-fourth cup fruit juice mixture may be substituted for wine.

Fruit Side Dishes   163

SCALLOPED PINEAPPLE

3 cups 1-inch cubes French bread
  (crusts removed)
1¼ cups sugar
⅓ cup butter or margarine,
  melted

3 large eggs, lightly beaten
1 (20-ounce) can crushed
  pineapple, undrained

Combine all ingredients in a large bowl; stir well. Spoon mixture into a
lightly greased 2-quart casserole. Bake at 350° for 45 to 50 minutes or until
golden and bubbly. Yield: 8 to 10 servings.

ASPARAGUS SOUFFLÉ

A soufflé is an airy mixture lightened by the addition of stiffly beaten egg whites or whipped cream. Soufflés may be hot or cold, savory or sweet. Baked soufflés are more delicate than chilled or frozen ones because the air trapped in a baked soufflé begins to escape as soon as the dish is removed from the oven, causing the soufflé to deflate. Be ready to serve a baked soufflé as soon as it comes out of the oven.

1 (10-ounce) package frozen
  asparagus
¼ cup butter or margarine
⅓ cup all-purpose flour
1½ cups milk
1 cup (4 ounces) shredded
  mozzarella cheese

½ teaspoon salt
¼ teaspoon black pepper
Dash of ground red pepper
4 large eggs, separated

Cut a piece of aluminum foil long enough to fit around a 2-quart soufflé
dish, allowing a 1-inch overlap; fold foil lengthwise into thirds. Lightly oil
1 side of foil and bottom of dish. Wrap foil around outside of dish, oiled side
against dish, allowing it to extend 3 inches above rim; secure with string.

Cook asparagus according to package directions, omitting salt; drain.
Position knife blade in food processor bowl; add asparagus. Process 1
minute or until smooth. Set aside.

Melt butter in a large heavy saucepan over low heat; add flour, stirring
until mixture is smooth. Cook, stirring constantly, 1 minute. Gradually add
milk; cook over medium heat, stirring constantly, until mixture is thickened
and bubbly. Add cheese and next 3 ingredients, stirring until cheese melts.

Beat egg yolks until thick and pale. Gradually stir about one-fourth of hot
mixture into yolks; add to remaining hot mixture, stirring constantly. Stir in
pureed asparagus. Beat egg whites at high speed of an electric mixer until
stiff peaks form; gently fold into asparagus mixture. Pour into prepared
dish. Bake at 350° for 50 minutes or until puffed and golden. Remove foil
collar, and serve immediately. Yield: 6 to 8 servings.

LEMON BROCCOLI

1½ pounds fresh broccoli
½ cup butter or margarine
2 tablespoons lemon juice
½ teaspoon dried oregano

¼ teaspoon garlic powder
¼ teaspoon freshly ground
  pepper

Remove broccoli leaves, and cut off tough ends of stalks; discard. Wash broccoli, and cut into spears. Arrange spears in a vegetable steamer over boiling water. Cover and steam 8 to 10 minutes or until crisp-tender.

Combine butter and remaining ingredients in a small saucepan; bring to a boil. Reduce heat, and cook until butter melts; pour over broccoli. Serve immediately. Yield: 6 servings.

BRANDIED CARROTS

2 pounds fresh baby carrots
  with tops
¼ cup honey
¼ cup brandy
2 tablespoons Grand Marnier or
  other orange-flavored liqueur

2 tablespoons lemon juice
1½ teaspoons cornstarch
1 tablespoon water
Chopped fresh parsley

Scrape and trim carrots, leaving ½ inch of green tops, if desired. Arrange carrots in a vegetable steamer over boiling water. Cover and steam 10 minutes or until crisp-tender. Set aside.

Combine honey and next 3 ingredients in a large skillet; cook over medium heat 5 minutes, stirring occasionally. Combine cornstarch and water, stirring until smooth; add to honey mixture. Cook, stirring constantly, 1 minute or until slightly thickened. Add carrots, and cook just until thoroughly heated, tossing gently. Transfer mixture to a serving bowl; sprinkle with chopped parsley. Yield: 6 to 8 servings.

Corn-and-Cheese Soufflé will make a stunning addition to your holiday dinner party. Two cheeses give the soufflé its creamy richness.

CORN-AND-CHEESE SOUFFLÉ

⅓ cup butter or margarine
¼ cup all-purpose flour
⅓ cup milk
1 (16½-ounce) can cream-style corn
1½ cups (6 ounces) shredded sharp Cheddar cheese

½ cup (2 ounces) shredded provolone cheese
⅛ teaspoon garlic powder
⅛ teaspoon ground red pepper
5 large eggs, separated
¼ teaspoon cream of tartar

A soufflé dish is round and has straight sides to help the mixture rise. Strips of foil are sometimes wrapped around the outside of the dish, with the top of the foil rising above the rim. This foil collar helps support a baked soufflé as it rises or acts as a mold for a chilled or frozen soufflé.

Cut a piece of aluminum foil long enough to fit around a 2-quart soufflé dish, allowing a 1-inch overlap; fold foil lengthwise into thirds. Lightly oil 1 side of foil and bottom of dish. Wrap foil around outside of dish, oiled side against dish, allowing it to extend 3 inches above rim; secure with string.

Melt butter in a large heavy saucepan over low heat; add flour, stirring until mixture is smooth. Cook, stirring constantly, 1 minute. Gradually add milk; cook over medium heat, stirring constantly, until mixture is thickened and bubbly. Add corn and next 4 ingredients, stirring until cheeses melt.

Beat egg yolks until thick and pale. Gradually stir about one-fourth of hot mixture into yolks; add to remaining hot mixture, stirring constantly. Beat egg whites and cream of tartar at high speed of an electric mixer until stiff peaks form; gently fold into corn mixture. Pour into prepared dish. Bake at 350° for 55 to 60 minutes or until puffed and golden. Remove foil collar, and serve immediately. Yield: 6 to 8 servings.

SAVORY GREEN BEANS

1½ pounds fresh green beans
2 tablespoons chopped onion
2 cloves garlic, halved
3 tablespoons vegetable oil
½ cup boiling water

1 teaspoon dried basil
½ teaspoon sugar
½ teaspoon salt
¼ teaspoon pepper

Wash beans; trim ends, and remove strings. Cut in half crosswise.

Cook onion and garlic in oil in a skillet over medium heat, stirring constantly, until onion is tender. Discard garlic. Add beans, boiling water, and remaining ingredients; cover and cook 25 minutes or until beans are tender. Add 1 to 2 tablespoons additional water, if necessary. Yield: 6 servings.

MUSHROOM NEWBURG

1 pound fresh mushrooms, sliced
3 tablespoons butter or
    margarine, melted
3 tablespoons dry sherry
1 tablespoon Cognac
¼ teaspoon salt

¼ teaspoon pepper
1 cup half-and-half
¼ cup whipping cream
2 egg yolks, lightly beaten
Patty shells or toast points

Cook mushrooms in butter in a large skillet over medium heat, stirring constantly, until liquid evaporates and mushrooms are tender. Add sherry and next 3 ingredients; cook until almost all liquid evaporates. Add half-and-half; simmer 5 minutes, stirring occasionally.

Combine whipping cream and egg yolks in a small bowl; stir well with a wire whisk. Add to mushroom mixture; cook over low heat, stirring constantly, until slightly thickened. Serve mushroom mixture in patty shells or over toast points. Yield: 6 servings.

A classic Newburg sauce contains butter, cream, egg yolks, sherry, and seasonings. Ingredients such as lobster, shrimp, or vegetables can be added to the basic sauce, and the combination is traditionally served in patty shells or over toast points.

SPICY BLACK-EYED PEAS

1 pound dried black-eyed peas
5 cups water
2 tablespoons minced green
  onions
1 tablespoon Creole seasoning

1 teaspoon dried parsley flakes
1 teaspoon garlic powder
1 teaspoon chili powder
3/4 teaspoon pepper
3 chicken-flavored bouillon cubes

Sort and wash peas; place in a Dutch oven. Cover with water 2 inches above peas. Let soak 8 hours. Drain peas; return to Dutch oven. Add 5 cups water and remaining ingredients. Bring to a boil; cover, reduce heat, and simmer 45 minutes or until tender. Serve with a slotted spoon. Yield: 8 to 10 servings.

MISSY POTATOES

We're not sure how the recipe for Missy Potatoes got its name, but we know you'll enjoy this variation of the traditional hash brown potato casserole.

1 (2-pound) package frozen hash
  brown potatoes, thawed
1 (16-ounce) carton sour cream
1 (10¾-ounce) can cream of
  celery soup, undiluted
1 cup (4 ounces) shredded sharp
  Cheddar cheese

½ cup butter or margarine,
  softened
1 teaspoon salt
1 teaspoon coarsely ground
  pepper
½ cup round buttery cracker
  crumbs

Combine first 7 ingredients in a large bowl; stir well. Spoon mixture into a lightly greased 13- x 9- x 2-inch baking dish; sprinkle with cracker crumbs. Bake at 350° for 55 minutes or until bubbly. Yield: 10 to 12 servings.

MAKE-AHEAD MASHED POTATOES

Make-Ahead Mashed Potatoes may be baked immediately after preparing. Bake, uncovered, at 350° for 25 minutes or until thoroughly heated.

3 pounds baking potatoes, peeled
  and quartered
2 (3-ounce) packages cream
  cheese, softened
⅔ cup sour cream
¼ cup milk

2 tablespoons butter or margarine
¾ teaspoon salt
1 tablespoon butter or margarine,
  melted
½ teaspoon paprika

Cook potato in boiling salted water to cover 15 minutes or until tender; drain and mash. Combine potato, cream cheese, and next 4 ingredients in a large mixing bowl; beat at medium speed of an electric mixer until smooth. Spoon mixture into a greased 11- x 7- x 1½-inch baking dish. Brush with melted butter, and sprinkle with paprika. Cover and chill up to 24 hours.

Remove from refrigerator; let stand, covered, 30 minutes. Uncover and bake at 350° for 30 minutes or until heated. Yield: 6 to 8 servings.

LEMON-BUTTERED NEW POTATOES

2 pounds new potatoes, quartered
¼ cup butter or margarine
2 tablespoons chopped fresh
  parsley
1 teaspoon grated lemon rind
2 tablespoons fresh lemon juice

½ teaspoon salt
¼ teaspoon pepper
⅛ teaspoon ground nutmeg
Garnishes: fresh parsley sprigs,
  lemon slices

Cook potato, covered, in boiling water to cover 10 minutes or just until tender; drain. Combine butter and next 6 ingredients in a small saucepan; cook over medium heat, stirring until butter melts. Pour butter mixture over potato; toss gently to coat. Garnish, if desired. Yield: 8 servings.

STREUSEL-TOPPED SWEET POTATO CASSEROLE

6 medium-size sweet potatoes
  (about 3 pounds)
¾ cup sugar
⅓ cup milk
¼ cup butter or margarine,
  melted
1 teaspoon vanilla extract
½ teaspoon ground cinnamon

½ teaspoon ground nutmeg
2 large eggs, lightly beaten
⅓ cup firmly packed brown sugar
⅓ cup finely chopped pecans
2 tablespoons all-purpose flour
2 tablespoons butter or
  margarine, softened

Cook sweet potatoes in boiling water to cover 30 to 40 minutes or until tender. Let cool to touch; peel and mash potatoes. Combine mashed sweet potato, sugar, and next 6 ingredients in a large mixing bowl; beat at medium speed of an electric mixer until smooth.

Spoon mixture into a lightly greased 2-quart casserole. Combine brown sugar and remaining ingredients; sprinkle over sweet potato mixture. Bake at 350° for 30 minutes or until thoroughly heated. Yield: 8 to 10 servings.

SPINACH-ARTICHOKE CASSEROLE

2 (14-ounce) cans artichoke
  hearts, drained and halved
2 (10-ounce) packages frozen
  chopped spinach
½ cup chopped onion
⅓ cup butter or margarine,
  melted
½ cup sour cream
¼ cup grated Parmesan cheese
¾ teaspoon salt
¾ teaspoon ground white pepper
Dash of ground red pepper
2 tablespoons grated Parmesan
  cheese

Arrange artichoke hearts in a lightly greased 8-inch square baking dish. Set aside.

Cook spinach according to package directions; drain well. Cook onion in butter in a large skillet over medium heat, stirring constantly, until tender. Stir in spinach, sour cream, and next 4 ingredients. Spoon spinach mixture over artichokes; sprinkle with 2 tablespoons Parmesan cheese.

Bake, uncovered, at 350° for 25 to 30 minutes or until thoroughly heated. Yield: 8 servings.

YELLOW SQUASH CASSEROLE

2 pounds yellow squash, sliced
1 cup water
2 small onions, minced
2 tablespoons butter or
  margarine, melted
1½ cups (6 ounces) shredded
  Cheddar cheese
1 cup round buttery cracker
  crumbs, divided
¼ teaspoon salt
¼ teaspoon pepper
4 slices bacon, cooked and
  crumbled
2 large eggs, lightly beaten
1 (2-ounce) jar diced pimiento,
  drained

Combine squash and water in a large saucepan; bring to a boil. Cover, reduce heat, and simmer 15 minutes or until squash is tender. Drain well, and mash. Drain again, and set aside.

Cook onion in butter in a large skillet over medium-high heat, stirring constantly, until tender. Combine squash, onion, cheese, ¾ cup cracker crumbs, and remaining ingredients; stir well. Spoon mixture into a lightly greased 2-quart casserole; sprinkle with remaining ¼ cup cracker crumbs. Bake at 350° for 45 minutes or until thoroughly heated. Yield: 6 servings.

APPLE AND PECAN-FILLED ACORN SQUASH

2 medium acorn squash (about
  1¼ pounds each)
1 cup peeled, chopped cooking
  apple
¼ cup firmly packed brown sugar

¼ cup butter or margarine,
  melted
¼ teaspoon apple pie spice
¼ cup chopped pecans, toasted

Cut squash in half crosswise, and remove seeds. Cut bottom of each squash half to sit flat, if necessary. Place squash halves, cut side up, in a 13- x 9- x 2-inch baking dish. Add hot water to dish to depth of 1 inch.

Combine apple and next 3 ingredients; spoon evenly into squash halves. Cover and bake at 350° for 1 hour or until squash is tender. Sprinkle with pecans. Yield: 4 servings.

TURNIPS AU GRATIN

9 medium turnips, peeled and
  diced (about 3 pounds)
1 teaspoon salt
1 teaspoon sugar
2 tablespoons butter or margarine
2 tablespoons all-purpose flour

1½ cups milk
¾ cup (3 ounces) shredded
  Cheddar cheese
1 teaspoon seasoned salt
⅛ teaspoon pepper
¼ cup fine, dry breadcrumbs

Gratin is a crisp, golden crust that often tops casseroles and potato dishes. The crust is typically composed of breadcrumbs and grated cheese and is browned in the oven or under the broiler.

Combine first 3 ingredients in a Dutch oven; add water to cover. Bring to a boil; cover, reduce heat, and simmer 10 to 12 minutes or until turnip is tender. Drain well, and set aside.

Melt butter in a large heavy saucepan over low heat; add flour, stirring constantly. Gradually add milk; cook over medium heat, stirring constantly, until slightly thickened. Add cheese, seasoned salt, and pepper, stirring until cheese melts. Remove from heat; stir in turnips.

Spoon turnip mixture into a lightly greased 1½-quart casserole; sprinkle with breadcrumbs. Bake at 350° for 20 to 25 minutes or until thoroughly heated. Yield: 6 servings.

Santa's Bread Shoppe

Whether drizzled with glaze, baked with fruit and nuts, or shaped into rolls or loaves, homemade breads fill Southern kitchens with holiday spirit. The inviting aromas they create while baking scent the whole house and revive special memories. Along with adding sparkle and old-fashioned appeal to meals, these breads offer another plus—versatility. Serve them with butter for breakfast, as a special treat with dinner, or with coffee for drop-in holiday visitors. You can even treat a special neighbor or friend with a basket of warm breakfast muffins or a loaf of fresh-from-the-oven bread.

From top: Cinnamon Twist Coffee Cake (page 188), Vienna Brioche Loaf (page 185), Buttered Rum-Nut Rolls (page 192).

FLUFFY BUTTERMILK BISCUITS

3 cups self-rising flour
2 teaspoons sugar
½ cup shortening

1 cup buttermilk
Melted butter or margarine

Combine flour and sugar in a large bowl; cut in shortening with a pastry blender until mixture is crumbly. Add buttermilk, stirring with a fork just until dry ingredients are moistened. (Dough will be sticky.) Turn dough out onto a heavily floured surface, and knead lightly 4 or 5 times.

Roll dough to ¾-inch thickness; cut with a 2½-inch biscuit cutter. Place biscuits on a lightly greased baking sheet; bake at 425° for 10 to 12 minutes or until golden. Remove from oven; brush with butter. Yield: 8 biscuits.

RISE-AND-SHINE BISCUITS

You'll be impressed with the light texture of Rise-and-Shine Biscuits. The addition of club soda causes the biscuits to be exceptionally fluffy and soft.

⅓ cup club soda
⅓ cup sour cream

1½ tablespoons sugar
2 cups biscuit mix

Combine first 3 ingredients in a medium bowl; add biscuit mix, stirring with a fork just until dry ingredients are moistened. Turn dough out onto a lightly floured surface, and knead lightly 10 to 12 times.

Shape dough into 6 (1-inch-thick) biscuits. Place 1 biscuit in the center of a lightly greased 8-inch round cakepan; arrange remaining biscuits around center biscuit. Bake at 425° for 12 to 14 minutes or until golden. Yield: 6 biscuits.

BREAKFAST SCONES

¾ cup buttermilk
⅓ cup currants
2 cups all-purpose flour
2 teaspoons baking powder
¼ teaspoon baking soda
⅛ teaspoon salt

2 tablespoons sugar
1 tablespoon grated orange rind
¼ cup plus 1 tablespoon butter or
  margarine
1 tablespoon milk
1 tablespoon sugar

Combine buttermilk and currants in a small bowl; set aside.

Combine flour and next 5 ingredients in a large bowl; cut in butter with a pastry blender until mixture is crumbly. Gradually add buttermilk mixture, stirring with a fork just until dry ingredients are moistened. Turn dough out onto a lightly floured surface, and knead lightly 4 or 5 times.

Roll dough to ½-inch thickness; cut with a 3-inch biscuit cutter. Place scones on a lightly greased baking sheet; brush with milk, and sprinkle with 1 tablespoon sugar. Bake at 400° for 14 to 16 minutes or until golden. Yield: 10 scones.

BACON-AND-CHEESE MUFFINS

1¾ cups all-purpose flour
2½ teaspoons baking powder
½ teaspoon salt
½ cup (2 ounces) shredded sharp
   Cheddar cheese
2 tablespoons sugar

10 slices bacon, cooked and
   crumbled
1 large egg, lightly beaten
¾ cup milk
⅓ cup vegetable oil

Combine first 6 ingredients in a large bowl; make a well in center of mixture. Combine egg, milk, and oil; add to dry ingredients, stirring just until moistened. Spoon batter into well-greased muffin pans, filling two-thirds full. Bake at 400° for 20 to 22 minutes or until golden. Remove from pans immediately. Yield: 1 dozen.

For perfect muffins, don't overstir the batter. After combining the ingredients, stir gently just until the dry ingredients are moistened. Overstirring creates holes or tunnels and makes the muffins tough and chewy.

BANANA-NUT MUFFINS

1¾ cups all-purpose flour
2½ teaspoons baking powder
½ teaspoon salt
½ cup sugar
1 large egg, lightly beaten

¾ cup mashed ripe banana
½ cup milk
⅓ cup vegetable oil
½ cup chopped pecans

Combine first 4 ingredients in a large bowl; make a well in center of mixture. Combine egg, banana, milk, and oil; add to dry ingredients, stirring just until moistened. Stir in pecans. Spoon batter into greased muffin pans, filling three-fourths full. Bake at 400° for 18 to 20 minutes or until golden. Remove from pans immediately. Yield: 1 dozen.

Jumbo Muffins: Prepare batter as directed above; spoon into 6 (3½-inch x 1¾-inch) greased muffin pans. Bake as directed above. Yield: 6 muffins.

The aroma of Cranberry-Walnut Streusel Muffins and Holiday Banana-Nut Bread (page 178) baking in the oven will draw even late-risers out of bed.

CRANBERRY-WALNUT STREUSEL MUFFINS

1 cup fresh cranberries
1 tablespoon all-purpose flour
1 tablespoon sugar
1¾ cups all-purpose flour
2¾ teaspoons baking powder
½ teaspoon salt
½ cup sugar

1 teaspoon ground nutmeg
1 teaspoon grated orange rind
1 large egg, lightly beaten
⅔ cup milk
⅓ cup vegetable oil
½ cup chopped walnuts
Streusel Topping

Combine first 3 ingredients in a small bowl; set aside.

Combine 1¾ cups flour and next 5 ingredients in a large bowl; make a well in center of mixture. Combine egg, milk, and oil; add to dry ingredients, stirring just until moistened. Fold cranberry mixture and walnuts into batter. Spoon batter into greased muffin pans, filling two-thirds full; sprinkle with Streusel Topping. Bake at 400° for 18 to 20 minutes or until golden. Cool in pans on a wire rack 5 minutes; remove from pans. Yield: 14 muffins.

Streusel Topping

⅓ cup firmly packed brown sugar
1 tablespoon all-purpose flour
1 tablespoon butter or margarine
¼ cup chopped walnuts

Combine sugar and flour in a small bowl; cut in butter with a pastry blender until mixture is crumbly. Stir in walnuts. Yield: 1 cup.

SPECIAL PUMPKIN BREAD

4 large eggs, lightly beaten
1 (16-ounce) can pumpkin
2 cups sugar
¾ cup vegetable oil
⅔ cup water
2 teaspoons vanilla extract
3⅓ cups all-purpose flour
2 teaspoons baking soda
½ teaspoon baking powder
¾ teaspoon salt
2 teaspoons pumpkin pie spice
1 teaspoon ground nutmeg
1 teaspoon ground cinnamon
1 cup chopped pecans
Cream Cheese and Gingered
  Peach Preserves

Looking for a quick appetizer or casual dessert? Serve Cream Cheese and Gingered Peach Preserves as a spread for an assortment of sweet crackers.

Combine first 6 ingredients in a large bowl; stir well. Combine flour and next 6 ingredients; add flour mixture to pumpkin mixture, stirring until well blended. Stir in pecans.

Spoon batter into 2 greased 9- x 5- x 3-inch loafpans. Bake at 350° for 1 hour or until a wooden pick inserted in center comes out clean. Cool in pans on wire racks 10 minutes; remove from pans, and let cool completely on wire racks. Serve with Cream Cheese and Gingered Peach Preserves. Yield: 2 loaves.

Cream Cheese and Gingered Peach Preserves

¼ cup peach preserves
¼ teaspoon ground ginger
1 (8-ounce) package cream cheese, softened

Combine peach preserves and ginger; spoon over block of softened cream cheese. Yield: enough for 2 loaves.

HOLIDAY BANANA-NUT BREAD

2 large eggs, lightly beaten
1 cup mashed ripe banana
½ cup butter or margarine,
   melted
1 teaspoon vanilla extract
1½ cups all-purpose flour

1 teaspoon baking soda
1 cup sugar
½ cup chopped pecans
¼ cup flaked coconut
¼ cup raisins

Combine first 4 ingredients in a large bowl; stir well. Combine flour, soda, and sugar; add to banana mixture, stirring until well blended. Stir in pecans, coconut, and raisins.

Spoon batter into a greased and floured 8½- x 4½- x 3-inch loafpan. Bake at 325° for 1 hour and 10 minutes or until a wooden pick inserted in center comes out clean. Cover with aluminum foil the last 15 minutes of baking, if necessary, to prevent overbrowning. Cool in pan on a wire rack 10 minutes; remove from pan, and let cool completely on wire rack. Yield: 1 loaf.

LEMON-CREAM CHEESE TEA LOAVES

1 (8-ounce) package cream cheese,
   softened
½ cup butter or margarine,
   softened
1¼ cups sugar
2 large eggs
2¼ cups all-purpose flour

1 tablespoon baking powder
½ teaspoon salt
¾ cup milk
⅔ cup chopped pecans
⅓ cup sifted powdered sugar
1 teaspoon grated lemon rind
2 tablespoons lemon juice

Beat cream cheese and butter at medium speed of an electric mixer until soft and creamy; gradually add 1¼ cups sugar, beating well. Add eggs, one at a time, beating after each addition.

Combine flour, baking powder, and salt; add to cream cheese mixture alternately with milk, beginning and ending with flour mixture. Mix after each addition. Stir in pecans.

Pour batter into 2 greased and floured 8½- x 4½- x 3-inch loafpans. Bake at 350° for 45 minutes or until a wooden pick inserted in center comes out clean. Combine powdered sugar, lemon rind, and lemon juice, stirring until smooth; pour slowly over hot loaves. Cool in pans on wire racks 10 minutes; remove from pans, and let cool completely on wire racks. Yield: 2 loaves.

OVERNIGHT COFFEE CAKE

2 cups all-purpose flour
1 teaspoon baking powder
1 teaspoon baking soda
½ teaspoon salt
1 cup sugar
½ cup firmly packed brown sugar
1 teaspoon ground cinnamon
1 cup buttermilk
⅔ cup butter or margarine, melted
2 large eggs
½ cup firmly packed brown sugar
½ cup chopped pecans
1 teaspoon ground cinnamon

Combine first 7 ingredients in a large mixing bowl; add buttermilk, butter, and eggs. Beat at low speed of an electric mixer until dry ingredients are moistened; beat at medium speed an additional 3 minutes.

Spoon batter into a greased and floured 13- x 9- x 2-inch pan. Combine ½ cup brown sugar, pecans, and 1 teaspoon cinnamon; sprinkle over batter. Cover and chill overnight. Bake, uncovered, at 350° for 30 minutes or until a wooden pick inserted in center comes out clean. Yield: 12 servings.

Overnight Coffee Cake may be baked immediately, if desired. Bake at 350° for 30 minutes or until a wooden pick inserted in the center comes out clean. To reheat, cover and bake at 350° for 5 to 10 minutes or until thoroughly heated.

BUTTERMILK CORNBREAD

2 cups self-rising cornmeal
1¾ cups buttermilk
¼ cup vegetable oil
1 tablespoon sugar
1 large egg, lightly beaten

Combine all ingredients, stirring just until dry ingredients are moistened. Place a well-greased 9-inch cast-iron skillet in a 450° oven for 5 minutes or until hot. Pour batter into hot skillet. Bake at 450° for 23 to 25 minutes or until golden brown. Yield: 6 to 8 servings.

Buttermilk Corn Muffins: Prepare batter as directed above. If using cast-iron muffin pans, place well-greased pans in a 450° oven for 5 minutes or until hot. Spoon batter into hot pans, filling three-fourths full. For regular muffin pans, spoon batter into greased pans, filling three-fourths full. Bake at 450° for 15 to 18 minutes or until golden brown. Yield: 1 dozen.

Buttermilk Corn Sticks: Prepare batter as directed above. Place a well-greased cast-iron corn stick pan in a 450° oven for 5 minutes or until hot. Spoon batter into hot pan, filling three-fourths full. Bake at 450° for 15 to 18 minutes or until golden brown. Yield: 1½ dozen.

Take a break from the holiday turkey-and-dressing routine and serve a bowl of steaming vegetable soup with Buttermilk Cornbread. The batter for perfect cornbread should be fairly thin and pourable. If it seems a little stiff, add more liquid.

BUTTERMILK PANCAKES WITH HOMEMADE SYRUP

For blueberry pancakes, fold one cup fresh or frozen blueberries into the batter just before cooking.

2 cups all-purpose flour
2½ teaspoons baking powder
1 teaspoon baking soda
¾ teaspoon salt
2 tablespoons sugar

2 large eggs, lightly beaten
2 cups buttermilk
¼ cup vegetable oil
Homemade Syrup

Combine first 5 ingredients; stir well. Combine eggs, buttermilk, and oil; add to flour mixture, stirring just until dry ingredients are moistened.

For each pancake, pour about ¼ cup batter onto a hot, lightly greased griddle. Cook pancakes until tops are covered with bubbles and edges look cooked; turn and cook other side. (Any unused batter may be refrigerated in a tightly covered container up to 1 week. If refrigerated batter is too thick, add milk or water to reach desired consistency.) Serve pancakes warm with Homemade Syrup. Yield: 19 (4-inch) pancakes.

Homemade Syrup

1 cup water
2 cups sugar

½ teaspoon maple flavoring

Bring water to a boil in a small saucepan; add sugar and flavoring. Boil, stirring constantly, 2 minutes; remove from heat. Serve warm, chilled, or at room temperature. (Leftover syrup may be refrigerated in a tightly covered container.) Yield: about 2 cups.

SOFT GINGER WAFFLES

Find it hard to tell when waffles are done? They're done when you no longer see steam coming from the sides of the waffle iron.

⅓ cup butter or margarine,
** softened**
¼ cup molasses
2 large eggs, separated
1¾ cups all-purpose flour
2¾ teaspoons baking powder
¼ teaspoon baking soda

¼ teaspoon salt
1¼ teaspoons ground ginger
¼ teaspoon ground cinnamon
¼ teaspoon ground nutmeg
½ cup plus 2 tablespoons milk
Lemon Hard Sauce

Beat butter at medium speed of an electric mixer until creamy. Add molasses; beat well. Add egg yolks, one at a time, beating after each addition.

Combine flour and next 6 ingredients; add flour mixture to butter mixture alternately with milk, beginning and ending with flour mixture. Mix after each addition.

Beat egg whites at high speed of an electric mixer until stiff peaks form; gently fold beaten whites into batter. Spoon 1 cup batter onto a preheated, oiled waffle iron; spread batter to edges. Bake until lightly browned. Repeat procedure with remaining batter. Serve waffles with Lemon Hard Sauce. Yield: 11 (4-inch) waffles.

Lemon Hard Sauce

⅓ cup butter or margarine,
  softened
¼ cup sifted powdered sugar

1 teaspoon grated lemon rind
1 tablespoon lemon juice

Beat butter at medium speed of an electric mixer until creamy; gradually add powdered sugar, lemon rind, and lemon juice, beating until light and fluffy. Serve at room temperature. Yield: ½ cup.

EASY OVERNIGHT FRENCH TOAST

4 large eggs, lightly beaten
¾ cup milk
1 tablespoon sugar
½ teaspoon vanilla extract
¼ teaspoon ground cinnamon

8 (¾-inch-thick) slices French
  bread
2 tablespoons butter or
  margarine, divided
Powdered sugar (optional)

Combine first 5 ingredients; stir well. Pour egg mixture into an 11- x 7- x 1½-inch dish. Arrange bread slices in dish over egg mixture, turning once to coat. Cover and chill 8 hours.

Melt 1 tablespoon butter in a medium skillet over medium heat. Arrange 4 bread slices in skillet; cook 3 to 4 minutes on each side or until browned. Repeat procedure with remaining butter and bread slices. Sprinkle with powdered sugar, if desired. Serve with syrup. Yield: 4 to 6 servings.

Don't rush the cooking of Easy Overnight French Toast by turning up the heat. French toast should cook at a lower temperature for a longer period of time so that the inside will be done but the outside won't be burned.

ANGEL BISCUITS

1 package active dry yeast
¼ cup warm water (105° to 115°)
2½ cups all-purpose flour
1½ teaspoons baking powder
¼ teaspoon baking soda

¾ teaspoon salt
2 tablespoons sugar
½ cup shortening
¾ cup buttermilk

Combine yeast and water; let stand 5 minutes. Combine flour and next 4 ingredients; cut in shortening with a pastry blender until crumbly. Add yeast mixture and buttermilk, stirring with a fork just until dry ingredients are moistened. Turn dough out onto a lightly floured surface, and knead lightly 10 to 15 times.

Roll or pat dough to ¾-inch thickness; cut with a 2½-inch round biscuit cutter. Place biscuits on an ungreased baking sheet. Cover and let rise in a warm place (85°), free from drafts, 35 minutes or until doubled in bulk. Bake at 400° for 12 to 14 minutes or until golden. Yield: 1 dozen.

PAN ROLLS

5 to 5½ cups all-purpose flour,
   divided
3 tablespoons sugar
2 teaspoons salt
1 package active dry yeast

1½ cups milk
½ cup water
¼ cup butter or margarine
Melted butter or margarine

Combine 3 cups flour, sugar, salt, and yeast in a large mixing bowl; stir well. Combine milk, water, and ¼ cup butter in a saucepan; heat until butter melts, stirring occasionally. Cool to 120° to 130°.

Gradually add liquid mixture to flour mixture, beating well at low speed of an electric mixer. Beat an additional 2 minutes at medium speed. Gradually stir in enough remaining flour to make a soft dough.

Turn dough out onto a floured surface; knead until smooth and elastic (8 to 10 minutes). Place in a well-greased bowl, turning to grease top. Cover and let rise in a warm place (85°), free from drafts, 1 hour or until dough is doubled in bulk.

Punch down dough; turn out onto a lightly floured surface, and knead lightly 4 or 5 times. Divide dough in half; shape each portion into 20 (1½-inch) balls. Arrange 20 balls in each of 2 greased 9-inch square pans.

Cover and let rise in a warm place, free from drafts, 40 minutes or until doubled in bulk. Bake at 375° for 15 minutes or until golden. Brush with melted butter. Yield: 40 rolls.

ITALIAN DINNER ROLLS

4½ cups all-purpose flour, divided
½ cup grated Parmesan cheese
2 tablespoons sugar
1½ teaspoons dried Italian
    seasoning
1 teaspoon salt
2 packages active dry yeast

1 cup milk
½ cup water
3 tablespoons butter or margarine
2 large eggs
2 tablespoons butter or
    margarine, melted
¼ cup grated Parmesan cheese

Combine 1½ cups flour, ½ cup Parmesan cheese, and next 4 ingredients in a large mixing bowl; stir well. Combine milk, water, and 3 tablespoons butter in a saucepan; heat until butter melts, stirring occasionally. Cool to 120° to 130°.

Gradually add liquid mixture to flour mixture, beating at low speed of an electric mixer. Beat an additional 2 minutes at medium speed. Add eggs; beat well. Gradually stir in enough remaining flour to make a soft dough.

Turn dough out onto a floured surface, and knead until smooth and elastic (8 to 10 minutes). Place in a well-greased bowl, turning to grease top. Cover and let rise in a warm place (85°), free from drafts, 45 minutes or until doubled in bulk.

Punch dough down; let rest 10 minutes. Turn dough out onto a lightly floured surface, and knead lightly 4 or 5 times. Divide dough into 16 equal portions; shape each piece into a ball. Dip tops of balls in 2 tablespoons melted butter, and then in ¼ cup Parmesan cheese. Arrange 8 balls in each of 2 greased 9-inch round pans. Cover and let rise in a warm place, free from drafts, 20 minutes or until doubled in bulk. Bake at 375° for 18 minutes or until golden. Yield: 16 rolls.

In some of our recipes, the yeast is dissolved in warm water (105° to 115°) before being added to any other ingredients. Other recipes follow the rapid-mix method used here in which the yeast is mixed with some of the dry ingredients before the warm liquid is added. With this method, the liquid ingredients should be 120° to 130° when added to the dry ingredients, unless otherwise specified.

BUTTERMILK WHEAT BREAD

Be sure to use the specified loafpan size when baking yeast bread. Otherwise, your loaf will not be shaped as pretty as you might like, and the baking time may not be right.

1¾ cups whole wheat flour
1 teaspoon salt
⅛ teaspoon baking powder
1 package active dry yeast
½ cup warm water (105° to 115°)
2 tablespoons sugar

1 cup buttermilk
¼ cup vegetable oil
2 tablespoons honey
1 large egg
2¼ to 2¾ cups bread flour

Combine first 3 ingredients in a small bowl; stir well, and set aside. Combine yeast and warm water in a 1-cup liquid measuring cup; stir in sugar, and let stand 5 minutes.

Combine yeast mixture, buttermilk, oil, honey, and egg in a large mixing bowl; beat at medium speed of an electric mixer until well blended. Add whole wheat flour mixture; beat an additional 3 minutes. Gradually stir in enough bread flour to make a soft dough.

Turn dough out onto a floured surface, and knead until smooth and elastic (about 10 minutes). Place in a well-greased bowl, turning to grease top. Cover and let rise in a warm place (85°), free from drafts, 1 hour or until doubled in bulk.

Punch dough down; turn out onto a lightly floured surface, and knead lightly 4 or 5 times. Divide dough in half. Roll 1 portion of dough into a 14- x 7-inch rectangle. Roll up dough, starting at short side, pressing firmly to eliminate air pockets; pinch ends to seal. Place dough, seam side down, in a well-greased 8½- x 4½- x 3-inch loafpan. Repeat procedure with remaining portion of dough.

Cover and let rise in a warm place, free from drafts, 45 minutes or until doubled in bulk. Bake at 350° for 25 minutes or until loaves sound hollow when tapped. Remove bread from pans immediately; let cool on wire racks. Yield: 2 loaves.

Note: Loaves may be prepared ahead and frozen. Bake loaves as directed; let cool. Wrap tightly in aluminum foil, and freeze up to 1 month. Let thaw, covered, at room temperature. Reheat in foil at 250° for 10 to 15 minutes, if desired.

VIENNA BRIOCHE LOAVES

4½ cups all-purpose flour, divided
¼ cup sugar
1 teaspoon salt
1 teaspoon grated lemon rind
1 package active dry yeast
1 cup butter
½ cup water
6 large eggs

3 tablespoons butter, softened
⅔ cup firmly packed brown sugar
2 tablespoons milk
¼ teaspoon vanilla extract
2 egg yolks, lightly beaten
2 cups finely chopped pecans
Melted butter
Powdered sugar (optional)

Combine 1¾ cups flour, ¼ cup sugar, and next 3 ingredients in a large mixing bowl; stir well. Combine 1 cup butter and water in a saucepan; heat until butter melts, stirring occasionally. Cool to 120° to 130°.

Gradually add liquid mixture to flour mixture, beating well at low speed of an electric mixer. Beat an additional 2 minutes at medium speed. Add 6 eggs; beat well. Gradually stir in remaining flour. Cover and let rise in a warm place (85°), free from drafts, 1 hour or until doubled in bulk. Cover and chill at least 8 hours.

Combine 3 tablespoons butter and next 4 ingredients in a medium bowl; stir well. Stir in pecans, and set aside.

Punch dough down; turn out onto a lightly floured surface, and knead lightly 4 or 5 times. Divide dough in half. Work with 1 portion of dough at a time, refrigerating other portion. Roll dough into a 14- x 9-inch rectangle; brush with melted butter. Spread half of pecan mixture over dough to within ½ inch of edge. Roll up 1 side of dough, starting at short side and ending at middle of dough. Roll up remaining side of dough until rolls meet in the middle. Place dough in a well-greased 9- x 5- x 3-inch loafpan, rolled side up. Gently brush loaf with melted butter. Repeat procedure with remaining portion of dough and pecan mixture.

Cover and let rise in a warm place, free from drafts, 45 minutes or until doubled in bulk. Bake at 350° for 20 minutes; cover with aluminum foil, and bake an additional 15 minutes or until golden. Remove bread from pans immediately; let cool on wire racks. Sprinkle with powdered sugar, if desired. Yield: 2 loaves.

Note: Loaves may be prepared ahead and frozen. Bake loaves as directed; let cool. Wrap tightly in aluminum foil, and freeze up to 1 month. Let thaw, covered, at room temperature. Reheat in foil at 250° for 10 to 15 minutes, if desired.

Brioche, a French specialty, is a yeast bread rich in butter and eggs. Although most often seen in its classic shape with a fluted base and little topknot, brioche may also appear as loaves or other shapes.

CINNAMON LOAVES

To shape the perfect yeast loaf, roll the dough to the dimensions specified in the recipe. Then roll the dough tightly in jellyroll fashion, beginning with the short side. As you roll the dough, press firmly to eliminate any air pockets.

4½ to 5 cups all-purpose flour, divided
½ cup sugar
1½ teaspoons salt
2 packages active dry yeast
1 cup milk
¼ cup butter or margarine

2 large eggs
¾ cup sugar
1 teaspoon ground cinnamon
2 tablespoons butter or margarine, melted and divided
⅔ cup raisins, divided
Powdered Sugar Glaze

Combine 2 cups flour, ½ cup sugar, salt, and yeast in a large mixing bowl; stir well. Combine milk and ¼ cup butter in a saucepan; heat until butter melts, stirring occasionally. Cool to 120° to 130°.

Gradually add liquid mixture to flour mixture, beating well at low speed of an electric mixer. Beat an additional 2 minutes at medium speed. Add eggs; beat well. Gradually stir in enough remaining flour to make a slightly stiff dough.

Turn dough out onto a floured surface, and knead until smooth and elastic (about 10 minutes). Place in a well-greased bowl, turning to grease top. Cover and let rise in a warm place (85°), free from drafts, 1 hour or until doubled in bulk.

Combine ¾ cup sugar and cinnamon; set aside. Punch dough down; turn out onto a lightly floured surface, and knead lightly 4 or 5 times. Divide dough in half. Roll 1 portion of dough into a 12- x 9-inch rectangle; brush with half of melted butter. Sprinkle half of cinnamon mixture over dough to within ½ inch of edge; sprinkle with half of raisins. Roll up dough, starting at short side, pressing firmly to eliminate air pockets; pinch ends to seal. Place dough, seam side down, in a well-greased 8½- x 4½- x 3-inch loafpan. Repeat procedure with remaining portion of dough, butter, cinnamon mixture, and raisins.

Cover and let rise in a warm place, free from drafts, 45 minutes or until doubled in bulk. Bake at 350° for 35 minutes or until loaves sound hollow when tapped. Cover with aluminum foil the last 10 minutes of baking, if necessary, to prevent overbrowning. Remove from pans immediately; let cool 10 minutes on wire racks. Drizzle with Powdered Sugar Glaze. Yield: 2 loaves.

Spread Christmas cheer with freshly baked Cinnamon Loaves. Give one loaf as a gift, and save one to enjoy with your family.

Powdered Sugar Glaze

1½ cups sifted powdered sugar   **¾ teaspoon vanilla extract**
2 tablespoons milk

Combine all ingredients, stirring until smooth. Yield: ½ cup.

CINNAMON TWIST COFFEE CAKE

Cinnamon Twist Coffee Cake may be prepared ahead and frozen. Prepare and bake as directed; let cool. Don't drizzle with glaze. Cover tightly with aluminum foil, and freeze up to one month. Let thaw, covered, at room temperature. Glaze and garnish as directed.

2 packages active dry yeast
½ cup warm water (105° to 115°)
1 cup boiling water
¾ cup instant potato flakes
1 teaspoon salt
½ cup sugar
½ cup instant nonfat dry milk powder
½ cup butter or margarine, softened
3 large eggs
5½ to 6½ cups all-purpose flour
⅔ cup sugar
1½ teaspoons ground cinnamon
½ cup butter or margarine, softened and divided
½ cup chopped pecans, divided
2 cups sifted powdered sugar
3 tablespoons milk
Garnishes: candied cherry halves, toasted sliced almonds

Combine yeast and warm water in a 1-cup liquid measuring cup; let stand 5 minutes. Combine boiling water, potato flakes, and salt in a large mixing bowl; beat at medium speed of an electric mixer until well blended. Add ½ cup sugar, milk powder, and ½ cup butter; beat well. Add eggs and yeast mixture; beat well. Stir in enough flour to make a soft dough.

Turn dough out onto a floured surface; knead until smooth and elastic (about 5 minutes). Place in a greased bowl, turning to grease top. Cover and let rise in a warm place (85°), free from drafts, 1 hour or until doubled in bulk.

Combine ⅔ cup sugar and cinnamon; set aside. Punch dough down; turn out onto a floured surface. Knead lightly 4 or 5 times. Divide dough into 6 portions; roll each portion into a 12-inch circle. Place 1 circle of dough on a well-greased 12-inch pizza pan. Spread 2 tablespoons butter over dough to within ½ inch of edge; sprinkle about 2½ tablespoons cinnamon mixture and 2 tablespoons pecans over dough. Place a second circle of dough on top of first. Repeat procedure with butter, cinnamon mixture, and pecans; top with a third circle of dough. Moisten outer edges of circles, and press firmly to seal edges. Repeat procedure with remaining portions of dough, butter, cinnamon mixture, and pecans, forming a second coffee cake.

Press a 2½-inch round biscuit cutter or glass into center of 1 coffee cake. (Do not cut through dough.) Cut dough into 8 wedges, using kitchen shears and cutting to biscuit cutter in center. Gently lift each wedge, and twist several times, forming a spiral. Remove biscuit cutter. Repeat procedure with remaining coffee cake. Cover and let rise in a warm place, free from drafts, 45 minutes or until doubled in bulk. Bake at 350° for 20 minutes or until golden. Cool 10 minutes. Combine powdered sugar and milk; drizzle over coffee cakes. Garnish, if desired. Yield: two 12-inch coffee cakes.

STOLLEN

1 cup raisins
1 cup mixed candied fruit
1 cup chopped blanched almonds
6½ to 7 cups all-purpose flour, divided
½ cup milk
½ cup orange juice
½ cup butter or margarine
2 packages active dry yeast
½ cup warm water (105° to 115°)
½ cup sugar
1½ teaspoons grated lemon rind
¾ teaspoon salt
½ teaspoon ground mace
2 large eggs
2 tablespoons butter or margarine, softened and divided
2 egg whites, lightly beaten
Red and green candied cherries
1 cup sifted powdered sugar
1½ tablespoons milk

Combine raisins, mixed candied fruit, almonds, and ½ cup flour, tossing to coat fruit mixture; set aside.

Combine ½ cup milk, orange juice, and ½ cup butter in a saucepan; heat until butter melts, stirring occasionally. Cool to 105° to 115°. Combine yeast and warm water in a 1-cup liquid measuring cup; let stand 5 minutes. Combine milk mixture, yeast mixture, 2 cups flour, ½ cup sugar, and next 4 ingredients in a large mixing bowl; beat at medium speed of an electric mixer until well blended. Stir in enough remaining flour to make a soft dough. Stir in fruit mixture.

Turn dough out onto a floured surface, and knead until smooth and elastic (about 8 minutes). Place in a greased bowl, turning to grease top. Cover and let rise in a warm place (85°), free from drafts, 2 hours or until doubled in bulk.

Punch dough down; turn out onto a floured surface. Knead lightly 4 or 5 times. Divide dough in half. Roll 1 portion of dough into a 1-inch-thick oval; brush with 1 tablespoon softened butter to within ½ inch of edge. Fold oval in half lengthwise, pressing edges to seal; place on a lightly greased baking sheet. Repeat procedure with remaining portion of dough and softened butter.

Cover and let rise in a warm place, free from drafts, 1 hour or until doubled in bulk. Gently brush loaves with egg whites; decorate with candied cherries. Brush again with remaining egg whites. Bake at 350° for 25 to 30 minutes or until golden. Combine powdered sugar and 1½ tablespoons milk; drizzle over warm loaves. Yield: 2 loaves.

Stollen is a traditional German Christmas yeast bread. It's packed with dried fruits and nuts and is often decorated with candied cherries and a powdered sugar glaze. Our version is shaped in the traditional fashion—a folded oval that closely resembles a giant Parker House roll.

Baba au Orange, a tender, syrup-soaked coffee cake, is easy and convenient to prepare using hot roll mix.

BABA AU ORANGE

Baba is a sweet, light-textured yeast cake that has been soaked in a rich syrup. Baba au Orange gets its moistness and refreshing flavor from a sinfully sweet orange syrup.

1 (16-ounce) package hot roll mix
⅓ cup sugar
1 cup hot water (120° to 130°)
¼ cup plus 2 tablespoons butter
  or margarine, melted
2 large eggs
1 cup sugar

1 cup water
1 (6-ounce) can frozen orange
  juice concentrate, thawed and
  undiluted
Toasted sliced almonds (optional)
Garnish: orange twists

Combine contents of hot roll mix package, yeast packet from mix, ⅓ cup sugar, hot water, and butter in a large mixing bowl, beating well at low speed of an electric mixer. Beat an additional 2 minutes at medium speed. Add eggs; beat well.

    Place dough in a well-greased bowl, turning to grease top. Cover and let rise in a warm place (85°), free from drafts, 45 minutes or until doubled in bulk. (Dough will be very soft.)

Stir dough down; spoon into a well-greased 12-cup Bundt pan. Cover and let rise in a warm place, free from drafts, 15 to 20 minutes or until doubled in bulk. (Dough will not fill pan completely.) Bake at 400° for 15 minutes or until loaf sounds hollow when tapped. Cover with aluminum foil the last 5 minutes of baking, if necessary, to prevent overbrowning. Invert bread onto a serving platter.

Combine 1 cup sugar, 1 cup water, and orange juice concentrate in a small saucepan. Bring to a boil over medium heat; reduce heat, and simmer, stirring constantly, until sugar dissolves. Spoon hot syrup mixture slowly over warm bread; brush bread with syrup mixture until most of the mixture is absorbed. Sprinkle with sliced almonds, if desired. Cool completely. Garnish, if desired. Yield: 10 to 12 servings.

LEMON BOWKNOTS

5½ to 6 cups all-purpose flour, divided
⅓ cup sugar
1 tablespoon grated lemon rind
1 teaspoon salt
1 package active dry yeast
1½ cups milk
½ cup butter or margarine
2 large eggs
1 cup sifted powdered sugar
1 to 2 tablespoons milk
1 teaspoon grated lemon rind

Combine 3 cups flour, ⅓ cup sugar, and next 3 ingredients in a large mixing bowl; stir well. Combine 1½ cups milk and butter in a saucepan; heat until butter melts, stirring occasionally. Cool to 120° to 130°.

Gradually add liquid mixture to flour mixture, beating at low speed of an electric mixer. Beat an additional 2 minutes at medium speed. Add eggs; beat well. Gradually stir in enough remaining flour to make a soft dough.

Turn dough out onto a lightly floured surface, and knead until smooth and elastic (about 5 minutes). Place in a well-greased bowl, turning to grease top. Cover and let rise in a warm place (85°), free from drafts, 1 hour or until doubled in bulk.

Punch dough down. Divide dough into 24 equal portions; roll each portion into a 10-inch rope. Tie ropes loosely into knots, and place on greased baking sheets. Cover and let rise in a warm place, free from drafts, 25 minutes or until doubled in bulk. Bake at 375° for 10 minutes or until golden.

Combine powdered sugar, 1 tablespoon milk, and 1 teaspoon lemon rind, stirring well. Add more milk, if necessary, to make glaze desired consistency. Brush glaze on rolls. Yield: 2 dozen.

It's easy to keep freshly grated citrus fruit rind on hand. Whenever you're about to juice a piece of fruit, grate the rind first, and store it in an airtight container in the freezer up to two months.

BUTTERED RUM-NUT ROLLS

Use a long strand of dental floss to make easy work of slicing the dough for sweet roll recipes. Just slide the floss under the roll, bring the ends of the floss up, and pull together slowly and tightly to cut the slice.

4 to 4½ cups all-purpose flour
2 tablespoons sugar
1 teaspoon salt
1 package active dry yeast
1¼ cups milk
¼ cup butter or margarine
2 large eggs
1 cup firmly packed dark brown sugar
½ cup butter or margarine

½ cup dark corn syrup
½ teaspoon ground cinnamon
½ teaspoon ground nutmeg
⅓ cup dark rum
1 cup chopped pecans
3 tablespoons butter or margarine, softened
2 tablespoons sugar
½ teaspoon ground cinnamon

Combine 2 cups flour, 2 tablespoons sugar, salt, and yeast in a large mixing bowl; stir well. Combine milk and ¼ cup butter in a saucepan; heat until butter melts, stirring occasionally. Cool to 120° to 130°.

Gradually add liquid mixture to flour mixture, beating well at low speed of an electric mixer. Beat an additional 2 minutes at medium speed. Add eggs; beat well. Gradually stir in enough remaining flour to make a soft dough.

Turn dough out onto a floured surface, and knead until smooth and elastic (about 10 minutes). Place in a well-greased bowl, turning to grease top. Cover and let rise in a warm place (85°), free from drafts, 1 hour or until doubled in bulk.

Combine brown sugar and next 4 ingredients in a saucepan; cook over medium heat, stirring constantly, until sugar dissolves and butter melts. Remove from heat; stir in rum. Spoon mixture into a buttered 13- x 9- x 2-inch pan; sprinkle evenly with pecans, and set aside.

Combine 3 tablespoons softened butter, 2 tablespoons sugar, and ½ teaspoon ground cinnamon; stir well. Punch dough down; turn out onto a lightly floured surface, and knead lightly 4 or 5 times. Roll dough into a 20- x 12-inch rectangle. Spread butter mixture over dough to within ½ inch of edge. Roll up dough, starting at long side; pinch seam to seal. (Leave ends open.) Cut into 1-inch slices; place slices, cut side down, in prepared pan.

Cover and let rise in a warm place, free from drafts, 45 minutes or until doubled in bulk. Bake at 375° for 20 to 25 minutes or until golden. Immediately invert pan onto a large serving platter. Let stand 1 minute; remove pan. Yield: 20 rolls.

SWEDISH LUCIA BUNS

2¼ cups milk
⅔ cup butter or margarine
2 packages active dry yeast
1½ cups sugar
½ teaspoon salt

½ teaspoon ground saffron
1 large egg
7½ to 8½ cups all-purpose flour
60 raisins
1 large egg, lightly beaten

Combine milk and butter in a saucepan; heat until butter melts, stirring occasionally. Cool to 105° to 115°. Add yeast to warm milk mixture, stirring well; let stand 5 minutes.

Combine yeast mixture, sugar, salt, saffron, 1 egg, and 3½ cups flour in a large mixing bowl; beat at medium speed of an electric mixer until well blended. Gradually stir in enough remaining flour to make a soft dough.

Turn dough out onto a floured surface, and knead until smooth and elastic (about 10 minutes). Place in a well-greased bowl, turning to grease top. Cover and let rise in a warm place (85°), free from drafts, 1 hour or until doubled in bulk.

Punch dough down; turn out onto a lightly floured surface, and knead 1 minute. Divide dough into thirds; shape each portion into 10 (9-inch) ropes. Place ropes 3 inches apart on greased baking sheets; curl ends of each rope in opposite directions, forming an "S" shape.

Cover and let rise in a warm place, free from drafts, 30 minutes or until doubled in bulk. Press a raisin into center of each curl. Gently brush rolls evenly with lightly beaten egg. Bake at 400° for 12 minutes or until golden. Yield: 2½ dozen.

Saffron is what gives the classic golden tint to Swedish Lucia Buns. It's an expensive spice generally used in small amounts to flavor and tint foods. Saffron is made from the yellow-orange stigmas of a small purple crocus. Each flower provides only three stigmas, which are carefully hand-picked and then dried. It takes more than 14,000 of these tiny stigmas to produce one ounce of saffron.

Sugar And Spice

Like shiny packages and twinkling Christmas lights, cookies and candies offer a special magic this time of year. Southerners have made an art of preparing these tiny confections using tattered recipes handed down from mother to daughter, with each generation adding its own personal touch. We offer a smorgasbord of sweet indulgences to help keep your cookie jars and candy tins filled. Our Fruitcake Cookies (page 197) remain as popular today as when the recipe was published in the first Christmas issue of **Southern Living** in 1966. And the dozens of requests we receive each fall for Orange Slice Cookies (page 198) signal the start of holiday baking and the countdown to the Christmas season.

On plate: Chocolate-Dipped Orange Logs (page 202), Old-Fashioned Praline (page 205), Almond Cream Confections (page 198).

JUMBO CHOCOLATE CHIP COOKIES

Let Jumbo Chocolate Chip Cookies cool slightly on the cookie sheets before removing them. The cookies are so large that they will break if you try to remove them immediately after baking. About one minute of cooling is sufficient.

½ cup butter or margarine, softened
½ cup shortening
1 cup firmly packed brown sugar
½ cup sugar
2 large eggs
2 teaspoons vanilla extract

2½ cups all-purpose flour
1 teaspoon baking soda
½ teaspoon salt
1 (12-ounce) package semisweet chocolate morsels
1 cup chopped pecans

Beat butter and shortening at medium speed of an electric mixer until soft and creamy; gradually add sugars, beating well. Add eggs and vanilla; beat well. Combine flour, soda, and salt; gradually add to butter mixture, beating well. Stir in chocolate morsels and pecans.

Drop dough by scant one-fourth cupfuls onto ungreased cookie sheets; flatten each cookie into a 3½-inch circle, making sure the flattened cookies are 2 inches apart. Bake at 350° for 12 minutes. Cool slightly on cookie sheets; remove to wire racks, and let cool completely. Yield: 2 dozen.

Chocolate Chunk Cookies: Substitute 1 (10-ounce) package chocolate chunks for chocolate morsels.

FORGET 'EM COOKIES

2 egg whites
½ teaspoon vanilla extract
¼ teaspoon cream of tartar
½ cup sugar

1 (6-ounce) package semisweet chocolate morsels
1 cup chopped pecans

Preheat oven to 350°. Beat first 3 ingredients at high speed of an electric mixer until foamy. Gradually add sugar, 1 tablespoon at a time, beating until stiff peaks form and sugar dissolves (2 to 4 minutes). Fold in chocolate morsels and pecans.

Drop mixture by heaping teaspoonfuls onto cookie sheets lined with aluminum foil. Place in oven, and turn off heat immediately. Do not open oven door for at least 8 hours. Carefully remove cookies from foil. Store cookies in an airtight container up to 1 week. Yield: 4½ dozen.

FRUITCAKE COOKIES

2 cups chopped pecans
½ pound candied pineapple,
   chopped
½ pound red and green candied
   cherries, chopped
½ pound golden raisins
¼ cup all-purpose flour

½ cup butter or margarine,
   softened
1 cup firmly packed brown sugar
4 large eggs
2½ cups all-purpose flour
1 teaspoon baking soda
¾ teaspoon ground cardamom

Combine first 5 ingredients in a large bowl, tossing to coat fruit and nuts with flour. Set aside. Beat butter at medium speed of an electric mixer until creamy; gradually add brown sugar, beating well. Add eggs; beat well. Combine 2½ cups flour, soda, and cardamom; gradually add to butter mixture, beating well. Stir in fruit mixture.

Drop dough by heaping teaspoonfuls 2 inches apart onto lightly greased cookie sheets. Bake at 350° for 12 minutes or until lightly browned. Cool slightly on cookie sheets; remove to wire racks, and let cool completely. Yield: 9½ dozen.

For drop cookies, allow at least two inches of space between each mound of dough on the cookie sheet. This will help prevent the cookies from running together as they bake.

WHITE CHOCOLATE–MACADAMIA NUT COOKIES

½ cup butter or margarine,
   softened
½ cup shortening
¾ cup firmly packed brown sugar
½ cup sugar
1 large egg
1½ teaspoons vanilla extract
2 cups all-purpose flour

1 teaspoon baking soda
½ teaspoon salt
1 (6-ounce) package white
   chocolate-flavored baking bars,
   cut into chunks
1 (7-ounce) jar macadamia nuts,
   coarsely chopped

Beat butter and shortening at medium speed of an electric mixer until soft and creamy; gradually add sugars, beating well. Add egg and vanilla; beat well. Combine flour, soda, and salt; gradually add to butter mixture, beating well. Stir in white chocolate chunks and nuts.

Drop dough by rounded teaspoonfuls 2 inches apart onto lightly greased cookie sheets. Bake at 350° for 8 to 10 minutes or until lightly browned. Cool slightly on cookie sheets; remove to wire racks, and let cool completely. Yield: 5 dozen.

One six-ounce package of vanilla-milk morsels may be substituted for the white chocolate-flavored baking bars.

ORANGE SLICE COOKIES

Use kitchen shears to snip orange slices into tiny pieces. Spray the shears with vegetable cooking spray to help prevent sticking.

1½ cups chopped candy orange slices
¼ cup all-purpose flour
1 cup butter or margarine, softened
1 cup firmly packed brown sugar
¾ cup sugar
2 large eggs
2 tablespoons milk
2 teaspoons vanilla extract
2 cups all-purpose flour
1 teaspoon baking soda
½ teaspoon salt
½ teaspoon ground cinnamon
½ teaspoon ground nutmeg
2½ cups quick-cooking oats, uncooked
1 cup flaked coconut

Combine chopped orange slices and ¼ cup flour in a medium bowl, tossing to coat candy. Set aside. Beat butter at medium speed of an electric mixer until creamy; gradually add sugars, beating well. Add eggs, milk, and vanilla; beat well. Combine 2 cups flour and next 4 ingredients; gradually add to butter mixture, beating well. Stir in candy mixture, oats, and coconut.

Drop dough by rounded teaspoonfuls 2 inches apart onto greased cookie sheets. Bake at 375° for 10 minutes or until lightly browned. Cool slightly on cookie sheets; remove to wire racks, and let cool completely. Yield: 9 dozen.

ALMOND CREAM CONFECTIONS

¼ cup sugar
2 tablespoons cocoa
¼ teaspoon salt
½ cup butter or margarine
1 large egg, lightly beaten
1¾ cups vanilla wafer crumbs
1 cup slivered almonds, toasted and chopped
½ cup flaked coconut
2 teaspoons vanilla extract
Cream Filling
2 (1-ounce) squares semisweet chocolate

Combine first 5 ingredients in a heavy saucepan; cook over low heat, stirring constantly, until butter melts and mixture begins to thicken. Remove from heat; stir in vanilla wafer crumbs, almonds, coconut, and vanilla. Press mixture firmly into an ungreased 9-inch square pan; cover and chill.

Spread Cream Filling evenly over almond mixture; cover and chill thoroughly. Cut into 1½-inch squares. Remove squares from pan; place ½ inch apart on wax paper.

Place chocolate in a small heavy-duty, zip-top plastic bag; seal bag. Submerge bag in hot water until chocolate melts. Snip a tiny hole in one corner of bag, using scissors; drizzle chocolate over squares. Yield: 3 dozen.

Cream Filling

⅓ cup butter or margarine, softened

3 cups sifted powdered sugar

½ teaspoon vanilla extract

2 to 2½ tablespoons milk

Beat butter at medium speed of an electric mixer until creamy; gradually add powdered sugar, beating well. Add vanilla and 2 tablespoons milk; beat well. Add additional ½ tablespoon milk, if necessary, to reach spreading consistency. Yield: 1½ cups.

CREAM CHEESE SWIRL BROWNIES

1 (4-ounce) package sweet baking chocolate

3 tablespoons butter or margarine

½ (8-ounce) package cream cheese, softened

2 tablespoons butter or margarine, softened

¼ cup sifted powdered sugar

3 large eggs, divided

1 tablespoon all-purpose flour

½ teaspoon vanilla extract

¾ cup sugar

½ cup all-purpose flour

½ teaspoon baking powder

¼ teaspoon salt

1½ teaspoons vanilla extract

Bake brownies and other bar cookies in the size pan that's indicated in the recipe. Otherwise, the baking time may be wrong and the texture of the finished product may be affected.

Melt chocolate and 3 tablespoons butter in a saucepan over low heat, stirring constantly. Set aside. Beat cream cheese and 2 tablespoons butter at medium speed of an electric mixer until creamy; gradually add powdered sugar, beating well. Add 1 egg, 1 tablespoon flour, and ½ teaspoon vanilla; beat well. Set aside.

Beat remaining 2 eggs at medium speed until thick and pale; gradually add ¾ cup sugar, beating until thickened. Combine ½ cup flour, baking powder, and salt; gradually add to egg mixture, beating well. Stir in chocolate mixture and 1½ teaspoons vanilla.

Spread 1 cup chocolate batter in a greased 8-inch square pan. Spoon cream cheese mixture over batter in pan; top with remaining chocolate batter. Swirl with a knife to create a marbled effect. Bake at 350° for 35 minutes or until done. Cool on a wire rack; cut into squares. Yield: 16 brownies.

The recipe for Rolled Sugar Cookies has been perfected in our kitchens, but the decorative touches you add in your own kitchen make these cookies unique.

ROLLED SUGAR COOKIES

1 cup butter or margarine,
  softened
1 cup sugar
1 large egg
1 teaspoon vanilla extract

2½ cups all-purpose flour
2 teaspoons baking powder
¼ teaspoon salt
Decorator sugar crystals

Beat butter at medium speed of an electric mixer until creamy; gradually add 1 cup sugar, beating well. Add egg and vanilla; beat well. Combine flour, baking powder, and salt; gradually add to butter mixture, beating just until blended. Shape dough into a ball; cover and chill at least 1 hour.

Divide dough into thirds. Work with 1 portion of dough at a time, storing remainder in refrigerator. Roll each portion to ⅛-inch thickness on a lightly floured surface. Cut with a 3-inch cookie cutter; place on lightly greased cookie sheets. Sprinkle with sugar crystals. Bake at 375° for 8 minutes or until edges are lightly browned. Cool slightly on cookie sheets; remove to wire racks, and let cool completely. Yield: 20 cookies.

RASPBERRY SWIRL COOKIES

½ cup butter or margarine,
  softened
1 cup sugar
1 large egg
1 teaspoon vanilla extract
2¼ cups all-purpose flour

1 teaspoon baking powder
¼ teaspoon salt
½ cup flaked coconut
½ cup raspberry jam
¼ cup finely chopped walnuts

Beat butter at medium speed of an electric mixer until creamy; gradually add sugar, beating well. Add egg and vanilla; beat well. Combine flour, baking powder, and salt; gradually add to butter mixture, beating well. Shape dough into a ball; cover and chill at least 2 hours.

Roll dough into a 12- x 9-inch rectangle on floured wax paper. Combine coconut, jam, and walnuts; spread evenly over dough to within ½ inch of edges. Roll up dough starting at long side, peeling wax paper from dough while rolling. Pinch side seam to seal. (Leave ends open.) Wrap roll in wax paper, and freeze until firm.

Unwrap dough, and cut into ¼-inch-thick slices; place 2 inches apart on cookie sheets lined with parchment paper. Bake at 375° for 10 to 12 minutes or until edges are lightly browned. Let cool 1 minute on cookie sheets; remove to wire racks, and let cool completely. Yield: 4 dozen.

It's easy to cut thin, perfectly round slices from the rolls of dough for Raspberry Swirl Cookies. Just freeze the rolls until firm, and slice them while frozen.

LEMON CRINKLE COOKIES

½ cup shortening
1 cup firmly packed brown sugar
1 large egg
1 tablespoon grated lemon rind
1½ cups all-purpose flour

½ teaspoon baking soda
Pinch of salt
½ teaspoon cream of tartar
¼ teaspoon ground ginger
2 tablespoons sugar

Beat shortening at medium speed of an electric mixer until creamy; gradually add brown sugar, beating well. Add egg and lemon rind, beating well. Combine flour and next 4 ingredients; gradually add to shortening mixture, beating just until blended. Cover and chill 15 minutes.

Shape dough into 1-inch balls. Roll balls in 2 tablespoons sugar; place 2 inches apart on ungreased cookie sheets. Bake at 350° for 12 minutes or until lightly browned. Cool slightly on cookie sheets; remove to wire racks, and let cool completely. Yield: 3 dozen.

Dark cookie sheets can cause cookies to burn on the bottom before they are done in the middle because the sheets absorb heat rather than reflect it. If you have only dark cookie sheets, lower the specified oven temperature by 25°.

CHOCOLATE-DIPPED ORANGE LOGS

1 cup butter or margarine,
  softened
½ cup sifted powdered sugar
1 teaspoon grated orange rind
1 teaspoon orange extract

2 cups all-purpose flour
6 (1-ounce) squares semisweet
  chocolate
¾ cup finely chopped almonds,
  toasted

Beat butter at medium speed of an electric mixer until creamy; gradually add powdered sugar, beating well. Stir in orange rind and orange extract. Gradually add flour, beating well. Cover and chill 1 hour.

Divide dough in half. Work with 1 portion of dough at a time, storing remainder in refrigerator. Divide each portion of dough into 24 pieces; shape each piece into a 2½- x ½-inch log on a lightly floured surface. Place logs on ungreased cookie sheets. Flatten three-quarters of each log lengthwise with tines of a fork to ¼-inch thickness. Bake at 350° for 12 minutes. Cool slightly on cookie sheets; remove to wire racks, and let cool completely.

Place chocolate squares in top of a double boiler; bring water to a boil. Reduce heat to low; cook until chocolate melts. Dip unflattened tips of cookies in chocolate; roll chocolate-coated tips in chopped almonds. Place on wire racks; let stand until chocolate is firm. Yield: 4 dozen.

BUTTER SPRITZ

Spritz are rich, buttery cookies that are shaped by forcing the dough through a cookie gun or cookie press. The name comes from spritzen, *which is German for "to squirt or spray."*

1½ cups butter, softened
1 cup sugar
1 large egg
1 teaspoon vanilla extract

½ teaspoon almond extract
4¼ cups all-purpose flour
1 teaspoon baking powder

Beat butter at medium speed of an electric mixer until creamy; gradually add sugar, beating well. Add egg and flavorings; beat well. Combine flour and baking powder; gradually add to butter mixture, beating well.

Use a cookie gun, following manufacturer's instructions, to shape dough as desired onto ungreased cookie sheets. Bake at 375° for 8 to 10 minutes or until edges are lightly browned. Cool slightly on cookie sheets; remove to wire racks, and let cool completely. Yield: about 6 dozen.

Florentine Lace Cookies are crisp and delicate, so handle with care.

FLORENTINE LACE COOKIES

¾ cup firmly packed brown sugar
½ cup butter
3 tablespoons whipping cream
1 cup minced pecans

¼ cup plus 2 teaspoons all-
    purpose flour
1 cup whipping cream
¼ cup sifted powdered sugar

Combine first 3 ingredients in a small saucepan; bring to a boil over medium heat, stirring constantly. Remove from heat; stir in pecans and flour.

Making 3 cookies at a time, drop batter by level tablespoonfuls 3 inches apart onto parchment paper-lined cookie sheets; flatten slightly into circles. Bake at 350° for 6 minutes or until edges are lightly browned. (Cookies will spread.) Remove from oven; let cool l minute on cookie sheets.

Quickly lift cookies with a spatula; flip cookies over, and roll each around the handle of a wooden spoon. Cool completely on wire racks while still wrapped around spoon handles. Carefully remove wooden spoons from cookies when cool. Repeat procedure with remaining batter.

Beat 1 cup whipping cream at high speed of an electric mixer until foamy; gradually add powdered sugar, beating until soft peaks form. Pipe whipped cream mixture into ends of each cookie; serve immediately. Yield: 22 cookies.

Store any unfilled Florentine Lace Cookies in an airtight container at room temperature up to one week.

CARAMEL CORN

Caramel Corn is perfect for gift giving because the recipe is simple to prepare and makes a large batch. Be sure to save some for the cook to enjoy!

6 quarts freshly popped corn
(about ⅔ cup unpopped corn)
1½ cups pecan halves
1½ cups raw peanuts
1½ cups firmly packed brown sugar

¾ cup butter or margarine
¾ cup light corn syrup
1 teaspoon vanilla extract
½ teaspoon baking soda

Combine popcorn and pecans in a lightly greased large roasting pan; set aside.

Combine peanuts and next 3 ingredients in a large saucepan. Bring to a boil over medium heat, stirring constantly. Boil 5 minutes, stirring occasionally. Remove from heat; stir in vanilla and soda.

Pour peanut mixture over popcorn mixture; stir with a lightly greased long-handled spoon until popcorn mixture is coated. Bake at 250° for 1 hour, stirring every 15 minutes. Remove from oven, and immediately pour mixture onto wax paper, breaking it apart as it cools. Store in airtight containers at room temperature. Yield: 6½ quarts.

DIVINITY

Divinity is a fluffy yet creamy candy made from a mixture that closely resembles boiled frosting. Nuts, candied fruits, coconut, and flavorings are often added for variety.

2½ cups sugar
½ cup water
½ cup light corn syrup

2 egg whites
1 teaspoon vanilla extract
1 cup chopped pecans, toasted

Combine first 3 ingredients in a large heavy saucepan; cook over low heat, stirring gently, until sugar dissolves. Bring to a boil over medium heat; cover and cook 2 to 3 minutes to wash down sugar crystals from sides of pan. Uncover and cook, without stirring, until mixture reaches hard ball stage or candy thermometer registers 260°. Remove from heat.

Beat egg whites in a large mixing bowl at high speed of an electric mixer until stiff peaks form. Pour hot sugar syrup in a thin stream over beaten egg whites while beating constantly at high speed. Add vanilla; beat just until mixture holds its shape (3 to 4 minutes). Stir in pecans. Drop by rounded teaspoonfuls onto wax paper. Cool completely. Yield: 1½ pounds.

Christmas Divinity: Substitute ½ cup finely chopped red candied cherries and ½ cup finely chopped green candied cherries for pecans.

PEANUT BRITTLE

2 cups sugar
1 cup light corn syrup
¾ cup boiling water

2 cups dry-roasted peanuts
1 tablespoon butter or margarine
1 teaspoon baking soda

Combine first 3 ingredients in a large heavy saucepan; cook over low heat, stirring gently, until sugar dissolves. Bring to a boil over medium heat; cover and cook 2 to 3 minutes to wash down sugar crystals from sides of pan. Uncover and add peanuts; cook until mixture reaches hard crack stage or candy thermometer registers 300°, stirring occasionally.

Add butter and soda, stirring until butter melts. Quickly pour mixture into a buttered 15- x 10- x 1-inch jellyroll pan, spreading evenly. Let cool completely, and break into pieces. Store in an airtight container at room temperature. Yield: 2 pounds.

OLD-FASHIONED PRALINES

2 cups coarsely chopped pecans
1 cup sugar
1 cup firmly packed brown sugar
¾ cup buttermilk

2 tablespoons butter or margarine
⅛ teaspoon salt
1 tablespoon vanilla extract
½ teaspoon baking soda

Butter the sides of a large heavy saucepan. Combine first 6 ingredients in prepared pan; cook over low heat, stirring gently, until sugar dissolves. Bring to a boil over medium heat; cover and cook 2 to 3 minutes to wash down sugar crystals from sides of pan. Uncover and cook, stirring constantly, until mixture reaches soft ball stage or candy thermometer registers 234°. Remove from heat, and stir in vanilla and soda. Beat with a wooden spoon just until mixture begins to thicken.

Working rapidly, drop mixture by tablespoonfuls onto greased wax paper; let stand until firm. Store in an airtight container at room temperature. Yield: 1½ to 2 dozen.

CHOCOLATE-COVERED CHERRIES

Don't be intimidated by the length of the recipe or the time involved for preparing Chocolate-Covered Cherries; some of the processes just can't be rushed. We know there's someone special on your Christmas list who deserves this sweet indulgence, and you can expect lots of compliments.

2½ cups sugar
¾ cup water
2½ tablespoons light corn syrup
2 (10-ounce) jars maraschino
   cherries with stems

1 (12-ounce) package semisweet
   chocolate morsels
1 tablespoon shortening

Combine first 3 ingredients in a large saucepan; cook over low heat, stirring gently, until sugar dissolves. Bring to a boil over medium heat; cover and cook 2 to 3 minutes to wash down sugar crystals from sides of pan. Uncover and cook, without stirring, until mixture reaches soft ball stage or candy thermometer registers 236°. Pour mixture onto a marble slab that has been sprinkled with cold water. (Do not scrape pan.) Let stand 4 minutes.

Using a dampened metal scraper, pull sides of mixture into center repeatedly to ensure mixture cools evenly. When mixture develops a yellowish tinge, continue working with dampened metal scraper, stirring mixture in a figure-8 motion. When mixture suddenly turns white and becomes too stiff to stir, knead with wet hands until smooth and creamy enough to form a firm ball (about 10 minutes). Place fondant in an airtight container, and let stand in a cool place at least 24 hours before using.

Drain cherries, reserving liquid; place cherries on paper towels to drain for several hours or overnight.

Place fondant in top of a double boiler; melt slowly over hot (not boiling) water, stirring constantly as it begins to melt. Stir in 1 tablespoon reserved cherry liquid. (Fondant should have the proper consistency for dipping when candy thermometer registers about 140°. Temperature should not rise above 140°.) If mixture seems too thick for dipping at this point, stir in 1 additional tablespoon reserved cherry liquid. Remove pan from heat, leaving fondant over hot water.

Working quickly and holding by the stem, dip each cherry in warm fondant, allowing excess to drain back into pan. Place cherries, stem up, on wax paper; let stand 1 hour or until firm.

Combine chocolate morsels and shortening in top of a double boiler; bring water to a boil. Reduce heat to low; cook until chocolate melts, stirring occasionally. Remove pan from heat, leaving chocolate mixture over hot water. Holding by the stem, dip each cherry in warm chocolate mixture, allowing excess to drain back into pan. Place cherries, stem up, on wax paper; let stand 2 hours or until firm. Store cherries in an airtight container at room temperature. Yield: about 5 dozen.

CHOCOLATE-PECAN FUDGE

2 cups sugar
⅔ cup half-and-half
¼ cup light corn syrup
2 (1-ounce) squares unsweetened
   chocolate, chopped

¼ cup unsalted butter
1 cup finely chopped pecans
2 teaspoons vanilla extract

Butter a large saucepan. Combine first 4 ingredients in pan; cook over low heat, stirring gently, until sugar dissolves. Bring to a boil over medium heat; cover and cook 2 to 3 minutes to wash down sugar crystals from sides of pan. Uncover and cook, without stirring, until mixture reaches soft ball stage or candy thermometer registers 234°. Remove from heat; without stirring, add butter, pecans, and vanilla. Cool to lukewarm (110°) without stirring.

   Beat with a wooden spoon just until mixture thickens and begins to lose its gloss (about 10 minutes). Quickly pour mixture into a buttered 8-inch square pan. Cool completely, and cut into squares. Yield: 1¼ pounds.

CHOCOLATE-ALMOND TOFFEE

2 cups sugar
1 cup butter
¼ cup water
2½ cups semisweet chocolate
   morsels, divided

2 cups finely chopped almonds,
   toasted and divided

Combine first 3 ingredients in a large heavy saucepan; cook over low heat, stirring gently, until sugar dissolves. Bring to a boil over medium heat; cover and cook 2 to 3 minutes to wash down sugar crystals from sides of pan. Uncover and cook, without stirring, until mixture reaches hard crack stage or candy thermometer registers 300°. Pour into a buttered 15- x 10- x 1-inch jellyroll pan; quickly spread to edges. Cool on a wire rack.

   Place 1¼ cups chocolate morsels in top of a double boiler; bring water to a boil. Reduce heat to low; cook until chocolate melts. Working quickly, spread chocolate over cooled candy. Sprinkle with 1 cup almonds, lightly pressing almonds into chocolate. Let stand until firm (about 2 hours).

   Carefully invert candy onto a cookie sheet lined with wax paper. Repeat procedure using remaining chocolate and almonds. Let stand until firm. Break candy into pieces. Yield: 2 pounds.

CHOCOLATE BOURBON BALLS

The flavor of Chocolate Bourbon Balls intensifies each day. If you prefer a stronger flavor, store the candies a couple of days before enjoying them.

1 (6-ounce) package semisweet chocolate morsels
½ cup bourbon
3 tablespoons light corn syrup

2½ cups vanilla wafer crumbs
1 cup finely chopped pecans
½ cup sifted powdered sugar
Sugar

Place chocolate morsels in top of a double boiler; bring water to a boil. Reduce heat to low; cook until chocolate melts. Add bourbon and corn syrup, stirring until smooth. Remove from heat.

Combine vanilla wafer crumbs, pecans, and powdered sugar in a large bowl; stir in chocolate mixture. Let stand 30 minutes. Shape chocolate mixture into 1-inch balls; roll in sugar. Store in an airtight container in refrigerator. Yield: 5½ dozen.

BUCKEYES

7 cups sifted powdered sugar
  (about 1½ pounds)
1¼ cups butter or margarine,
  softened
1 (18-ounce) jar crunchy peanut
  butter

3 cups semisweet chocolate
  morsels
1½ tablespoons shortening

Position knife blade in food processor bowl; add half each of first 3 ingredients. Process until thoroughly blended. Shape mixture into 1-inch balls; cover and chill. Repeat procedure with remaining powdered sugar, butter, and peanut butter.

Combine chocolate morsels and shortening in top of a double boiler; bring water to a boil. Reduce heat to low; cook until chocolate melts. Dip each ball in chocolate, coating three-fourths of ball; place on wax paper, and let stand until chocolate hardens. Store in an airtight container in refrigerator. Yield: 7½ dozen.

Good luck keeping Buckeyes and Roasted Pecan Clusters on hand for gift giving and holiday visitors—these chocolate-coated goodies will disappear quickly!

ROASTED PECAN CLUSTERS

3 tablespoons butter or margarine
3 cups pecan pieces

6 (2-ounce) squares chocolate-
flavored candy coating

Melt butter in a 15- x 10- x 1-inch jellyroll pan; spread pecans evenly in pan. Bake at 300° for 25 minutes, stirring every 10 minutes.

Place candy coating in top of a double boiler; bring water to a boil. Reduce heat to low; cook until candy coating melts. Remove pan from heat, leaving candy coating over hot water; cool 2 minutes. Stir in pecans. Drop by rounded teaspoonfuls onto wax paper; let stand until firm. Store in an airtight container at room temperature. Yield: 4½ dozen.

And Everything Nice

Some of our most vivid holiday memories revolve around the luscious desserts that accompany special meals. Such extravagancies as fresh coconut cake smothered with fluffy white frosting and sinfully rich chocolate cheesecake glazed with even more chocolate are a highlight of Christmas in the South. Although many of our recipes are impressive once-a-year undertakings, others are so popular that they are prepared throughout the year. And the occasions at which these traditional delicacies appear range from cozy family gatherings to lavish celebrations. But no matter what the event, your holiday meals just won't be complete without one of our grand finales.

Italian Cream Cake (page 215), Praline Cheesecake (page 220).

APPLE CAKE WITH BROWN SUGAR GLAZE

2 cups sugar
1 cup vegetable oil
3 large eggs
3 cups all-purpose flour
1 teaspoon baking soda
½ teaspoon salt

1 teaspoon ground cinnamon
3 cups peeled, finely chopped
   cooking apple
½ cup chopped pecans
Brown Sugar Glaze

Beat first 3 ingredients at medium speed of an electric mixer until creamy. Combine flour and next 3 ingredients; add to sugar mixture, beating well. Stir in apple and pecans.

Pour batter into a greased and floured 12-cup Bundt pan. Bake at 350° for 1 hour and 20 minutes or until a wooden pick inserted in center comes out clean. Cool in pan on a wire rack 10 to 15 minutes; remove from pan, and let cool completely on wire rack. Drizzle Brown Sugar Glaze over cake. Yield: one 10-inch cake.

Brown Sugar Glaze

½ cup firmly packed brown sugar
¼ cup butter or margarine

2 tablespoons evaporated milk

Combine all ingredients in a small saucepan; cook over high heat, stirring constantly, 2 minutes or until butter melts. Cool to lukewarm. Yield: ½ cup.

CHOCOLATE-ALMOND CAKE

Standard round cakepans measure eight and nine inches in diameter. You'll probably want to have three of each size on hand because most traditional layer cakes have at least three layers.

½ cup cocoa
½ cup boiling water
⅔ cup shortening
1¾ cups sugar
2 large eggs
2¼ cups all-purpose flour
1½ teaspoons baking soda

¼ teaspoon salt
1½ cups buttermilk
1 teaspoon vanilla extract
Almond Cream Filling (facing page)
Chocolate Frosting (facing page)
Garnishes: toasted sliced almonds,
   candied violets

Grease 3 (8-inch) round cakepans. Line bottoms of pans with wax paper; grease wax paper. Flour wax paper and sides of pans. Set aside. Combine cocoa and boiling water in a small bowl; stir until smooth. Set aside.

Beat shortening at medium speed of an electric mixer until creamy; gradually add sugar, beating well. Add eggs, one at a time, beating after each addition. Combine flour, soda, and salt; add to shortening mixture alternately with buttermilk, beginning and ending with flour mixture. Mix after each addition. Stir in cocoa mixture and vanilla.

Pour batter into prepared pans. Bake at 350° for 25 minutes or until a wooden pick inserted in center comes out clean. Cool in pans on wire racks 10 minutes; remove from pans, and let cool completely on wire racks.

Spread Almond Cream Filling between layers to within ½ inch of edge. Reserve 1 cup Chocolate Frosting; spread remaining frosting on top and sides of cake. Using a star tip, pipe reserved frosting on top of cake. Garnish, if desired. Yield: one 3-layer cake.

Almond Cream Filling

2 tablespoons all-purpose flour
¼ cup plus 1 tablespoon milk
¼ cup shortening
2 tablespoons butter or margarine, softened

½ teaspoon almond extract
⅛ teaspoon salt
2 cups sifted powdered sugar

Combine flour and milk in a small saucepan; cook over low heat, stirring constantly with a wire whisk, until mixture is thick enough to hold its shape and resembles a soft frosting. (Do not boil.) Remove from heat; let cool completely.

Beat shortening and butter at medium speed of an electric mixer until soft and creamy; add flour mixture, almond extract, and salt, beating well. Gradually add powdered sugar, beating at high speed 4 to 5 minutes or until fluffy. Yield: 1½ cups.

Chocolate Frosting

½ cup butter or margarine, softened
3 (1-ounce) squares unsweetened chocolate, melted

½ cup milk
1 teaspoon vanilla extract
1 (16-ounce) package powdered sugar, sifted

Beat butter at medium speed of an electric mixer until creamy. Add melted chocolate, milk, and vanilla; beat well. Gradually add powdered sugar, beating at high speed about 5 minutes or until mixture is spreading consistency. Yield: enough for one 3-layer cake.

FRESH COCONUT CAKE

Snow Peak Frosting is more commonly known as boiled frosting or Italian meringue. This creamy confection is made by slowly beating a hot sugar syrup into beaten egg whites. The syrup actually cooks the meringue, creating a very dense, glossy mixture.

¾ cup shortening
1½ cups sugar
3 large eggs
2¼ cups sifted cake flour
2½ teaspoons baking powder
½ teaspoon salt

¾ cup milk
1 teaspoon vanilla extract
Custard Filling
Snow Peak Frosting
2 cups freshly grated coconut

Beat shortening at medium speed of an electric mixer until creamy; gradually add sugar, beating well. Add eggs, one at a time, beating after each addition. Combine flour, baking powder, and salt; add to shortening mixture alternately with milk, beginning and ending with flour mixture. Mix after each addition. Stir in vanilla.

Pour batter into 2 greased and floured 9-inch round cakepans. Bake at 375° for 20 minutes or until a wooden pick inserted in center comes out clean. Cool in pans on wire racks 10 minutes; remove from pans. Cool on wire racks.

Split cake layers in half horizontally to make 4 layers. Spread Custard Filling between layers. Spread Snow Peak Frosting on top and sides of cake. Sprinkle top and sides of cake with coconut. Yield: one 4-layer cake.

Custard Filling

2 cups milk
½ cup sugar
⅓ cup cornstarch
4 egg yolks, lightly beaten

3 tablespoons Grand Marnier or other orange-flavored liqueur
1 cup freshly grated coconut

Combine first 4 ingredients in a medium saucepan; cook over medium heat, stirring constantly, 10 minutes or until thickened. Stir in liqueur. Transfer to a medium bowl; cover and chill. Stir in coconut. Yield: 3 cups.

Snow Peak Frosting

1 cup sugar
⅓ cup water
2 tablespoons light corn syrup

½ teaspoon cream of tartar
3 egg whites
¾ teaspoon vanilla extract

Combine first 4 ingredients in a medium-size heavy saucepan. Cook over low heat, stirring gently, until sugar dissolves. Bring to a boil over medium heat; cook, without stirring, until mixture reaches soft ball stage or candy thermometer registers 240°.

Beat egg whites at high speed of an electric mixer until soft peaks form; continue to beat, adding hot syrup mixture in a slow, steady stream. Add vanilla; beat until stiff peaks form and frosting is spreading consistency. Yield: enough for one 4-layer cake.

ITALIAN CREAM CAKE

½ cup butter or margarine, softened
½ cup shortening
2 cups sugar
5 large eggs
2 cups all-purpose flour

1 teaspoon baking soda
1 cup buttermilk
1 teaspoon vanilla extract
1 (3½-ounce) can flaked coconut
1 cup chopped pecans
Cream Cheese Frosting

Grease 3 (9-inch) round cakepans. Line bottoms of pans with wax paper; grease wax paper. Flour wax paper and sides of pans. Set aside. Beat butter and shortening at medium speed of an electric mixer until soft and creamy; gradually add sugar, beating well. Add eggs, one at a time, beating after each addition. Combine flour and soda; add to butter mixture alternately with buttermilk, beginning and ending with flour mixture. Mix after each addition. Stir in vanilla, coconut, and pecans.

Pour batter into prepared pans. Bake at 350° for 30 minutes or until a wooden pick inserted in center comes out clean. Cool in pans on wire racks 10 minutes. Remove from pans; peel off wax paper. Cool on wire racks. Spread Cream Cheese Frosting between layers and on top and sides of cake. Store in refrigerator in an airtight container. Yield: one 3-layer cake.

Cream Cheese Frosting

1 (8-ounce) package cream cheese, softened
1 (3-ounce) package cream cheese, softened

⅓ cup butter or margarine, softened
6½ cups sifted powdered sugar
1½ teaspoons vanilla extract

Beat first 3 ingredients at medium speed of an electric mixer until soft and creamy. Gradually add powdered sugar, beating until smooth. Stir in vanilla. Yield: enough for one 3-layer cake.

Use shiny metal cakepans to produce cakes with pale golden, tender crusts. Dark metal or enamel pans can cause uneven and excessive browning.

CHOCOLATE PECAN TORTE

A torte is a rich cake in which ground nuts or breadcrumbs replace some of the flour. Tortes are often composed of several thin layers spread with buttercream, jam, or other filling.

4 large eggs, separated
½ cup sugar
⅔ cup all-purpose flour
½ teaspoon baking soda
¼ teaspoon salt
¾ cup ground pecans
⅓ cup cocoa

¼ cup water
1 teaspoon vanilla extract
¼ cup sugar
Chocolate Frosting
¾ cup chopped pecans, toasted
Chocolate Glaze (facing page)
Garnish: chocolate leaves

Grease bottoms only of 2 (9-inch) round cakepans. Line bottoms of pans with wax paper; grease wax paper. Set aside.

Beat egg yolks at high speed of an electric mixer; gradually add ½ cup sugar, beating until mixture is thick and pale. Combine flour and next 4 ingredients; add to yolk mixture alternately with water, beginning and ending with flour mixture. Stir in vanilla.

Beat egg whites at high speed of an electric mixer until foamy; gradually add ¼ cup sugar, beating until stiff peaks form. Fold into batter. Pour batter into prepared pans. Bake at 375° for 16 to 18 minutes or until a wooden pick inserted in center comes out clean. Cool in pans on wire racks 10 minutes; remove from pans, and let cool completely on wire racks.

Split cake layers in half horizontally to make 4 layers. Place 1 cake layer on a serving plate; spread 1 cup Chocolate Frosting on top of layer. Repeat procedure with second and third cake layers and 2 additional cups Chocolate Frosting. Top stack with fourth cake layer. Spread remaining ½ cup Chocolate Frosting on sides of cake; gently press chopped pecans into frosting. Spread Chocolate Glaze over top of cake. Garnish, if desired. Yield: one 9-inch cake.

Chocolate Frosting

⅔ cup sifted powdered sugar
⅓ cup cocoa

2 cups whipping cream
1½ teaspoons vanilla extract

Combine powdered sugar and cocoa in a large mixing bowl; gradually stir in whipping cream. Add vanilla; beat at low speed of an electric mixer until blended. Beat at high speed until stiff peaks form. Yield: 3½ cups.

Chocolate Glaze

2 tablespoons cocoa
2 tablespoons water
1 tablespoon butter or margarine

1 cup sifted powdered sugar
¼ teaspoon vanilla extract

Combine first 3 ingredients in a small saucepan; cook over medium heat, stirring constantly, until mixture thickens. Remove from heat; stir in powdered sugar and vanilla. Yield: ⅓ cup.

A rich, fluffy frosting separates the layers of Chocolate Pecan Torte, while a shiny glaze tops off this extraordinary masterpiece.

YULE LOG

A yule log, or bûche de Noël, is a traditional French Christmas cake shaped to resemble a log. A fork is pulled through the frosting to create the appearance of bark.

¾ cup sifted cake flour
¼ teaspoon salt
¼ cup cocoa
5 large eggs, separated
1 cup sugar
1 tablespoon lemon juice

2 to 3 tablespoons powdered sugar
1 cup whipping cream, whipped
Creamy Chocolate Frosting
Garnish: red and green candied
  cherries

Grease a 15- x 10- x 1-inch jellyroll pan. Line bottom of pan with wax paper; grease wax paper. Flour wax paper and sides of pan. Set aside.

Sift together first 3 ingredients; set aside. Beat egg yolks in a large mixing bowl at high speed of an electric mixer 5 minutes or until thick and pale. Gradually add 1 cup sugar, beating well. Stir in lemon juice. Set aside.

Beat egg whites at high speed of electric mixer until stiff peaks form. Gently fold beaten whites into egg yolk mixture. Gradually fold in flour mixture. Spread batter evenly in prepared pan. Bake at 350° for 15 minutes.

Sift powdered sugar in a 15- x 10-inch rectangle on a cloth towel. When cake is done, immediately loosen from sides of pan, and turn out onto sugared towel. Peel off wax paper. Starting at narrow end, roll up cake and towel together; let cool completely on a wire rack, seam side down.

Unroll cake, and remove towel. Spread cake with whipped cream; carefully reroll cake. Cover and chill at least 1 hour. Cut a 1-inch-thick diagonal slice from 1 end of cake roll. Place cake roll on a serving plate, seam side down; position cut piece against side of cake roll to resemble a knot. Spread Creamy Chocolate Frosting over cake. Score frosting with the tines of a fork or a cake comb to resemble tree bark. Garnish, if desired. Yield: 10 to 12 servings.

Creamy Chocolate Frosting

¾ cup semisweet chocolate
  morsels
⅔ cup butter or margarine

⅓ cup plus 1 tablespoon half-
  and-half
2 cups sifted powdered sugar

Combine first 3 ingredients in a large heavy saucepan; cook over medium heat, stirring frequently, until chocolate melts. Remove from heat; stir in powdered sugar. Set saucepan in a large bowl of ice, and beat at low speed of an electric mixer 8 minutes or until frosting holds its shape and loses its gloss. Yield: 2 cups.

LIGHT FRUITCAKE

1½ pounds yellow, green, and red candied pineapple, chopped (about 3¾ cups)
1 pound red and green candied cherries, halved (about 2½ cups)
¼ pound diced citron (about ½ cup)
3 cups pecan halves
1½ cups golden raisins
1 cup walnuts, coarsely chopped
½ cup all-purpose flour
1½ cups butter, softened
1½ cups sugar
1 tablespoon vanilla extract
1 tablespoon lemon extract
7 large eggs, separated
3 cups all-purpose flour
¼ cup brandy
Additional brandy (optional)

Draw a 10-inch circle on a piece of brown paper using a 10-inch tube pan as a guide. (Do not use recycled paper.) Cut out circle. Set tube pan insert in center of circle, and draw around inside tube; cut out smaller circle. Grease 1 side of paper circle, and set aside. Heavily grease and flour 10-inch tube pan; set aside.

Combine first 6 ingredients in a large bowl; sprinkle with ½ cup flour, tossing to coat fruit and nuts. Set aside.

Beat butter at medium speed of an electric mixer until creamy; gradually add sugar, beating well. Stir in flavorings. Beat egg yolks; add yolks to butter mixture alternately with 3 cups flour, beginning and ending with flour. (Batter will be very thick.) Stir fruit mixture into batter. Beat egg whites until stiff peaks form; fold into batter.

Spoon batter into prepared pan. Cover pan with paper circle, greased side down. (This will prevent cake from overbrowning during extended baking time.) Bake at 250° for 4 hours or until a wooden pick inserted in cake comes out clean. Remove cake from oven; remove and discard paper circle. Slowly pour ¼ cup brandy evenly over warm cake; let cool completely in pan on a wire rack.

Remove cake from pan; wrap in brandy-soaked cheesecloth, if desired. Store in an airtight container in a cool place at least 1 week before serving. Cake may be stored up to 3 weeks before serving, if desired. Pour a small amount of brandy over cake each week, if desired. Yield: one 10-inch cake.

The title of this recipe, Light Fruitcake, refers to the cake's color, not its calorie content. Light fruitcakes generally are made with light-colored ingredients such as granulated sugar or light-colored corn syrup, golden raisins, walnuts or almonds, and brandy. Dark fruitcakes generally are made with dark-colored ingredients such as brown sugar or molasses, dates, prunes, pecans, and bourbon.

PEACH BRANDY POUND CAKE

Original pound cakes were made with one pound each of flour, butter, eggs, and sugar, with a little extract added for flavor. But as recipe development has evolved, leavening agents such as baking powder and baking soda and flavorings such as coconut, nuts, and raisins have been added.

1 cup butter or margarine, softened
3 cups sugar
6 large eggs
3 cups all-purpose flour
¼ teaspoon baking soda
⅛ teaspoon salt

1 (8-ounce) carton sour cream
½ cup peach brandy
2 teaspoons dark rum
1 teaspoon orange extract
1 teaspoon vanilla extract
½ teaspoon lemon extract
¼ teaspoon almond extract

Beat butter at medium speed of an electric mixer 2 minutes. Gradually add sugar, beating at medium speed 5 minutes. Add eggs, one at a time, beating just until yellow disappears. Combine flour, soda, and salt; add to butter mixture alternately with sour cream, beginning and ending with flour mixture. Mix at low speed just until blended after each addition. Stir in brandy and remaining ingredients.

Pour batter into a greased and floured 10-inch tube pan. Bake at 325° for 1½ hours or until a wooden pick inserted in center comes out clean. Cool in pan on a wire rack 10 to 15 minutes; remove from pan, and let cool completely on wire rack. Yield: one 10-inch cake.

PRALINE CHEESECAKE

1 cup graham cracker crumbs
¼ cup finely chopped pecans
3 tablespoons sugar
⅓ cup butter or margarine, melted
3 (8-ounce) packages cream cheese, softened

1 cup firmly packed brown sugar
3 large eggs
2 teaspoons vanilla extract
Garnishes: whipped cream, toasted chopped pecans

Combine first 4 ingredients; stir well. Press mixture into bottom and 1 inch up sides of a 9-inch springform pan. Bake at 350° for 8 minutes. Set aside.

Beat cream cheese at high speed of an electric mixer until creamy. Add brown sugar; beat well. Add eggs, one at a time, beating after each addition. Stir in vanilla. Pour mixture into prepared crust.

Bake at 325° for 40 minutes. Turn oven off; leave cheesecake in oven, with oven door partially opened, 30 minutes. Cool; cover and chill at least 8 hours. Remove from pan; garnish, if desired. Yield: one 9-inch cheesecake.

CHOCOLATE-GLAZED TRIPLE-LAYER CHEESECAKE

1 (8½-ounce) package chocolate wafer cookies, crushed
¾ cup sugar, divided
¼ cup plus 1 tablespoon butter or margarine, melted
2 (8-ounce) packages cream cheese, softened and divided
3 large eggs, divided
¼ teaspoon vanilla extract
2 (1-ounce) squares semisweet chocolate, melted

1⅓ cups sour cream, divided
⅓ cup firmly packed dark brown sugar
1 tablespoon all-purpose flour
½ teaspoon vanilla extract
¼ cup chopped pecans
5 ounces cream cheese, softened
¼ teaspoon vanilla extract
¼ teaspoon almond extract
Chocolate Glaze
Garnish: chocolate leaves

For optimum flavor and texture, allow chilled cheesecakes to stand at room temperature about 30 minutes before serving.

Combine cookie crumbs, ¼ cup sugar, and butter; stir well. Press mixture into bottom and 2 inches up sides of a 9-inch springform pan. Set aside.

Combine 1 package cream cheese and ¼ cup sugar; beat at medium speed of an electric mixer until creamy. Add 1 egg and ¼ teaspoon vanilla; beat well. Stir in melted chocolate and ⅓ cup sour cream; spoon into crust.

Combine remaining package cream cheese, brown sugar, and flour; beat until creamy. Add 1 egg and ½ teaspoon vanilla; beat well. Stir in pecans. Spoon over chocolate layer. Combine 5 ounces cream cheese and remaining ¼ cup sugar; beat until creamy. Add remaining egg; beat well. Stir in remaining 1 cup sour cream, ¼ teaspoon vanilla, and almond extract; spoon over pecan layer.

Bake at 325° for 1 hour. Turn oven off; leave cheesecake in oven, with oven door closed, 30 minutes. Partially open oven door; leave cheesecake in oven an additional 30 minutes. Cool on a wire rack. Cover and chill at least 8 hours. Remove cheesecake from pan; spread with warm Chocolate Glaze. Garnish, if desired. Yield: one 9-inch cheesecake.

Chocolate Glaze

6 (1-ounce) squares semisweet chocolate
¼ cup butter or margarine

¾ cup sifted powdered sugar
2 tablespoons water
1 teaspoon vanilla extract

Combine chocolate and butter in top of a double boiler; bring water to a boil. Reduce heat to low; cook until chocolate melts. Remove from heat. Add powdered sugar, water, and vanilla; stir until smooth. Yield: 1 cup.

Add a taste of the tropics to your holiday dessert selection by offering Macadamia Christmas Pie. It's packed with macadamia nuts and coconut.

MACADAMIA CHRISTMAS PIE

2 (3½-ounce) jars macadamia nuts
⅓ cup flaked coconut
1 unbaked 9-inch pastry shell
4 large eggs, lightly beaten
1 cup light corn syrup

½ cup sugar
1½ teaspoons vanilla extract
¼ teaspoon salt
1½ tablespoons cream of coconut
½ cup whipping cream, whipped

Rinse nuts with hot water; drain and pat dry with paper towels. Coarsely chop nuts; set aside. Press coconut into bottom and up sides of pastry shell; set aside.

Combine eggs and next 4 ingredients; stir in nuts. Pour filling into prepared pastry shell. Bake at 350° for 15 minutes. Reduce oven temperature to 325°, and bake an additional 35 minutes or until set.

Fold cream of coconut into whipped cream; serve whipped cream mixture with pie. Yield: one 9-inch pie.

PECAN PIE

1 cup sugar
1 cup light corn syrup
⅓ cup butter or margarine
4 large eggs, lightly beaten

1 teaspoon vanilla extract
¼ teaspoon salt
1 unbaked 9-inch pastry shell
1¼ cups pecan halves

Combine first 3 ingredients in a medium saucepan; cook over low heat, stirring constantly, until sugar dissolves and butter melts. Remove from heat; let cool slightly. Stir in eggs, vanilla, and salt. Pour filling into pastry shell, and top with pecan halves. Bake at 325° for 50 to 55 minutes or until mixture is set. Yield: one 9-inch pie.

Rum Pecan Pie: Prepare recipe as directed above, adding 3 tablespoons dark rum with vanilla extract.

PUMPKIN PIE

3 cups canned pumpkin
1 cup sugar
½ teaspoon salt
½ teaspoon ground ginger
½ teaspoon ground allspice
½ teaspoon ground nutmeg

½ teaspoon ground cinnamon
3 large eggs, lightly beaten
1 (12-ounce) can evaporated milk
1 unbaked 10-inch pastry shell
Frozen whipped topping, thawed
  (optional)

Combine first 9 ingredients; stir well. Pour filling into pastry shell. Bake at 425° for 15 minutes. Reduce oven temperature to 350°, and bake an additional 40 to 45 minutes or until a knife inserted near center comes out clean. Serve with whipped topping, if desired. Yield: one 10-inch pie.

Sweet Potato Pie: Prepare recipe as directed above, substituting 3 cups cooked, mashed sweet potato for canned pumpkin.

BREAD PUDDING WITH WHISKEY SAUCE

Bread pudding is a simple, old-fashioned dessert made with cubes or slices of bread that have been soaked in a mixture of milk, eggs, sugar, and vanilla. Bread pudding may be served hot or cold with a dessert sauce or heavy cream.

1 (16-ounce) loaf French bread
3 cups milk
1 cup cream sherry
3 large eggs, lightly beaten
2 cups sugar
1 cup raisins

¼ cup butter or margarine, melted and divided
2 tablespoons vanilla extract
½ cup honey
Whiskey Sauce

Break bread into small chunks, and place in a large bowl. Add milk and sherry; stir well. Let stand 10 minutes.

Combine eggs, sugar, raisins, 2 tablespoons butter, and vanilla; add to bread mixture, stirring well. Spoon mixture into a lightly greased 13- x 9- x 2-inch baking dish. Combine honey and remaining 2 tablespoons butter; pour over bread mixture. Bake at 350° for 45 minutes or until set and lightly browned. Serve warm with Whiskey Sauce. Yield: 10 to 12 servings.

Whiskey Sauce

1 cup sugar
1 cup milk
½ cup butter or margarine

2 tablespoons cornstarch
¼ cup cold water
¾ cup bourbon

Combine first 3 ingredients in a heavy saucepan; cook over medium heat, stirring frequently, until sugar dissolves and butter melts. Combine cornstarch and water; add cornstarch mixture and bourbon to milk mixture. Bring to a boil; cook 1 minute, stirring occasionally. Yield: 3 cups.

BROWNIE TRIFLE

1 (19.8-ounce) package fudge brownie mix
¼ cup praline or coffee-flavored liqueur (optional)
1 (3.9-ounce) package chocolate fudge instant pudding mix

8 (1.4-ounce) toffee-flavored candy bars, crushed
1 (12-ounce) container frozen whipped topping, thawed
Garnish: chocolate curls or grated chocolate

Prepare brownie mix according to package directions. Bake according to package directions in a 13- x 9- x 2-inch pan. Prick top of warm brownies at

1-inch intervals with a wooden pick, and brush with liqueur, if desired. Cool; crumble into small pieces.

Prepare chocolate fudge pudding mix according to package directions, omitting chilling procedure.

Place half of crumbled brownies in bottom of a 3-quart trifle bowl or large glass bowl; top with half each of pudding, crushed candy bars, and whipped topping. Repeat layers with remaining half of crumbled brownies, pudding, candy bars, and whipped topping. Cover and chill at least 8 hours. Garnish, if desired. Yield: 16 to 18 servings.

Chocolate lovers will adore Brownie Trifle. This make-ahead delight features fudgy brownies layered with chocolate pudding, crushed toffee bars, and whipped topping.

CHOCOLATE DECADENCE

The intense flavor and creamy texture of Chocolate Decadence closely resembles that of a rich chocolate truffle.

16 (1-ounce) squares semisweet chocolate
⅔ cup butter
5 large eggs
2 tablespoons sugar
2 tablespoons all-purpose flour
2 cups fresh raspberries

2 cups water
¼ cup sugar
2 tablespoons cornstarch
2 tablespoons water
Whipped cream
Garnish: fresh raspberries

Line the bottom of a 9-inch springform pan with parchment paper; set aside.

Combine chocolate and butter in top of a double boiler; bring water to a boil. Reduce heat to low; cook until chocolate melts. Gradually add chocolate mixture to eggs, beating at medium speed of an electric mixer 10 minutes. Fold in 2 tablespoons sugar and flour. Pour mixture into prepared pan. Bake at 400° for 15 minutes. (Cake will not be set in center.) Remove from oven; cover and chill thoroughly.

Combine 2 cups fresh raspberries, 2 cups water, and ¼ cup sugar in a large saucepan; bring to a boil over medium-high heat. Reduce heat, and simmer 30 minutes, stirring occasionally. Pour raspberry mixture through a wire-mesh strainer into a bowl, discarding seeds. Return raspberry mixture to pan.

Combine cornstarch and 2 tablespoons water; add to raspberry mixture. Cook over medium heat, stirring constantly, until mixture comes to a boil; boil, stirring constantly, 1 minute. Cool completely.

To serve, spoon 2 to 3 tablespoons raspberry sauce onto each individual dessert plate; place wedge of chocolate dessert on sauce. Top each wedge with a dollop of whipped cream. Garnish, if desired. Yield: 10 to 12 servings.

MIXED FRUIT AMBROSIA

2 (20-ounce) cans pineapple chunks
1½ tablespoons sugar
2 teaspoons grated orange rind

6 medium oranges
3 medium-size pink grapefruit
4 medium bananas
1 (3½-ounce) can flaked coconut

Drain pineapple chunks, reserving 1 cup juice. Set pineapple chunks aside. Combine reserved juice, sugar, and orange rind in a large bowl, stirring until sugar dissolves; set aside.

Peel and section oranges and grapefruit, catching juice in a medium bowl. Set sections aside. Slice bananas; add banana slices to orange juice mixture, tossing gently to coat. (This prevents banana slices from turning brown.) Add banana mixture, pineapple chunks, orange sections, and grapefruit sections to pineapple juice mixture; toss gently to combine. Cover and chill thoroughly. Just before serving, add coconut and toss gently to combine. Yield: 10 to 12 servings.

HOLIDAY SORBET

1½ cups orange juice
1 cup water
⅔ cup sugar
1 (12-ounce) package fresh
   cranberries
2 tablespoons Grand Marnier or
   other orange-flavored liqueur
   (optional)

1¾ cups water
⅓ cup sugar
1½ teaspoons lemon juice
1 (6-ounce) can frozen limeade
   concentrate, thawed and
   undiluted
Garnishes: fresh cranberries,
   fresh mint sprigs

A sorbet is usually served as dessert or as a palate refresher between courses. Unlike some sherbet, sorbet never contains milk, and it is often softer in texture than sherbet.

Combine first 4 ingredients in a large saucepan; bring to a boil. Cover, reduce heat, and simmer 6 to 8 minutes or until cranberry skins pop. Remove from heat, and let cool 10 minutes.

Position knife blade in food processor bowl; add half of cranberry mixture. Process until smooth, stopping once to scrape down sides. Repeat procedure with remaining cranberry mixture. Pour cranberry mixture through a large wire-mesh strainer into a bowl, discarding pulp. Stir in liqueur, if desired. Pour mixture into a 13- x 9- x 2-inch pan; cover and freeze until mixture is firm.

Combine 1¾ cups water and ⅓ cup sugar in a saucepan; cook over medium heat, stirring constantly, until sugar dissolves. Remove from heat, and stir in lemon juice and limeade concentrate. Pour mixture into an 8-inch square pan; cover and freeze until firm.

Position knife blade in processor bowl; add frozen limeade mixture, and process until smooth. Set aside. Process half of frozen cranberry mixture until smooth; spread evenly into a 9- x 5- x 3-inch loafpan. Spoon limeade mixture over cranberry mixture in pan, spreading evenly. Process remaining frozen cranberry mixture until smooth; spread over limeade mixture. Cover and freeze until firm. Remove from pan; cut into slices. Garnish, if desired. Yield: 8 servings.

Christmas Memories

Praline Sauce

To The
Hooper
Family—
Merry Christmas

Jeweled Pepper
Chutney

To Mary Ann
Happy Holidays

Gifts From the Kitchen

 There's no better way to capture the holiday spirit than with gifts from the kitchen. For a favorite aunt, stir up a batch of Brandied Fruit Starter (page 239), one of **Southern Living**'s most sought-after recipes from years past.  Start early to make Coffee-Flavored Liqueur (page 234) for a hostess gift, or bake several batches of Monster Cookies (page 236) for the neighborhood children.  For other gift giving, try our recipes for potpourris with fragrances reminiscent of magical Christmases past.  And when it comes to packaging these personalized presents, use your imagination. Your selection of unique containers will double the surprise and can be enjoyed long after the contents are fond memories.

Clockwise from bottom: Cheese Ball with Sun-Dried Tomatoes (page 232), Praline Sauce (page 237), French Market Soup Mix (page 240), Cinnamon-Stick Ornament (page 240), Jeweled Pepper Chutney (page 238).

BEEF STICKS WITH HOT-SWEET MUSTARD

Hot-Sweet Mustard makes a prized gift even without the beef sticks. Tuck a jar of this tangy spread into a basket along with crackers and a unique spreader. Save some for yourself to enjoy with ham or egg rolls.

5 pounds ground beef
2 tablespoons meat-cure mix
1 tablespoon dry mustard
1 tablespoon coarsely ground
  pepper
1 tablespoon Worcestershire sauce
2½ teaspoons garlic powder
2 teaspoons hickory-smoked salt
1½ teaspoons seasoned salt
Hot-Sweet Mustard

Combine first 8 ingredients, stirring well. Cover and chill at least 8 hours.

Shape mixture into 5 (10-inch) logs; place on a rack in a shallow pan. Bake at 225° for 5 hours, turning occasionally. Drain on paper towels; let cool. Refrigerate beef sticks in an airtight container up to 3 weeks. Slice and serve with crackers and Hot-Sweet Mustard. Yield: five 10-inch beef sticks.

Hot-Sweet Mustard

2 (2-ounce) cans dry mustard
1 cup cider vinegar
1 cup sugar
⅓ cup butter or margarine
3 egg yolks, lightly beaten

Combine mustard and vinegar in a small glass bowl, stirring until smooth. Cover and let stand at room temperature 8 hours.

Combine mustard mixture, sugar, and butter in top of a double boiler; bring water to a boil. Reduce heat to low; cook, stirring frequently, until butter melts. Gradually stir about one-fourth of hot mixture into yolks; add to remaining hot mixture. Cook, stirring constantly, until mixture is thickened and thermometer registers 160°.

Remove from heat, and let cool. Spoon mustard into jars. Cover and refrigerate up to 1 month. Yield: 2 cups.

CHEESE BALLS WITH SUN-DRIED TOMATOES

3 (8-ounce) packages cream
  cheese, softened
1 (7-ounce) jar oil-packed sun-
  dried tomatoes, drained
2 teaspoons dried basil
1 clove garlic, halved
½ cup coarsely chopped almonds
  or pine nuts, toasted

Position knife blade in food processor bowl; add first 4 ingredients. Process until smooth. Cover and chill thoroughly.

Divide cheese mixture into 6 equal portions; shape each portion into a ball. Roll cheese balls in almonds, lightly pressing almonds into cheese balls. Wrap each cheese ball in plastic wrap; refrigerate up to 5 days. Serve with unsalted crackers. Yield: six 3-inch cheese balls.

HOT SPICED TEA MIX

2 cups orange-flavored breakfast beverage crystals
2 cups sugar
½ cup instant tea
1 teaspoon ground cinnamon

1 teaspoon ground cloves
1 (.31-ounce) package unsweetened lemon-flavored drink mix

Combine all ingredients; stir well. Store in an airtight container. To serve, place 2 tablespoons mix in a cup or mug. Add ¾ cup boiling water, stirring well. Yield: 4 cups mix or 32 servings.

For a special friend, fill a box with a jar of Hot Spiced Tea Mix, a package of gourmet cookies, and a paperback best-seller.

AMARETTO

1 lemon
3 cups sugar
2 cups water
3 cups vodka

3 tablespoons brandy
2 tablespoons almond extract
2 teaspoons vanilla extract
1 teaspoon chocolate flavoring

Peel lemon, leaving inner white skin on fruit; reserve lemon for another use. Cut lemon rind into 2- x ¼-inch strips.

Combine lemon rind strips, sugar, and water in a medium saucepan. Bring to a boil; cover, reduce heat, and simmer 30 minutes. Remove from heat; remove and discard lemon rind strips. Cover and chill thoroughly. Add vodka and remaining ingredients to chilled mixture; stir well. Store in an airtight container at room temperature at least 1 week before serving. Use in any recipe calling for amaretto. Yield: 6 cups.

Dress up your present of Amaretto or Coffee-Flavored Liqueur (page 234) with a decorative bottle. You can find the bottles at specialty cook's shops and crafts stores.

COFFEE-FLAVORED LIQUEUR

Drop a piece of vanilla bean into each bottle of Coffee-Flavored Liqueur to infuse it with flavor. If you vary the bottle size, similarly vary the piece of vanilla bean.

5 cups sugar
1 (2-ounce) jar instant coffee granules

4 cups boiling water
1 (1-liter) bottle vodka
1 vanilla bean

Combine sugar and coffee granules in a large metal or glass bowl; add boiling water, stirring until sugar and coffee granules dissolve. Cool to room temperature. Stir in vodka.

Pour mixture into 3 (1-quart) jars or decorative bottles. Cut vanilla bean into thirds; place 1 piece in each jar or bottle. Cover and let stand at room temperature at least 12 days before serving. Use in any recipe calling for coffee-flavored liqueur. Yield: 11 cups.

CHOCOLATE SWIRL LOAVES

6¾ to 7¼ cups all-purpose flour, divided
½ cup sugar
2 teaspoons salt
2 packages active dry yeast
1½ cups milk

½ cup butter or margarine
4 large eggs
¼ teaspoon ground cinnamon
2 (1-ounce) squares unsweetened chocolate, melted and cooled
Amaretto Glaze (facing page)

Combine 2½ cups flour, sugar, salt, and yeast in a large mixing bowl; stir well. Combine milk and butter in a saucepan; heat until butter melts, stirring occasionally. Cool to 120° to 130°.

Gradually add liquid mixture to flour mixture, beating at low speed of an electric mixer until blended. Beat an additional 5 minutes at medium speed. Add eggs; beat well. Stir in enough remaining flour to make a soft dough.

Divide dough in half; set 1 portion aside. Turn 1 portion of dough out onto a lightly floured surface; sprinkle with cinnamon, and knead until dough is smooth and elastic (8 to 10 minutes). Place in a well-greased bowl, turning to grease top. Cover and let rise in a warm place (85°), free from drafts, 1 hour or until doubled in bulk.

Turn remaining portion of dough out onto a lightly floured surface; pour melted chocolate over dough, and knead until dough is smooth and elastic and chocolate is incorporated (about 8 to 10 minutes). Place in a well-greased bowl, turning to grease top. Cover and let rise in a warm place, free from drafts, 1 hour or until doubled in bulk.

Punch each portion of dough down, and divide each portion in half. Roll 1 portion of chocolate dough and 1 portion of plain dough into 15- x 9-inch rectangles. Position chocolate rectangle on top of plain rectangle. Roll up, starting at short side, pressing firmly to eliminate air pockets; pinch ends to seal. Place dough, seam side down, in a well-greased 9- x 5- x 3-inch loafpan. Repeat procedure with remaining portions of chocolate and plain doughs.

Cover and let rise in a warm place, free from drafts, 1 hour or until doubled in bulk. Bake at 350° for 45 minutes or until loaves sound hollow when tapped. Cover with aluminum foil the last 20 minutes, if necessary, to prevent excessive browning. Remove from pans immediately; transfer to wire racks. Cool 15 minutes. Drizzle Amaretto Glaze over warm loaves. Yield: 2 loaves.

Amaretto Glaze

2 cups sifted powdered sugar   **1 tablespoon amaretto**
2 tablespoons milk

Combine all ingredients, stirring until smooth. Yield: about 1 cup.

Delight your hostess or a next-door neighbor with a gift of Chocolate Swirl Loaf or Christmas Potpourri (page 241).

MONSTER COOKIES

½ cup butter or margarine, softened

1 cup plus 2 tablespoons firmly packed brown sugar

1 cup sugar

3 large eggs

¾ teaspoon light corn syrup

¼ teaspoon vanilla extract

2 cups creamy peanut butter

4½ cups regular oats, uncooked

2 teaspoons baking soda

¼ teaspoon salt

1 cup candy-coated chocolate pieces

1 (6-ounce) package semisweet chocolate morsels

Beat butter at medium speed of an electric mixer until creamy; gradually add sugars, beating well. Add eggs, corn syrup, and vanilla; beat well. Add peanut butter; beat until smooth. Combine oats, soda, and salt; gradually add to butter mixture, stirring well. Stir in chocolate pieces and chocolate morsels.

Drop dough by one-fourth cupfuls onto lightly greased cookie sheets; flatten each cookie into a 3½-inch circle, making sure flattened cookies are 2 inches apart. Bake at 350° for 12 to 14 minutes or until lightly browned. (Centers of cookies will be slightly soft.) Cool slightly on cookie sheets; remove to wire racks, and let cool completely. Yield: 2½ dozen.

LEMON CURD

Lemon curd is a rich, creamy sauce made from lemon juice, sugar, butter, and eggs. It is traditionally used as a bread spread, as a dessert sauce, or to fill pastries. Fresh lemon juice is the secret to intense flavor.

2 cups sugar

1 cup butter or margarine

¼ cup grated lemon rind

⅔ cup fresh lemon juice

4 large eggs, lightly beaten

Combine first 4 ingredients in top of a double boiler; bring water to a boil. Reduce heat to low; cook until butter melts. Gradually stir about one-fourth of hot mixture into eggs; add to remaining hot mixture, stirring constantly. Cook over medium-low heat, stirring constantly, until mixture thickens and coats a spoon (about 15 minutes). Remove from heat; cool. Cover and refrigerate up to 2 weeks.

Serve chilled as a topping for pound cake, angel food cake, or gingerbread. Yield: 3¼ cups.

HOT FUDGE SAUCE

1½ cups semisweet chocolate
   morsels
⅔ cup sugar

2 (5-ounce) cans evaporated milk
1 tablespoon butter or margarine
1 teaspoon vanilla extract

Combine first 3 ingredients in a medium saucepan. Bring to a boil over medium heat, stirring frequently. Boil, stirring constantly, 1 minute. Remove from heat; stir in butter and vanilla. Cool completely. Cover and refrigerate up to 2 weeks. Serve warm over ice cream or cake. Yield: 2¼ cups.

PRALINE SAUCE

¼ cup butter or margarine
1¼ cups firmly packed light
   brown sugar
¾ cup light corn syrup

3 tablespoons all-purpose flour
1½ cups chopped pecans, toasted
1 (5-ounce) can evaporated milk

Melt butter in a medium saucepan; add brown sugar, corn syrup, and flour, stirring until smooth. Bring to a boil; reduce heat, and simmer, stirring constantly, 5 minutes. Remove from heat, and let cool 20 minutes. Stir in pecans and evaporated milk. Cool completely. Cover and refrigerate up to 2 weeks. Serve warm over ice cream or plain cheesecake. Yield: 3 cups.

To toast chopped pecans, spread them in a single layer on a baking sheet. Bake at 300° for 15 minutes or until lightly toasted, stirring once or twice.

JEZEBEL SAUCE

1 (16-ounce) jar pineapple
   preserves
1 (16-ounce) jar apple jelly
1 (5-ounce) jar prepared
   horseradish

3 tablespoons dry mustard
1 tablespoon coarsely ground
   pepper

Combine all ingredients; stir well. Cover and refrigerate up to 2 weeks. Serve as an appetizer with cream cheese and crackers, or as a sauce with pork or beef. Yield: 3⅔ cups.

PUMPKIN BUTTER

Pumpkin Butter really isn't butter but a thick, dark spread made by slow-cooking pumpkin, sugar, and spices.

2¼ cups sugar
3 tablespoons powdered fruit
   pectin

1 teaspoon ground cinnamon
½ teaspoon ground allspice
1 (16-ounce) can pumpkin

Combine all ingredients in a medium saucepan; bring to a boil over medium heat, stirring constantly. Boil, stirring constantly, 1 minute. Remove from heat, and let cool; spoon into jars. Cover and refrigerate up to 3 weeks or freeze up to 3 months. Serve with biscuits. Yield: 3 cups.

JEWELED PEPPER CHUTNEY

2 cups sugar
2 cups firmly packed brown sugar
2 cups golden raisins
2½ cups cider vinegar
8 large sweet red peppers, seeded
   and cut into ¼-inch cubes

8 cloves garlic, finely chopped
4 jalapeño peppers, finely
   chopped
1 (2-ounce) jar crystallized ginger,
   finely chopped

Combine all ingredients in a large Dutch oven; bring to a boil. Reduce heat, and simmer, uncovered, 1 hour and 45 minutes, stirring occasionally.

Pack hot mixture into hot jars, leaving ½-inch of headspace. Remove air bubbles; wipe jar rims. Cover at once with metal lids, and screw on bands. Process in boiling-water bath 10 minutes. Store in refrigerator after opening. Serve with pork, chicken, or turkey. Yield: 6 half pints.

FIRE-AND-ICE PICKLES

2 (32-ounce) jars medium-size
   whole dill pickles, drained
4 cups sugar
2 tablespoons hot sauce

½ to ¾ teaspoon dried crushed
   red pepper flakes
3 cloves garlic, peeled

Cut pickles into ¼-inch-thick slices. Combine pickles, sugar, hot sauce, and pepper flakes in a large bowl; stir well. Cover and let stand 2 hours, stirring occasionally. Spoon pickles into 3 (1-pint) canning jars, adding 1 garlic clove to each jar. Cover and refrigerate up to 1 month. Yield: 3 pints.

Brandied Fruit Starter is a gift that can be enjoyed year-round by simply keeping the starter fed. Serve the kicky fruit mixture over ice cream or pound cake.

BRANDIED FRUIT STARTER

1 (16-ounce) can sliced peaches, drained

1 (16-ounce) can apricot halves, drained

1 (15¼-ounce) can unsweetened pineapple chunks, drained

1 (10-ounce) jar maraschino cherries, drained

1¼ cups sugar

1¼ cups brandy

Apricot or peach brandy may be substituted for regular brandy, if desired.

Combine all ingredients in a large glass bowl, stirring gently. Cover and let stand at room temperature 3 weeks before serving, stirring twice a week. Serve over ice cream or pound cake. Reserve at least 1 cup starter at all times.

To replenish starter, add 1 cup sugar and one of the first 4 ingredients every 1 to 3 weeks, alternating fruit each time. Cover and let stand at room temperature at least 3 days before serving each time starter is replenished. Yield: 6 cups.

FRENCH MARKET SOUP MIX

Package two cups of French Market Soup Mix in a decorative bag tied with colorful ribbon, and attach a copy of the recipe for French Market Soup. The recipe for the soup mix makes enough for 13 gifts.

1 pound dried black beans
1 pound dried Great Northern beans
1 pound dried navy beans
1 pound dried pinto beans
1 pound dried red beans
1 pound dried black-eyed peas

1 pound dried green split peas
1 pound dried yellow split peas
1 pound dried lentils
1 pound dried baby limas
1 pound dried large limas
1 pound barley pearls

Combine all ingredients in a very large bowl. Divide mixture into 13 (2-cup) packages to give with recipe for French Market Soup. Yield: 26 cups.

French Market Soup

1 (2-cup) package French Market Soup Mix
2 quarts water
1 large ham hock
1 (16-ounce) can whole tomatoes, undrained and coarsely chopped

1½ cups chopped onion
3 tablespoons lemon juice
1 chile pepper, coarsely chopped
1 clove garlic, minced
1¼ teaspoons salt
¼ teaspoon pepper

Sort and wash soup mix; place in a Dutch oven. Cover with water 2 inches above soup mix; let soak 8 hours.

Drain soup mix, and return to Dutch oven; add 2 quarts water and ham hock. Bring to a boil; cover, reduce heat, and simmer 1½ hours or until beans are tender. Stir in tomato and next 4 ingredients. Bring to a boil; reduce heat, and simmer, uncovered, 30 minutes. Remove ham hock; remove meat from bone. Chop meat, and return to soup. Stir in salt and pepper. Yield: 3 quarts.

CINNAMON-STICK ORNAMENT

8 to 10 (3-inch) sticks cinnamon
1 yard (¼-inch-wide) red satin ribbon

Craft glue
Small decorative red bow

Place a cinnamon stick in center of length of ribbon; tie ribbon around cinnamon stick. Add a dab of glue between cinnamon stick and ribbon to secure. Place next cinnamon stick on top of previous stick at a 90° angle; tie with ribbon. Repeat with remaining cinnamon sticks and additional glue. Knot ribbon to hold cinnamon sticks securely. Glue decorative bow to ornament to conceal knot. Knot ends of ribbon to form a hanger. (Not to be eaten or used in food preparation.) Yield: 1 ornament.

CHRISTMAS POTPOURRI

Bark pieces
Bay, eucalyptus, and patchouli leaves
Beechnut husks
Cinnamon sticks, broken into 2- to 3-inch pieces
Coriander seeds
Dried acorns and chestnuts
Dried rose hips and red strawflower petals
Gingerroot pieces
Lotus pods
Sandalwood pieces
Small pinecones and pine needles
Star anise
Sweet gum balls
Tulip wings
Whole cloves
Whole nutmegs, cracked
Evergreen oil
Patchouli oil
Pine or spruce oil
Sandalwood oil

You'll find most of the ingredients for Christmas Potpourri at a large crafts store. Package the potpourri in bags for gifts. You may want to include an attractive bowl for displaying the fragrant mixture.

Combine various amounts of first 16 ingredients in a large glass bowl to achieve desired amount of potpourri. For every 4 cups of mixture, add 2 drops of each oil, tossing to distribute oils. Place mixture in an airtight container; let stand 4 to 6 weeks at room temperature before using. To preserve scent, place potpourri in a glass container with a lid, and uncover only when you want to freshen the air. (Not to be eaten or used in food preparation.)

ORANGE-AND-CINNAMON POTPOURRI

6 oranges
Whole cloves
2 ounces orange oil
6 drops cinnamon oil
10 (3-inch) sticks cinnamon

The recipe for Orange-and-Cinnamon Potpourri may be doubled or tripled. Should the scent diminish, reapply the oil mixture to the potpourri.

Peel oranges in long strips, leaving white skin on fruit; reserve oranges for another use. Stud peel with cloves, placing cloves ½ inch to 1 inch apart.

Combine oils in a small bowl; dip peel and cinnamon sticks in oil mixture, allowing excess to drip off. Arrange peel and cinnamon sticks in a glass or ceramic bowl. (Not to be eaten or used in food preparation.)

Children's Workshop

Remember Christmas when you were young? How the chance to cut out star-shaped sugar cookies or create edible ornaments filled the season with fun and excitement? Well, you can bring back that special magic by spending an afternoon in the kitchen with your children or grandchildren. If you're called upon to make treats for your child's school or church parties, select one of these recipes and get your child to help. Most are simple to prepare and require minimal cooking. As children wait for Christmas with boundless enthusiasm, turn your kitchen into a holiday workshop. You'll have volunteers begging to help make Jolly Reindeer Cookies (page 246) and Chocolate-Peanut Butter Cups (page 247). Such an occasion guarantees plenty of warm memories.

Chocolate Chip Tub Cookies, Hot Cocoa Mix (page 244).

HOT COCOA MIX

Hot Cocoa Mix is the perfect gift for teachers. Let the children help measure and stir the mix, and don't forget to attach the recipe!

2 cups sifted powdered sugar
2 cups instant nonfat dry milk
  powder
2 cups powdered nondairy coffee
  creamer

2 cups powdered chocolate
  milk mix
2 cups miniature marshmallows

Combine all ingredients; stir well. Store in an airtight container. To serve, place ¼ cup mix in a mug or cup. Add ¾ cup boiling water, stirring well. Yield: 8 cups mix or 32 servings.

Minted Hot Cocoa Mix: Add 1 cup mint chocolate morsels to mix; stir well. Prepare as directed above. Yield: 8¾ cups mix or 35 servings.

CHOCOLATE CHIP TUB COOKIES

½ cup butter or margarine,
  softened
½ cup shortening
¾ cup firmly packed brown sugar
½ cup sugar
1 large egg
1 teaspoon vanilla extract

2 cups all-purpose flour
1 teaspoon baking soda
½ teaspoon salt
1 (12-ounce) package semisweet
  chocolate morsels
1 cup chopped pecans

Beat butter and shortening at medium speed of an electric mixer until mixture is smooth and creamy; gradually add sugars, beating well. Add egg and vanilla; beat well.

Combine flour, soda, and salt; gradually add flour mixture to butter mixture, beating well. Stir in chocolate morsels and pecans.

Divide dough in half, and place each portion in a 2½-cup airtight container. Store in refrigerator. Yield: 2 gift tubs or 5 dozen cookies.

Directions for recipe gift card for 1 tub: Dough for Chocolate Chip Tub Cookies may be refrigerated up to 2 weeks or frozen up to 1 month. When ready to bake, drop dough by level tablespoonfuls 2 inches apart onto ungreased cookie sheets. Bake at 350° for 12 to 14 minutes or until lightly browned. Cool on cookie sheets 1 minute; remove to wire racks, and let cool completely. Yield: 2½ dozen.

Little bakers can prepare and package the mix for Brown Sugar Brownies.

BROWN SUGAR BROWNIE MIX

2 cups self-rising flour
2 cups chopped pecans

1 (16-ounce) package dark brown
sugar

Combine all ingredients; stir well. Divide mixture in half, and place each portion in an airtight container to give with recipe for Brown Sugar Brownies. Yield: 2 gift packages or 32 brownies.

Brown Sugar Brownies

½ cup butter or margarine
2 large eggs, lightly beaten
1 teaspoon vanilla extract

1 package Brown Sugar Brownie
Mix

Melt butter in a large saucepan over low heat. Remove from heat; let cool slightly. Stir in eggs and vanilla. Add brownie mix; stir well. Pour batter into a greased and floured 9-inch square pan. Bake at 350° for 25 minutes. Cool completely on a wire rack; cut into squares. Yield: 16 brownies.

EASY GINGER CRINKLES

Easy Ginger Crinkles are quick to prepare using a commercial cake mix. Chill the dough for at least eight hours to make it firm enough for little hands to roll into balls.

1 (18.25-ounce) package spice cake mix without pudding
1 teaspoon ground ginger
2 large eggs, lightly beaten
¼ cup vegetable oil
¼ cup molasses
Sugar

Combine cake mix and ginger in a large bowl; stir well. Combine eggs, oil, and molasses; add to dry ingredients, stirring until blended (dough will be sticky). Shape dough into a ball; cover and chill at least 8 hours.

Divide dough in half. Work with 1 portion of dough at a time, storing remaining portion in refrigerator. Shape dough into 1-inch balls; roll each ball in sugar. Place 2 inches apart on lightly greased cookie sheets. Bake at 375° for 14 minutes. Cool 2 minutes on cookie sheets; remove to wire racks, and let cool completely. Repeat procedure with remaining portion of dough and sugar. Yield: about 3½ dozen.

JOLLY REINDEER COOKIES

Children of all ages will love the whimsical appearance of Jolly Reindeer Cookies. The frosting holds the decorations on the graham crackers. Let the cookies dry on wire racks to make them crisp.

1 cup sifted powdered sugar
2 tablespoons whipping cream
1 teaspoon vanilla extract
12 (2½-inch-square) graham crackers
24 semisweet chocolate mini-morsels
12 red cinnamon candies
12 miniature pretzels, broken in half

Combine first 3 ingredients in a small bowl; stir well. Set frosting aside.

Have a grown-up cut graham crackers in half diagonally with a serrated knife, using a sawing motion. Spread a small amount of frosting over 1 side of half the crackers. Top with remaining cracker halves, forming triangles. Spread a small amount of frosting to cover top crackers.

Press 2 chocolate morsels into each frosted cracker for eyes, 1 cinnamon candy for a nose, and 2 pretzel halves for antlers. Let dry on a wire rack. Yield: 1 dozen.

CHOCOLATE-PEANUT BUTTER CUPS

1 (20-ounce) package refrigerated sliceable peanut butter cookie dough

48 miniature peanut butter cup candies, unwrapped

Cut cookie dough into ¾-inch slices; cut each slice into quarters. Place quarters in greased miniature (1¾-inch) muffin pans (do not shape). Bake at 350° for 9 minutes (dough will puff during baking). Remove from oven, and immediately press a peanut butter cup candy gently into each cookie cup. Cool completely before removing from pans. Chill until firm. Yield: 4 dozen.

ORANGE-COCONUT BALLS

1 (12-ounce) package vanilla wafers
1 (16-ounce) package powdered sugar
½ cup butter or margarine, melted

1 (6-ounce) can frozen orange juice concentrate, thawed and undiluted
1 (3½-ounce) can flaked coconut

Powdered sugar may be substituted for the flaked coconut in Orange-Coconut Balls.

Position knife blade in food processor bowl; add vanilla wafers. Process until ground. Combine vanilla wafer crumbs, powdered sugar, butter, and orange juice concentrate; stir well. Shape mixture into 1-inch balls; roll balls in coconut. Cover and freeze. Serve frozen. Yield: about 4½ dozen.

WHITE CHOCOLATE CRUNCH

1 pound vanilla-flavored candy coating
2 cups miniature pretzels

1 cup corn-and-rice cereal
2 (3-ounce) packages salted peanuts

For a festive present, wrap White Chocolate Crunch in colored plastic wrap, and tie with lots of curling ribbon.

Trace 2 (6-inch) circles on wax paper. Turn paper over, and place on a large baking sheet; set aside.

Place candy coating in a 2-quart glass bowl; microwave at MEDIUM (50% power) 3 to 4 minutes or until melted, stirring after 2 minutes. Stir in pretzels, cereal, and peanuts. Spoon mixture evenly into centers of prepared circles, spreading to edges. Cool completely. Remove from wax paper; wrap each portion in plastic wrap. Yield: 1½ pounds.

PEPPERMINT CANDY CUPS

Petit four paper cups with a holiday design are perfect containers for Peppermint Candy Cups.

12 ounces vanilla-flavored candy coating

¾ cup crushed hard peppermint candy

Place candy coating in a 2-quart glass bowl; microwave at MEDIUM (50% power) 3 to 4 minutes or until melted, stirring after 2 minutes. Stir in candy. Spoon mixture evenly into petit four paper cups, filling ¾ full. Chill until firm. Store in an airtight container. Yield: 3 dozen.

Peppermint Candy Cups are fun and safe to make because the vanilla-flavored candy coating melts in the microwave oven, not on the stove.

248 Children's Workshop

SNACK MIX

1 (16-ounce) jar dry-roasted
  peanuts
1 (15-ounce) package raisins
1 (12-ounce) package butterscotch
  or peanut butter morsels

1 (11½-ounce) package milk
  chocolate morsels

Combine all ingredients in a large bowl; stir well. Store in an airtight container at room temperature. Yield: 10 cups.

No measuring is involved in making Snack Mix. Whole packages are used, making it simple for children to help prepare the mix.

EDIBLE ORNAMENTS

¼ cup butter or margarine,
  softened
⅓ cup light corn syrup
1 teaspoon vanilla extract
1 (16-ounce) package powdered
  sugar, sifted and divided

Green food coloring
Red cinnamon candies
Powdered sugar
1 (4¼-ounce) tube white
  decorator frosting

Combine first 3 ingredients in a large mixing bowl; beat at medium speed of an electric mixer until blended. Gradually add half the package of powdered sugar, beating until smooth. Stir in enough of the remaining package of powdered sugar to make a stiff dough, kneading with hands, if necessary.

Divide dough in half; wrap 1 portion in plastic wrap, and set aside. Knead green food coloring into remaining portion of dough. To make wreaths, shape green dough into 18 (1-inch) balls. Roll each ball into a 5-inch rope, and connect ends of rope to form a circle. Decorate circles with red cinnamon candies to resemble wreaths.

To make cutout ornaments, roll out remaining portion of dough on a surface lightly dusted with powdered sugar. Cut into desired shapes using 3-inch cookie cutters. Punch a hole in the top of each ornament using a drinking straw. Decorate with frosting.

Lay wreaths and ornaments flat on wax paper; set aside to partially dry (about 4 hours). Remove from wax paper; transfer to wire racks. Let dry 24 hours. To hang, tie ornaments with ribbon. Yield: about 3 dozen ornaments.

The dough for Edible Ornaments is safe for children to eat and is pliable enough that small hands should have no problem shaping it. The ornaments become firm when allowed to dry on wire racks.

Recipe Index

Credits

Oxmoor House wishes to thank the following merchants and individuals:

Bridges Antiques, Birmingham, AL

Bromberg's, Birmingham, AL

Cassis & Co., New York, NY

Christine's, Birmingham, AL

Department 56, Inc., Eden Prairie, MN

Fitz and Floyd/Omnibus International, Dallas, TX

Frankie Engel Antiques, Birmingham, AL

Goldsmith/Corot, Inc., New York, NY

N.S. Gustin, Atlanta, GA

The Holly Tree, Birmingham, AL

House Parts, Inc., Atlanta, GA

Mesa International, Elkins, NH

Midori, Inc., Seattle, WA

Old World Pewter, Gainesville, GA

A Touch of Ivy, Inc., New York, NY

Union Street Glass, Oakland, CA

Vietri, Hillsborough, NC

Photographers

Ralph Anderson: front cover, back cover, pages 7 (bottom), 8, 10, 18, 22, 32, 46, 48, 51, 53, 54, 60, 86, 89, 98, 100, 105, 110, 115, 120, 127, 130, 147, 156, 159, 172, 176, 190, 194, 200, 203, 209, 228, 230, 242, 245, 248

Jim Bathie: pages 2, 7 (top), 12, 24, 31, 40, 64, 70, 75, 76, 78, 82, 85, 90, 94, 143, 150, 152, 162, 166, 187, 210, 217, 222, 225, 235, 239

J. Savage Gibson: page 138

Photo Stylists

Kay E. Clarke: pages 2, 7 (top), 12, 24, 31, 40, 64, 70, 75, 76, 78, 82, 85, 90, 94, 143, 150, 152, 162, 166, 187, 210, 217, 222, 225, 235, 239

Virginia R. Cravens: front cover, back cover, pages 8, 10, 18, 22, 32, 46, 48, 51, 53, 54, 60, 86, 89, 98, 100, 105, 110, 115, 120, 127, 130, 138, 147, 156, 159, 172, 176, 190, 194, 200, 203, 209, 228, 230, 242, 245, 248